LIFE'S END
Technocratic Dying in an Age of Spiritual Yearning

DAVID WENDELL MOLLER
Indiana University

Routledge
Taylor & Francis Group
LONDON AND NEW YORK

First published 2000 by Baywood Publishing Co., Inc.

Published 2018 by Routledge
2 Park Square, Milton Park, Abingdon, Oxon OX14 4RN
52 Vanderbilt Avenue, New York, NY 10017

First issued in paperback 2018

Routledge is an imprint of the Taylor & Francis Group, an informa business

Library of Congress Catalog Number: 99-33740

Library of Congress Cataloging-in-Publication Data

Moller, David Wendell.
    Life's end : technocratic dying in an age of spiritual yearning /
David Wendell Moller.
        p.   cm.
    Includes bibliographical references and index.
    ISBN 0-89503-202-3 (Cloth : alk. paper)
    1. Death--Social aspects.   2. Thanatology.   I. Title.
HQ1073.M66   1999
304.6'4--dc21   99-33740
                                                                 CIP

ISBN 13: 978-0-415-78458-0 (pbk)
ISBN 13: 978-0-89503-202-7 (hbk)

Printed in the United Kingdom
by Henry Ling Limited

For Binky,
in honor of the
beauty that she is
and radiates.
I Love You!

Preface

One indispensable measure of the human condition is how humanity responds to suffering, tragedy, and death. Dying is not just a personal experience or medical process. It is a part of life that has enormous symbolic and social significance. Patterns by which individuals die are created by and reflective of patterns by which they live. Thus, the ways of dying embody meanings that reveal the place of mortality in cultural life. Moreover, modern patterns of dying symbolize and contain many dreaded conditions of human existence: fear, loneliness, pain, unrelieved suffering, physical deterioration, helplessness, and meaninglessness. In this way, the prevailing icons of modern death are not only permeated with threatening and catastrophic images, they also represent and inform us about both the present state of living and dying in the culture.

Ironically, death teaches much about life. The specific arrangements of personal and social life lay the foundation for certain forms of dying. In this way, my indictment of the suffering-infused pattern of modern death which fills the pages of this book is, at the same time, an indictment of the conditions of modern life. Hence, a critique of the patterns of death is simultaneously a critique of the patterns of life. Death cannot be distinguished from life. Rather, it is a mirror and reflection of life's meanings, values, and folkways. Taking that into consideration, it is essential to explore the experience of dying in explicit connection to the values, institutions, and patterns of behavior which organize modern society.

At its simplest, the quality of dying is indicative of the quality of living; a measure of the condition and worth of the life of dying persons. On a deeper level, the styles of dying are suggestive of perplexing and complex psychosocial issues that characterize the contemporary cultural context. In this regard, the study of death has tremendous existential and social significance. It facilitates insight into the conditions of our lives and establishes a foundation upon which life can be transformed. In this way, despite its seemingly morbid aura, thanatology is potentially emancipating, life affirming, and life empowering.

On a personal note, the individuals whose voices so ennoble this book have been my greatest teachers about life. In their confrontation with mortality, I have seen them at their most vulnerable and perhaps most unflattering moments. I have been impressed with the courage it took for them to face bodily deterioration and death steadily. The real strength of this book lies not in my analysis and interpretation. Instead, it resonates from the words, expressions, suffering, and lives of the seriously sick persons whose stories are profound but mostly ignored. As one patient told me just yesterday: *We have been cast aside, disregarded, and forgotten about!* The needs and concerns of the patients in this study, like most dying people, are largely unrecognized and neglected. Their experience is virtually invisible and concealed by a society that has enormous difficulty in openly confronting mortality. All too often, consistent with values and patterns of modern life, they lived and suffered in isolation.

This book is an attempt to tell part of their story. By doing so, I hope to bring their suffering and tribulations out of the deep freeze of silence and avoidance. Their story, all the more crucial for not typically being told, is an important one. My work in this book is commensurately important because these sick and dying persons have allowed me to speak for them. They honor me with their trust, and I am privileged to try to serve as their voice. If I am able to portray the urgency and extremity of their sufferings with candor, sensitivity, and advocacy I will have served as their representative successfully. And if I succeed, perhaps some value will be derived from their sufferings, dying, and deaths. As one patient emphatically let it be known:

> Maybe some good can come of this effort for others. You know, not for me, but for those who come after me. That's why I'm participating in this study with you . . .

My deepest gratitude is extended to these patients. They have made this book possible. More importantly, they have touched me deeply as a person and as a professional. They will never be forgotten!

Acknowledgments

I am grateful to the many colleagues who have recognized and supported my passion for teaching about life through death. I would especially like to thank Robert White, Linda Haas, Bill Gronfein, Eric Wright, Carol Gardner, David Ford, and Ain Haas. I am grateful to Herman Saatkamp, Jr., for his support. I am honored to have him as an advocate and colleague. My colleagues in the School of Medicine and Program in Medical Ethics serve as exemplary role models for me, for their students, and for other colleagues. My belief in the value of ethics and humanities in the healthcare professions is continually reinforced by the everyday role they play as the ethical soul and conscience of the Indiana University School of Medicine. They are: Greg Gramelspacher, Meg Gaffney, Richard Gunderman, Gary Mitchell, and David Orentlicher. I would like to thank Bill Schneider of the Program in Medical Humanities for his support of this project and other related efforts in the area of thanatology. A special debt of gratitude is owed to Doris Merritt for her belief in the value of my work, and for her faith in me. I thank the Indiana Health Ethics Network for their interest in and support of my efforts to understand and improve the care of the dying. My colleagues in the Living with Dying project are vital sources of support and collegiality. In addition to those already mentioned in other capacities, I want to thank David Smith, Jenny Girod, Betsy Fife, and Dan Pesut for their support of me, and of our continuing effort to improve the care of dying persons. Jerry K. Shepherd, Tina Wiesert, Alice Wong, and Jaime Van Zant have worked hard and provided invaluable assistance in the preparation of this manuscript.

Writing is a solitary endeavor. I am indebted to Linguine, Sambuca, Tubettini, Minestrone, and Spumone for their constant companionship, on my desk, throughout the writing of this book. They are virtually co-authors. Certainly, it is their feline humility and utter absence of need for fame or recognition that prevents their names from appearing on the title page of this manuscript.

I am grateful to my students at Indiana University. They are very special, make my job of teaching enormously rewarding, and have taught me much in return. I am very appreciative of their support and recognition of my efforts on their behalf.

It was Camus and Dostoyevsky who advanced the theme that the path to joy leads through suffering. While this book is clearly about human suffering, I hasten to emphasize that my intellectual and professional passions are driven by a love of and respect for life. It may very well be that, on a personal and societal level, the folkways of dying are the richest representation of human self-expression. It may also very well be that the ways in which human beings face up to the mystery that is the end of life is the final and greatest statement about the value and meaning of life itself. In this way, candid awareness and understandings of mortality and of the life experience of dying persons are essential to understanding the pathways to joy and the means of achieving authenticity in living. Listen carefully to the words of the sick and dying persons throughout the pages of this book. They express two very important messages. One indicts the horribleness of the modern experience of dying; the other loudly affirms the sweetness and essential goodness of living. Thus, this study of death is a study of life. It is motivated by a personal and professional belief in the value and intrinsic beauty of life. It is also driven by my conviction that in facing mortality and committing ourselves to the relief of suffering, the splendor and meaning of life is deepened and enriched.

David Wendell Moller, Ph.D.

Précis

"Are you dying?" . . . "Why? Can't you see I am?" . . . "Well, get on with your dying; don't raise a blamed fuss over that job. We can't help you" [1, p. 331].

Joseph Conrad

In the twentieth-century rush to technologize medicine, the hospital has become an inappropriate place to die. The earlier fear of hospitals as the place where poor people went to die has been overcome. Most people admitted to hospitals are now discharged alive. Thanks to biomedical inventiveness a few remain dying for a long time. When the brain ceases to function, the heart muscle can be kept beating. Quaternary care has become awesome.

Caught up with new medical knowledge—mostly, with halfway technologies—physicians, always uncomfortable with failure, are more reluctant than ever to give up. Technologies are applied beyond reasonable expectations that patients can be restored to functioning human beings. So long as the heart muscle can be kept beating, there is a wish, almost unconscious, that the body ensemble will achieve a recognizably living condition. Who knows? Tomorrow a new biomedical discovery may bring the patient around.

Yet, even as more and more people die in the hospital, it is less and less considered to be an appropriate place to die. Other institutions called hospices have sprung up, to better serve the dying. Hospices are not yet so plentiful, however, that they can take over the dying from the hospitals. Physicians in hospitals are dedicated to the prevention of dying. Physicians do not define themselves as ministering to the dying. So long as physicians maintain their authority in hospitals, dying patients will be kept from death by available technology.

Yet dying patients do eventually die, and for some this may take a long time. How does the hospital, particularly the attending physician, deal with this? Not very well, according to medical ethicist and sociologist David Moller. Applying a sociomedical perspective to complement the biomedical perspectives of hospital physicians, Moller critically examines medical folkways in the hospital with respect to dying. He finds that physicians see no purpose in dying. He argues that if we understood more about dying we would gain in our power to "design personal and social systems of living, that are creative, constructive and meaningful." By way of the intensive, scholarly study he reports here, Moller has become an advocate of the dying, seeking to reduce their socially enforced isolation.

Dying is not only rejected by hospital physicians as a condition they feel prepared to deal with professionally, but is also neglected in the larger social sphere. How does society respond? Dying is avoided as a subject for conversation. Attention is directed to doing physically possible things. We are lacking in socially acceptable routines in dealing with dying. There are no standards, guidelines, or codes. The subject is suppressed as being too depressing. It becomes a totally private phenomenon with which few of us are prepared to deal. Technological concerns displace or, at least, dampen social and emotional involvement. Dying is a reflection on the failure of technology; and modern medicine is nothing if not technology.

Lest he be misunderstood as attacking how physicians respond to dying, Moller does not single out modern medicine as unique or even peculiar in its technological orientation. Rather, he places it in the broader society with its technological emphasis. Technologizing is one of two major social forces which has led to the isolating and falsely hopeful experience of the dying. The second is the cultural value of individualism as manifested in the human potential movement. These two powerful and pervasive social forces are merged in the managing, packaging, and containment of dying as an individual experience subject to unrealistically indefinite, technological postponement. The dying role decimates individual dignity and identity, converting the individual to the "low status of a second-class citizen."

Moller calls for a more candid, open approach to dying which will recognize dying as a normal, social phenomenon as well as a deeply personal, individual experience. He counsels us to abandon technologic intimations of immortality. The creative efforts of individuals, heroic and moving as they may be when confronting dying, need to be buttressed by social legitimization in the form of "prescribed societal rituals, folkways and meaning sets." Individuals and their social networks should not be left entirely to their own resources in coping with dying. Moller wants social recognition of the meanness of dying, especially oncological dying in the hospital, the subject of his empirical observations, with its "experiences of alienation, stigma, helplessness, pain, suffering, normlessness and turbulence."

The current societal approach to dying is silent avoidance. Cultural variation in funeral arrangements is a social response to the actual occurrence of death, not to dying. There are no dying "images and themes" in ordinary social intercourse. This is a twentieth-century phenomenon, unlike preceding centuries. Dying is now shameful, dirty, improper, and a social evil since it is outside of technological control. It is disinfected by medicalization in the hospital technocracy. As Glaser and Strauss have shown, the reality of dying is hidden by conspiratorial interaction of doctors, nurses, patients, and their families [2].

Moller identifies dehumanization of medical care as a structural force, rooted in the way physicians are trained and perpetuated by the peer culture and organization of medical work. With Renée Fox he recognizes the importance of the human anatomy laboratory with its cadavers as the place where medical students learn detached concern, even callousness. In the case of the dying, physicians' priorities are activities which medically benefit patients. When doctors note that death is imminent, Moller observed "a formal and regular rush to move on to the next patient and on to another floor." He concludes that there is increasing normlessness with respect to how physicians should relate to dying patients. As medical technology becomes more rational, more uncertainty is introduced into interactions between physicians and dying patients, leaving this to individual physicians and patients.

The ultimate powerlessness of the dying is reflected in the behavior not only of the patient, but also in that of the physician and the hospital. Family and friends are limited in their experience with dying as a social phenomenon. Society has as yet failed to provide the necessary rules for processing the inevitable ultimate failure of science and technology to prevent what is, after all, a universal social as well as biological event.

Moller is not content with phenomenological description and analysis. He further provides us not only with social diagnosis, but also calls for social prescriptions. Social rules and behavior need to be invented for the social phenomenon of oncological dying and put into practice in order to respond to:

- the sense of isolation of dying patients and loved ones
- the feelings of powerlessness of dying patients and loved ones
- the devaluation of the dying experience
- the downward path of pain, suffering, and deterioration experienced by the dying person
- the stigma of dying
- the hopelessness, helplessness, ugliness, anxiety, and frustration of the dying process
- the unrelieved pain of oncological dying
- the feelings of vulnerability when emotional and social needs are inadequately met
- the feelings of self-blame, guilt, and dependency
- the feelings of rejection as a sexual being
- undignified dying patient behavior, such as anger, cantankerousness, and behavioral expression of private, negative feelings
- romantic, sentimental, and overly-inflated expressions of grief.

Such social rules and behavior could, according to Moller:

- re-introduce a peaceful sense of harmony between dying people and the process of dying
- provide the support of community participation in dying rituals
- be a force for the harmonious acceptance of the coming of death as ordinary and natural process as opposed to a social evil
- emphasize the comforting roles of fellowship, ritual, and ceremony
- facilitate, even mandate, the notion that dying should be a culturally shared community experience
- culturally legitimate the pain and suffering that often typifies the experience of dying
- provide a common base of participation and sense of belonging; attach the dying person to the community of the living.

This prescriptive catalogue of social rules and behavior could, in David Moller's view, transform and retrieve the process of dying from a medicalized technology to a natural social experience. As plausible and rational as his analysis, diagnosis, and prescription seem, it remains to be seen how compliant society will be. In any case, he has vividly reminded us that dying is a social phenomenon as well as an individual event; and that attention to its social components may provide us with social dignity when faced with an inevitable biological occurrence.

REFERENCES

1. J. Conrad, The Nigger of Narcissus, in *The Portable Conrad* (Revised Edition), M. D. Zabel (ed.), Penguin Books, New York, reprinted 1977.
2. B. Glaser and A. Strauss, *Awareness of Dying,* Aldine, New York, 1965.

Jack Elinson

Table of Contents

Introduction

There is no love of life without despair of life [1, p. 56].

Albert Camus

A man in his mid-fifties sat on the edge of his hospital bed, holding onto his IV pole. He had extensive involvement of cancer in his kidneys, and his healthy cell tissue was rapidly being replaced by the accumulation of water in the abdominal area. The twenty or twenty-five pounds of fluid which had accumulated in his stomach provided an absurd contrasting image to his otherwise frail frame. His oncologist walked into the room in midafternoon and found him disoriented, slightly hallucinatory, in danger of falling out of bed and toppling over onto his IV connection, and very much alone. The bed-tray had been pushed to one corner of the room, where it remained with medicines that were not administered and with food that had not been eaten.

When the oncologist returned later that evening, the man's wife had come to visit him after work. The patient was lying securely in his bed, but his bed-tray was still full with uneaten food and unadministered medicines. The doctor began talking to the man's wife, telling her that her husband would not be released over the weekend. He told her that she simply would not be able to manage him at home, so it would be best if he stayed where he was. He also commented that they would have to wait and see how he was progressing, and then begin to think about letting him go home during the middle of the following week. (The physician, however, had fully anticipated that this patient would die sometime over the weekend, if not that very night.) He also expressed his belief that the patient should have someone attend him around the clock. While voicing some concern over whether or not this could be managed financially, he felt it would be best for the patient's safety, given his worry about the patient's disorientation and newly-developed inclination of trying to get out of bed. The patient's wife responded that if it needed to be done, she would go ahead and make the necessary arrangements with the hospital cashier. The oncologist informed the wife that one of his associates would be making rounds over the weekend and he wished her good night.

1

The physician, upon leaving the patient's room, summoned one of the floor nurses and gave her verbal instructions (which were also appropriately written into the patient's chart) on what needed to be done for the patient, including making sure that his medications were fully administered.

In this brief case example, there are many ordinary processes related to modern dying that are taking place. There are no medical heroics involved, there is no extraordinary machinery in place, and the patient was admitted onto a general medical floor. In a certain sense, the situation of this dying patient is quite normative and commonly found in modern hospital settings. The patient had been treated for his disease for nine months, and he had been in and out of the hospital several times. He was still getting chemotherapy, and was receiving additional medical treatment for the symptoms that occurred from his disease. At this point, the patient was basically in an "auto-pilot" situation, a medical holding pattern where his symptoms would be actively treated, and a wait-and-see attitude had developed on whether he would live for days, a week, a month, or die very soon.

Death, of course, is present in this holding pattern, but then again it is very much absent. In terms of physician interaction with the patient and his wife, the idea or possibility of death—not to mention the reality that the patient was dying—was never discussed. Indeed, dying was isolated from conversations that took place, and the conversations which took place steered attention away from death. It was clear, though, that the issue of dying was very much in the heart, mind, and tearful eyes of the patient's wife. However, the physician masterfully orchestrated the course of interaction away from dying and guided it toward practical, technical, medical matters. It is in this way that dying becomes very difficult to detect; it is disguised as the need for physical management and symptom treatment, and thereby is excluded from the regular, ongoing flow of doctor-patient, doctor-family interaction.

The absence of culturally established guidelines and moral codes to preside over dying leaves patients and loved ones confused and anxious. They frequently feel that they are inadequate participants in their own experience, often not knowing how to act or what to say. Physicians typically ignore the personal chaos experienced by patients and their families. They instead focus on technical and physical concerns. This process whereby the personal issues of dying are redefined into technical matters is not only consistent with their training and social organization of work, it also serves to reshape the human experience of dying into disease focus and treatment options. As we will see, this enables healthcare professionals to work each day in an environment where dying and death abound without having to deal with the emotions and social issues of dying and death. Dying, as a messy, complex, and profoundly meaningful personal experience, is consequently isolated in the private world of patients and loved ones. While patients and their loved ones are understandably concerned with the overriding question, "Is this dying or death?," the personal issues of dying are not an agreeable topic of conversation with physicians. Thus, patients, families, and physicians approach the experience of dying from sharply divergent perspectives. Patients and families experience deep personal and social implications of dying, whereas physicians adopt a preeminently technical approach in their patterns of care.

It is this pattern of interaction that invokes a deafening silence about dying and death, which is a penultimate source of social isolation for the dying patient. The emotional neutrality and objective-technical emphasis of the medical caretakers facilitate the isolation of emotional and social needs of dying patients. This often means that patients live in a private, personal, isolated, and encapsulated world. In this way, one of the major consequences of the technological management of the process of dying is to remand and banish the human meanings of dying to the private, isolated milieu of patients and their loved ones.

The theme of controlling the experience of dying through technological manipulation and through the social isolation of individuals is central to this book. I will explore how the American value of individualism and the widespread commitment to technology have given rise to particular forms of governing the process of dying that are unique to the professional dominance of death in the hospital setting. I will focus attention on how the values of technology in the broader society are applied in the framework of medicalized care of dying patients, and discuss the consequences this has for their lives. Additionally, I will analyze how the value of individualism, so ubiquitous in the broader society, influences the treatment of dying patients and their definition of the meanings of their own dying. In this way, I will show how the dominant values of the American cultural system are institutionalized in the medical treatment of dying patients.

My explicit purpose is to analyze dying and death in the cosmopolitan, modern setting. There is, however, an additional theme that is implicit in my analysis and observations. The portrait of dying, which is provided in the pages to follow, also tells us a great deal about life. It demonstrates that the foundation for the medicalization of death that piercingly shapes the life experience of dying persons and loved ones is a product of the ways of life in the broader culture. As emphasized in the Preface, the styles and patterns of dying and death are reflective of the styles and patterns of life in a particular historical and cultural circumstance. Indeed, the more I study and learn about death and dying, the more I am convinced that the way one dies is a reflection of the way one lives. This is not just relevant for the personal, private lives of individuals. It is also true on a societal level. In particular, the circumstances of an individual's private life—the quality of relationships, spirituality, personality characteristics, etc.—are significant to the unique way each person will endure his or her own dying experience. More broadly, the dominant patterns of life and socialization in the larger society will significantly shape and define the contours of the collective dying experience in American society. In addition, the values and institutional arrangements of the broader society significantly influence how individuals craft their own personalized meanings and response to dying. Thus, an interesting reciprocal relationship between life and death is apparent: the styles of death are a reflection of the ways of life, and the ways of life establish the styles of death [2, p. 236]. Hence, the study of death ultimately is a study of life.

It is precisely for these reasons that the study of death, which on the surface appears to be morbid, is one of the deepest pronouncements of the love of life. First and foremost, I have rarely witnessed more appreciation of life than I have observed in those individuals who are coming to the end of life. They truly are inspirational teachers about life and its joys. In addition, on a more scholarly level, the issues raised by the study of death are seminal to the study of life. Issues such as meaning, the significance of suffering, the need for social support and intimacy, integrity of the body, and yearnings for spiritual connection are not just narrowly related to death and dying. They are central to the human condition and are major issues defining patterns of life in America today.

The study of death also offers possibilities for transforming the conditions of life. The study of the suffering, agony, dilemmas, pain, and terrors of dying persons can lead to explanations and understandings that have the potential for improving their lives. In a corollary vein, the life experience of dying persons and loved ones is a signal indicator of how the quest for meaning, satisfaction, and joy in living is being fulfilled on a daily basis for all citizens. By approaching the study of dying as a cultural and structural reflection of living, we can obtain insight into dying and living which is sensitive to and affirms the value of life for all human beings—healthy, disabled, sick, or dying. If there was one dominant unspoken message which I read in the eyes of the dying patients whose lives and sufferings so enrich this book, it ran something like this:

> Tell your students, your readers that despite the incomprehensibility of our sufferings, this is truth, not fiction. Revel in the joy and goodness of life. For as we, the dying, thirst for health, normalcy, and a future those of you with all of these gifts at your doorstep owe it to us not to take life and its splendor for granted. Appreciate each breath that you draw, for someday soon, each of us is going to be dead for an awfully long time.

The most important message of these dying patients was not about death. It was about life.

This book, with the landscape of modern life and death which it portrays, is devoted to understanding and honoring the lives and sufferings of all dying persons—both present and future.

REFERENCES

1. A. Camus, *Lyrical and Critical Essays*, Random House, New York, 1968.
2. D. W. Moller, *Confronting Death: Values, Institutions, and Human Mortality*, Oxford University Press, New York, 1996.

CHAPTER
1

Encountering Mortality:
Preliminary Reflections

And now lying and listening in the darkness, he understood his life [1, p. 15].
Herman Broch

Cholera! The thought flashed through Kitty's mind and then a deathlike feeling came over her; she was seized with terror, she struggled for a moment against the night that seemed agonizingly to run through her veins; she felt horribly ill; and then darkness [2, p. 151].
W. Somerset Maugham

Death is the great instrument and facilitator of life! For it is death above all else which makes life precious and irreplaceable. Within the impossible knowledge that our lives will end lies both terror at the prospects of dying, and an opportunity for resurrection and renewal of life. It is ironic that death, which curdles the human heart with fear and constantly shadows each life with the possibility of extinction, is our unyielding companion throughout life's journey. For those who love life and yearn for its experiences, life cannot and does not exist independently from death. There can be no escaping the knowledge that life is temporary, and can be lost at any moment. In this regard, one of the most profound and universal challenges of humanity lies in our personal and collective confrontation with mortality. As we are summoned to meet this challenge, which is uniquely at the center of the human experience, it is important to recognize that the struggle for meaningful and fulfilling life must come face-to-face with the realities of suffering, of pain, of sorrow, and of death.

Perhaps the human spirit, with great influence from contemporary values and folkways, can avoid and "conquer" death through pretense and denial. This avoidance, however, is more illusion than productive accomplishment. In truth, we never fully escape the knowledge that we are destined someday to grieve the loss of loved ones as well as die ourselves. It is within this framework of knowing that a serious and successful passage through life must come to terms with death.

The mysteries of mortality are integral to the mysteries of life. The pursuit of self-knowledge and self-acceptance must reconcile the facts of death with the facts of life. It may be ironic that the process of nurturing and caring for life must include preparations for endings of life. The ongoing attempt to avoid the confrontation and encounter with mortality only serves to deepen our fears and heighten our anxieties. In this way, freedom from death in life is only obtained by active engagement with death throughout life. As Sherwin Nuland advises, it is only by frank discussions of the very details of dying can we best deal with those aspects that frighten us the most. It is by knowing the truth and being prepared for it that we rid ourselves of that fear of the terra incognita of death that leads to self-deceptions and disillusions [3, p. XVII].

Today, dying is filled with images of unmitigated suffering and horror. As we have progressed throughout the twentieth century, the styles of everyday life have become increasingly incompatible with facing the burden of mortality. Suffering, dying, and death have lost their presence in modern cultural life, and have been systematically separated from visible and public patterns of social activity. Of course, the confrontation with death remains an inevitable part of human experience. In the modern context, however, encounters with mortality have become increasingly concealed and privatized. Coinciding with this trend toward invisibility and privatization is the vanishing of norms and rituals that once helped to guide individuals through the dying process. In the contemporary milieu, where the cultural devaluation of death has given rise to pervasive patterns of avoidance, the human drama of dying is often sequestered in hospitals and redefined into a clinical and technological matter.

Images of denial have replaced images of familiarity and acceptance. Anxiety about the indignities of hi-tech, medicalized death continues to grow. In this regard, the intersection between the facts of modern life and the facts of modern dying has become increasingly strained and shaped by a gnawing sense of unease and confusion. Consider, for example, how difficult it is to talk openly and comfortably about death. Although very simple to pronounce, dying-death-dead are words which are difficult to say and to hear. When we must talk about mortality, our utterances are usually shrouded in euphemisms such as: "passed away," "kicked the bucket," "bought the farm," and "is with God now." Medically based euphemisms are also widespread, reflecting both clinical detachment and duplicity: "the patient has expired," "respirations have ceased," "the patient is no longer with us," and "the patient has gone sour." For many people, even more unsettling than talking openly about death is the actual confrontation with dying. Families are typically overwhelmed with unease and anxiety when witnessing a loved one die. They regularly complain about not knowing what to do or say. They frequently feel impotent and helpless in the face of suffering that seems so alien to the rest of their lives. And individuals, when faced with the diagnosis of life-threatening illness, are often paralyzed with fear upon receiving the news. We can only imagine the terror that grips the heart when a malignancy is discovered, as if the disease itself was an incarnation of evil. As we will see, not only does the encounter with mortality elicit feelings of fear and anxiety, it often results in patients being outraged by and ashamed of what is happening to them.

This growing unease in the face of life-threatening disease stems from the inability of the modern styles of life to establish sanctity, solace, and meaning in death. Our popular culture is filled with illusions of life and beauty eternal. The worldly and physical icons of exciting and dynamic lifestyles, sexy bodies, and materialistic comfort are tied to the development of immortal longings. This environment, which oozes with media-fed images of physical beauty and shiny new products, creates and disseminates the pipe-dream that our earthly bodies will never shrivel with sickness, die, disintegrate, or decompose. Indeed, it is the energy, folkways, and the organization of modern life that conceal the personal, social, and physical realities of death, rendering the human encounter with mortality all the more difficult to ponder. In this way, suffering, dying, and death disappear from everyday life, and the certainty of dying, death, and decomposition of our bodies becomes unfathomable and inapplicable to the self-reflections and cultural experiences of most persons.

Additionally, in a world where we amass and jealously guard our possessions, the tendency is to believe that our lives and relationships can be preserved indefinitely. Despite widespread evidence to the contrary, our cultural conceptions of love and intimacy often promote the fantasy that our relationships will last forever—and are forever exciting and dynamic. In this regard, despite rationally knowing that our relationships are finite, we imagine that our lives will be spared the horror and sorrow of the deaths of those we love. This is part of our reluctance to speak freely and comfortably about such matters and contributes to our inability to productively accompany our loved ones through the ending of their lives. In this way, the prevailing styles of life leave us typically unprepared for and inept at coping with sorrow and devastating loss. They also reinforce our personal and collective need to continually reinvent strategies for denial and avoidance.

La Rochefoucauld may be correct in observing that death and the sun are not to be looked at steadily. Goëthe may also be on target in observing that death is, to a certain extent, an impossibility that becomes a reality. Historically, however, Western society went to great lengths to enable humankind to confront mortality in direct and open ways. Despite variations in form throughout the ages, the community gathered around the deathbed and death was celebrated through solemn and meaningful ceremony. The patterns of traditional death provided for moral guidance and social support, and established death as a public and community affair. The individual dying person was anchored by traditions and cultural expectations that enabled him to prepare for death and to face mortality with dignity. In this context, the individual dying person and those who loved her were successfully escorted through the dying process. The looming terror of death and the grip it has on the human experience was confronted directly and openly, thereby allowing the community to assert a meaningful sense of mastery over the ending of life.

This enduring tradition of dealing with death openly, which the historian Philippe Ariès brilliantly chronicles in the *Hour of Our Death* [4], meant that death was a regular and public part of social and cultural life. For example, for many hundreds of years in traditional Western society, large mass graves were used to bury the dead. Bodies were piled on top each other in enormous holes that could accommodate six hundred to fifteen hundred bodies. Of special interest is the fact that in the cemetery there was always one or perhaps two of these mass graves that were fully open and visible. Additionally, a significant amount of social activity typically occurred in the cemetery—in the presence of the open graves and their decomposing bodies. This may seem surprising and even disgusting to modern persons who are accustomed to the facts of death being banished from their eyesight, but it was a matter of indifference and pervasive acceptance in traditional folkways of life. Of great importance in this ultimate connection between death and life is the fact that death, by being public and noticeable, was seen as being both familiar and normal.

The widespread presence of visible and public icons of death continued, in differing ways and manifestations, until the twentieth century. It is not that the dawning of this century instantaneously transformed the ways of dying, eliminating death as a normal and recognizable part of the life of the community. Rather, it is the metamorphosis and culmination of changes in social, political, and industrial life that transfixed the styles of death. Specifically, the emergence of fear and meaninglessness in modern dying is directly associated with two related processes of historical evolution: the abdication of community to individualism and the emergence of a technological and secular worldview. These changes, while essentially originating in the late eighteenth century, proved to have watershed consequences that dramatically altered not just the ways of life but the ways of death. As we shall see repeatedly, individualism and technological reliance have become central forces in the making of death into a meaningless and monstrous experience.

It is my contention that the struggle to confront mortality has become all the more difficult and precarious because the prevailing ways of life are intrinsically hostile to the relief of suffering and the acceptance of finitude. Dying in the modern context has become perceived as an evil; a cultural evil that is not only feared but is morally and socially injurious. Dying terrorizes not only individual dying persons and their loved ones. It also dramatically undermines the legitimacy of prevailing values around which modern living is organized. The forces of individualism, technology, and materialism, which are so prevalent in daily life, are often dysfunctional when they appear in the dying process. In the modern cultural context, we have lost both our collective and personal ability to support dying persons through the devolution of their bodies and the ending of their lives. The dying experience is consequently filled with an enormous sense of abandonment, isolation, and loneliness. As we shall also see, tenuous connections of family and community in the broader society play a significant role in the modern isolation of dying persons. Of equal or perhaps even greater importance is the cultural tendency to exclude death from the threshold of daily life. As dying has become increasingly invisible and vanquished from the collective cultural experience we have become increasingly inept as a nation, as families, and as individuals to tend to the needs of dying persons. In this way, the process of dying has become disconnected from community, family, ceremony, and purpose. As a result, the modern experience of dying is filled with social isolation and emotional estrangement that becomes a source of suffering for dying persons and for loved ones.

One of the reasons dying individuals seem so profoundly unsettled in the modern era is that their sufferings are pushed out of sight and rendered insignificant in the freneticism of everyday activity. Our busy and demanding lifestyles leave little time for facing the demands and complexities of suffering-relief. Cheerfulness, efficiency of activity, and productivity are some of the prevailing behavioral norms that disconnect suffering from the mainstream parameters of cultural life. Their dominant place in the culture often leaves dying persons and loved ones in a private, turbulent world of avoidance and indifference.

In modern death, not only are dying persons separated from systems of social support, they are often plagued by an overwhelming sense of meaninglessness. Our abilities to face death openly and accompany others into their deaths have been impaired because dying and suffering are the exact opposite of the forces that ignite and organize so much of contemporary culture and social life. Dying has become a source of great worry, and its associated sufferings are exacerbated by the absence of ritual, meaningfulness, and social support. As dying has become more difficult and worrisome during the preceding three decades, the tendency has been to turn to hi-tech intervention as a means of controlling and managing the dying process. Hi-tech medical organization of death is safe and emotionally protective as a means of controlling and regulating death. But, to put it simply, from a humanistic standpoint the technologization of dying has also been an abysmal failure! Despite some moderate success in controlling physical pain, medicalization of dying has precipitated a frightening increase in emotional pain and suffering. In fact, within the milieu of hi-tech dying, the deathbed has become a place where suffering rages. It has also evolved into a place of enormous expense, agonizing conflict and moral choice. Presently, one-half of all Americans die entangled in a web of anxiety provoking tubes and machines. It is this prevailing trend toward never ending procedures and shameless technological attacks upon disease that leaves families emotionally and financially drained. It also leaves patients filled with anxiety while longing for equanimity, relief of suffering, and dignity. Thus the burden of care, once reserved for loved ones in a communal setting, has been transferred to the technical arena of the hospital and is now placed under the jurisdiction of physicians. Trained in a technologically predominate manner, physicians themselves are often the last to accept the idea that good patient care often means summoning the courage not to begin or extend treatment in order to prolong life. In addition, as we will painfully witness in subsequent chapters, physicians frequently do not listen to what patients want, communicate inadequately and with half-truths about bad news, and are oblivious to the profound personal suffering of dying persons. In this framework, the organization and culture of technologically-based medicine are frequently at war with patient wishes, needs, and comfort [5, p. 2457].

This process which seeks to exert technological control over death is consistent with the prevailing ideology of industrial progress, namely, that technology adequately developed and properly applied is the most effective way of addressing the problems that afflict the human condition. We live in an age where "new and improved" products and technological "quick fixes" promise to make life more fulfilling and livable. However, as we will see, emotional suffering and the complex connection between life, disease, and dying are neither reducible to nor compatible with the "identify and fix the problem" mindset of technological progress.

THINKING ABOUT THE END OF LIFE: IMAGES AND METAPHORS

It is not accidental that the patient who reveals her experience in Mortality Narrative One (see Chapter 2) begins by filtering the human encounter with cancer and mortality through the lyrics of David Bowie's song "A Space Oddity." She describes herself and her experience through personally meaningful metaphor and analogy:

> I am on a mission that has taken me to a new dimension and I will never be the same. My oncology team—is my Ground Control, always there to give me my "protein pills" and to pat me on the shoulder when I "made the grade." My alienation causes me to feel like I'm floating above the earth.

As this person so perceptively puts it, life-threatening illness spectacularly changes the world for individuals and loved ones. It brings to the forefront, despite even the most aggressive attempts at denial, the confrontation with the growing awareness of the possibility of non-being. In this regard, as Goëthe's "impossible occurrence" becomes increasingly probable one is forced to ponder the imponderable: non-existence, non-consciousness, non-being. As theologian Paul Tillich observes, it is only humans that are aware that non-being is an unavoidable part of being [6]. As he and others have explained, enormous anxiety is produced when humans are forced to think about the self—in both mind and body—not being. It is the incomprehensibility of non-existence, and the inherent disparity between consciousness in life and absence of consciousness in death, that require humanity to ponder and speak about death through images and metaphors.

Symbolism and imagery serve as a buffer which makes the inaccessible accessible, and the unimaginable imaginable. In order to understand the human attempt to comprehend dying and death, it is important to pay attention to the craft of metaphor and image construction. It is for this reason that references to great literature appear throughout this book. It is my belief that insights into the moral, emotional, and social meanings of death lie in both the soul and the genius of the literary artist. I am convinced that as the study of death is of great importance to the study of life, the genius of the artist's insight into suffering, dying, and death is similarly genius of insight into the dynamics of meaningful life and the well-being of humanity.

My goal in this section is to sample some of the images in novels on illness and death in order to explore how physical, psychological, emotional, and moral change occur. These images are not just relevant to the ways in which individuals perceive, experience, and cope with their illness, dying, and death. They are also a barometer of the prevailing culture, and reflect how culturally anchored experiences of illness and death are a product of the values and patterns of life in the broader society.

One of the salient themes that characterize literary images of death is the profound and central role that death plays in life. In *The River Why,* David James Duncan explores the deterioration of the natural environment and the spiritual emptiness of the modern world. Gus Orviston, James' central character, was born and raised to flyfish by messianic parents whose marriage was dominated by the conflict in their contrasting approaches to the art of fishing. When Gus comes of age, with his passion and skills for flyfishing finely honed, he embarks on a personal quest that will consummate his life's persistent desire: to abandon himself to the activity and the environs of flyfishing. Gus pursues his quest with the fervor of a fanatic: relentlessly and obsessively. Yet when his lifelong dream becomes a reality, it quickly proves vapid and meaningless:

> I proceeded to fish all day, everyday, first light to last. All my life I'd long for such a marathon—
> And I haven't one happy memory of it. All I recall is stream after stream, fish after fish, cast after cast, and nothing in my head but the low cunning required the hoodwink my mindless quarry. Each night my log entries read like tax tables or grocery receipts, describing not a dream come true, but a drudgery of double shifts on a creekside assembly line [7, p. 75].

The story of Gus Orviston is an allegory of modern life and modern individuals who, achievement after achievement, deal after deal, acquisition after acquisition, are ultimately left spiritually and humanly barren. The good news for Gus—and the challenge for all of us as we journey through our lives—is that he used his emerging sense of emptiness as an opportunity for self-reflection and transformation. In fact, even in the frenzy of his daily activity, questions about the purpose of life slosh and seethe in his mind:

What is Death/ What is life/ Why am I here? What am I here for stuff. What use were such questions? Hobgoblins—that's all they were—noisy abstract—good for nothing but scaring and depressing hell out of everybody they occurred to. . . . *But . . . everyone I knew would be dead. This was no abstraction. What could it mean? What should I do about it? Was there equipment to purchase to protect myself from it? Was there reference material to peruse that would make it comprehensible? Pills to pop to make it bearable? . . . I didn't know. I didn't know anything about anything. Everything in my head came from fishing magazines, fishing manuals, and fishing novels. And what did these works have to say about the meaning of Life and Death?* [7, p. 108].

The very process of pondering the meaning of mortality was an epiphany of sorts for Gus. All the while he continued in his frenzy of fishing he was bombarded with "unstoppable," "unanswerable," "unbearable" questions about death and its place in human life. Despite the inclination to resort to familiar patterns of avoidance and denial, Gus resists and musters the courage to face his sense of personal and spiritual hollowness squarely. And then suddenly:

. . . all thought and pain and awareness came to a standstill. I wasn't miserable anymore. I wasn't anything anymore . . . I was aware of one thing only: **NEXT TO THE GAPING FACT CALLED DEATH, ALL I KNEW WAS NOTHING, ALL I DID MEANT NOTHING, ALL I FELT CONVEYED NOTHING** [7, p. 112] (emphasis added).

Gus' realization was profound. He came to see how death transforms the essence of life like nothing else. In his new found comprehension he not only understands that someday he would die, but also that the inevitability of death created a special urgency to find ways of living that are sane and meaningful. This quest, David James Duncan argues, is the only way to free ourselves from the prison of death's certainty and terror. For Gus, the search for meaningful life led to fellowship, love, and intimacy. It was by embracing and nurturing the ability to love that the cold emptiness of modern, materialistic life could be transformed and filled with joy. And, not only does the capacity for love offer possibilities for peaceful and joyful life, it is love, and "love alone," which enables us to reach and touch God, and achieve the fulfillment of spiritual meaning.

The yearning for spiritual fulfillment in an era that fosters materialism and technological pursuits is also a central theme in the literature on dying, suffering, and death. In his brilliantly crafted novel *After Many a Summer Dies The Swan*, Aldous Huxley argues that the gravest error a person can make is to accept the world the way it is and submit to the prevailing culture of materialism. Mr. Stoyle, Huxley's central figure in the novel, did exactly this:

> Like all the others he had allowed the advertisers to multiply his wants; he had learnt to equate happiness with possessions, and prosperity, with money to spend in a shop [8, p. 107].

Huxley argues that the underpinning of Western Capitalism stimulates an endless desire for possessions and entices and enslaves people in a tyranny of materialism and narcissism. Yet, when we probe beyond the surface of life, people yearn for more:

> They want their lives to have some sense [8, p. 175].

As Huxley observes, the task of creating meaning in our lives is universal to humanity. The contemporary inability to successfully find meaning, however, is connected to the value of materialism and the controlling social impact of technological development. If meaning in life is to be achieved, it must be connected to the human capacity for love and development of the soul. Soulful living, according to Huxley, stems not from worldly accomplishments. Rather, it is a creation of spiritual experience and triumph which emphasizes qualities such as:

- Knowledge
- Wisdom
- Empowerment of self and others
- Peace
- Joy
- Freedom
- Goodness
- Mind
- Meaningfulness of experience
- Connectedness between persons

While these qualities do exist in the contemporary arrangement of life, Huxley's point is that they are not dominant qualities nor do they define the structural foundation of present day values and patterns of activity. The degree to which individuals are capable of achieving these qualities is a matter of individualized effort, not dominant social trend. In fact, prevailing patterns of life not only hinder the development of these qualities, which are the center of soulful and spiritual living. They actually encourage the development of social patterns that are hostile to soulful and meaningful life. In this soulless social context, driven by materialistic values, the following become major ingredients in contemporary life:

- Information (not to be confused with wisdom or understanding)
- Technique
- Control

- Efficiency
- Fear of others
- Anger
- Feelings of being trapped
- Self-interest
- Emphasis on physical beauty
- Greed and materialism
- Disconnection and isolation
- Power over others

Huxley's portrait of Mr. Stoyle is recognizable as a modern icon of success. He was rich, sophisticated, "owned a showcase in California," and was able to capitalize on progress and technology in order to amass enormous profit. Yet, despite having achieved the kind of life so many dream about, he was haunted by nagging whispers of discontent and was possessed by a terror of death. Especially important is the fact that these values, which Mr. Stoyle had relied on to give energy and significance to his life, began to fail him as he was forced to confront his own mortality. Not only did the devaluation of his materialistic belief system leave him bewildered and yearning for meaning, it increasingly made his personal experience with disease, suffering, and mortality all the more impossible to endure. Even the news of a major financial conquest, which years ago would have thrilled and inspired him to desire more, seemed vapid and unproductive:

> Good news, good news! A year or two from now he would be richer by another million. But the millions were in one world and the old unhappy man was in another, and there was no communication between the two [8, p. 242].

Stoyle's success, power, and wealth were inversely proportionate to his ability to find spiritualism, peace, and meaning in his life. Huxley's point is that the modern, materialistic styles of life ill prepare us to confront our mortality. They also establish ways of death that leave us feeling incomplete and regretful about the ways in which we have lived. And, ultimately, the ways of life and death create and exacerbate enormous suffering and tension when modern individuals are brought face-to-face with their own deaths or the deaths of loved ones. As Huxley opines:

> On the human level, men live in ignorance, craving, and fear. Ignorance, craving and fear result in some temporary pleasures, in many lasting miseries, in final frustration. The nature of the cure is obvious: the difficulties in the way of achieving it, almost insuperable. We have to choose between almost insuperable difficulties on the one hand and absolute misery and frustration on the other [8, p. 324].

The great challenge for humanity is to stand up to the seductive and powerful forces of materialism and narcissism; that is to say, to resist the urge to continually seek refuge in temporary pleasures. Clearly, this is a daunting and difficult task in a culture of materialism. It is, however, essential for meaningful life and for peaceful, meaningful death. To remain steeped in materialistic ways is to live in a manner that promotes both fear of death and enormous suffering while dying. Thus, for Huxley, good death presupposes good life. And, good life requires that we defer the enticements of physical, worldly pleasure in preference to ways of living that cultivate our spirits and souls.

One of the most extraordinary accounts of the meaning of dying and death in life is contained in Herman Broch's *The Death of Virgil*. Not only can the careful reader glean from its 500 pages unforgettable images and metaphors of dying, but the forever haunting impact of Broch's experience in the Nazi concentration camps and its effect on his vision of life and death. The novel is about the last days of life of the Latin poet Virgil, and probes the significance of deathbed turmoil, reflection, and awakenings. In a manner similar to Duncan, Broch illuminates, through Virgil's agony on the deathbed, that an open encounter with mortality transforms the significance and perception of life. Similar to Huxley, Broch forcefully critiques materialism and the pervasive social and human drive for self-indulgence, self-centeredness, and self-seeking. He begins by describing how the world is increasingly given over to greed and the gluttony of materialism, and how in this context humanity is:

> . . . dedicated to a horrible self-imprisoned lust, insatiably desirous of having, desirous of bargaining for goods, money, place and honors, desirous of the bustling idleness of possession . . . everywhere smoldered in avarice and lust . . . the whole ship was lapped in a wave of greed [1, p. 15].

Of special significance for Broch, as revealed by the deathbed reflections of Virgil as he ponders his life and wrestles in anguish about whether to publish the Aenid, is the connection of the love of possessions and the pursuit of wealth to the inability to live meaningfully and to die peacefully. In his deathbed meditation and awakening, Virgil contemplates the ramifications of shallow, self-absorbed living and becomes aware of:

> People's profound capacity for evil . . . and their reversion therewith to the antihuman, brought to pass by a hollowing out of existence, by turning existence toward a mere thirst for superficialities . . . so that nothing remained but the dangerous isolated life of self, a sad, sheer exteriority pregnant with evil [1, pp. 23-24].

This pattern of life is destined to fail. Materialism, greed, and superficiality are at odds with the universal and inescapable yearnings of humanity: to make our lives and deaths make sense. Clearly, although suffering and dying have little place in the materialistic culture they are powerful human experiences that strip away the delusory comfort of materialistic trappings. While suffering at the threshold of death is both naked and agonizing, it also offers opportunity for reflection and transformation. In this regard, despite the fact that death in an era where narcissism and love of material things prevail is seemingly unbearable, dying can give birth to life. Simply, Virgil comes to recognize that his dying is an illumination of his life. On the deathbed he comes face-to-face with how he has lived and the consequences of that life. Thus, Virgil arrives at an understanding that confronting death and exploring its meaning is essential to enlightened, conscious life:

> In truth, only he who is able to perceive death is also able to perceive life [1, p. 325].

It is for this reason, as Virgil lies dying and faces the ending of life, that life's meaning is revealed to him:

> And now, lying and listening in the darkness, he understood his life [1, p. 80].

Specifically, in the throes of death, Virgil has two revolutionary insights: 1) the prevailing ways of life make dying all the more difficult, painful, and horrible; 2) peaceful death can only be achieved by meaningful life, and this requires communion and fellowship with others.

Materialism is not only inherently antagonistic to the yearnings of the soul, it also seeks denial of death. Make no bones about it, materialism offers little sanctuary in the face of extinction. Death renders the power of affluence and status impotent. And, once wealth and narcissism's trappings are debilitated by suffering and dying all that remains is emptiness. Virgil comes to understand that life lived in and squandered by materialism ultimately and painfully proceeds to the point of meaninglessness where:

> Nothing [is] left but icy horror, this crippling and breathtaking horror of death [1, p. 93].

The way out of a squandered life and horrifying death, the triumph over emptiness is in the tending to the soul, especially in connection to the ability to love:

He saw and he knew it would have to pass, because the true law of reality revenged itself irresistibly on mankind . . . when being greater than any manifestation of beauty, it was bartered beauty—plainly affronted by this, despised by being overlooked, high above. . . . there was the law of reality . . . there was the law of the heart, and woe to a world which had forgotten this last reality [1, p. 249].

In his dying, Virgil grasps what so many others in their blindness have failed to grasp:

Love is the reality [1, p. 250].

It is in love, brotherhood, and fulfilling the duty to be of help to others, and not through materialistic indulgence, selfishness, and greed that one can prepare for "eternal salvation," thereby making physical death tolerable and peaceful.

Despite tremendous variation in contextual framework and frame of reference, Duncan, Huxley, and Broch develop similar themes and understandings. In their novels, they commonly explore:

- How dying and death transform life
- How crises of mortality are a cure for living
- The relationship between spiritual yearnings and worldly existence
- The role of love and fellowship in transforming life and death and how one comes to value love through suffering, disease, and dying
- How prevailing styles of life render the ways of death horrific and unbearable.

In these novels, there is severe criticism of having renounced life by becoming inert and submissive to dominant cultural values and folkways. When living a life full of self-indulgence, pursuit of power, wealth, the acquisition of things, self-centeredness, and self-seeking, all of these efforts become fruitless and empty when the self is standing on the threshold of annihilation. It is precisely for this reason that the materialistic cravings of modern society create a need for widespread denial of death. As death is reduced to an experience of irretrievable and icy horror, avoidance of death becomes crucial to protecting and maintaining the prevailing ways of life. A seemingly vicious cycle is begun. As the patterns by which we live our lives exacerbate spiritual longings and ill prepare us for death, resistance to and fear of death increases, eliciting deeper, more pervasive means of denial.

A SUMMARY STATEMENT

Excessive avoidance of suffering, dying, and death can precipitate enormous trouble on both a cultural and personal level. As we will see in the chapters that follow, the inability to confront mortality directly is not just related to the abstract philosophical problem of meaninglessness which is so perceptively captured by

Huxley, Duncan, and Broch. It is also unmistakably tethered to unrelieved and exacerbated suffering in real life. As the voices of dying persons throughout this book will reveal, real people know how hard their dying is and how omnipresent their suffering is. Consequently, while the geniuses of great literature often see disease, suffering, dying, and death as a stimulus for enlightenment and life, real dying individuals typically endure their life in anguish, without the benefit of the insight of the genius, or the deathbed conversions and triumphs that often occur in great literature.

Goëthe says: Misery too has its virtues. I have learned much in illness that I could have learned nowhere else in my life [9]. Thomas Mann similarly echoes the sentiment that suffering and disease offer opportunity for transformation and renewal of life:

Disease has two faces and a double relation to man and his human dignity. On the one hand, it is hostile: by overstressing the physical, by throwing man back upon his body, it has a dehumanizing effect. On the other hand, it is possible to think and feel about illness as a highly dignified human phenomenon . . . In disease resides the dignity of man; and the genius of disease is more human than the genius of health [10, pp. 29-30].

In the framework of literary genius and social philosophy, suffering and dying are catalysts for self-reflection and transcendence. While there can be no doubt that suffering, dying, and death are universally part of the human experience and touch the human heart as nothing else can, enlightenment and metamorphosis in real dying are never as neat and tidy as they are in art and intellectual observation. When they do occur, as the life experiences of real persons will illuminate in following chapters, it is often secondary to and overpowered by misery and distress. And, as also will be shown, the modern dying experience is typically so difficult and horrible that it is bereft of the growth in wisdom and understanding that is portrayed by many artists and intellectuals.

Theory and metaphor provide a framework for examining the meaning of mortality in the human experience. However, they are meaningful beyond the intellectual arena only when they are reflective of and connected to the lives of seriously sick persons as they attempt to confront disease and mortality. Thus, although images from great literature will continue to appear throughout this book because they are a valuable part of the human effort to contemplate dying and death, they are not the heart and soul of my portrait of the modern dying experience. Rather, the real experiences of sick people as they reflect upon and confront their own mortality are the most important part. When theory and metaphor enter into the discussion they do so only in ways that are illustrative and reflective of the lives of real human beings as they attempt to cope with disease; suffer; and die.

REFERENCES

1. H. Broch, *The Death of Virgil,* North Point Press, San Francisco, 1945.
2. W. Somerset Maugham, *The Painted Veil,* Penguin Books, London, 1925.
3. S. Nuland, *How We Die: Reflections on Life's Final Chapter,* Vintage Books, New York, 1993.
4. P. Ariès, *The Hour of Death,* Alfred Knopf, New York, 1981.
5. D. W. Moller, Death, Societal Attitudes Toward, *Encyclopedia of Applied Ethics,* Academic Press, New York, 1997.
6. P. Tillich, *The Courage To Be,* Yale University Press, New Haven, 1952.
7. D. J. Duncan, *The River Why,* Sierra Club Books, San Francisco, 1993.
8. A. Huxley, *After Many a Summer Dies the Swan,* Ivan R. Dee, Chicago, 1993.
9. *Goëthe's World View,* trans, Heinz Norden, New York, p. 157, 1963.
10. T. Mann, Goëthe and Tolstoy, in *Three Essays,* trans. H. T. Howe-Porter, New York, 1929.

CHAPTER
2

Contemplating Death:
Human Voices

"For the fact is, I'm going to die. In six months I'll be dead, gone, no longer here," he kept saying to himself over and over again. . . . the very "idea" was unbearable. Period [1, p. 4].

Françoise Sagan

Now I knew it for sure, he was worse than a dog, he couldn't conceive of his own death [2, p. 9].

Céline

The hope of getting better was only a dream. . . . We must have done something very wicked before we were born, or else we must be going to be very happy indeed when we are dead, for God to let this life have all the textures of expiation and all the sorrows of an ordeal. [3, p. 242].

Alexandre Dumas fils

During the twentieth century, not only have the styles of dying been transformed, but so has the relationship between human beings and mortality. As indicated in Chapter 1, dying, suffering, and death have lost their cultural meaning. As a consequence, these unavoidable facts of human existence have become invisible and isolated from social life. Contemporary images of the deathbed reflect the enormous dread and suffering that has become emblematic of modern death. And, as we will see in rather dramatic fashion in the following chapters, the processes of hi-tech, medicalized death which have become a standard response to the problem of dying emerge from, coincide with, and contribute to the growing inability to cope with suffering and dying in the broader culture. Thus, despite the recent outpouring of literature on death and dying, a deafening silence still remains. Dying persons regularly journey toward their deaths severed from self and self-understandings of what is happening to them. They are also typically alienated from healthcare professionals, loved ones, and community support. Families and loved ones are often withdrawn spectators of the dying process, and overwhelmed by chaotic feelings of frustration, anger, and helplessness.

It is my contention that the humanity in the cultural organization of life, and the test of any system of medical care, lies in the ability to relieve suffering. In this regard, present day cultural and medical systems are failing that test abysmally, especially when it comes to mitigating the suffering of dying persons and loved ones. If and when "dignity" in dying is achieved it tends to be an isolated occurrence of heroic personal effort, not systematic process of care. It is for this reason that successful relief of sorrow and suffering in the shadow of dying have been rendered not just personal and private, but scant. The result is that dying individuals are frequently left to endure their sufferings in an unsupported state of isolation, loneliness, and unexpressed need.

In the present system, dying persons have been cut off from prevailing norms and patterns of life. As one patient told me quite recently: *I feel like I've very much been pushed aside and forgotten about.* As a result of this distancing and its associated disempowerment, the concerns of dying persons have been pushed to the periphery and their voices have been muffled. If suffering is to be relieved and the terrors of dying eased THESE VOICES MUST BE HEARD! The snapshot case narratives which follow express the life experiences of persons coming face-to-face with their own mortality. In some ways they confirm the insights of the literary geniuses' view of death. In other ways, they are different. But most importantly, they establish a venue by which the voices of humans confronting death can be heard, and their needs and concerns can be expressed, not metaphorically or thematically, but directly.

GROUND CONTROL TO MAJOR TOM:
INSIGHTS INTO THE ABYSS OF MORTALITY

The Human Voice of Mortality

I have directly and indirectly found myself starving for sources of nourishment . . . for feelings of support and affirmation . . . but it always seemed to be overshadowed by the elements that they could not control and those that eventually defeated them.

I feel like Major Tom. I feel like I am on a mission that has taken me to a new dimension and I will never be the same. My oncology team is my Ground Control, always there to give me my "protein pills" and to pat me on the shoulder when I "make the grade." My alienation causes me to feel like I'm "floating above the Earth." I don't see my position above being indicative of betterment, so to say, or as indicating superiority. I see my position as a placement into a lonely dimension that causes me to view things differently than most around me. Many times, this position feels like a "tin can." Where my alienation is concerned, I feel there's nothing I can do.

One thing cancer is, is all-encompassing . . . This is something I had to get used to. I think getting used to it happens when I don't give energy to thinking about its constant presence . . . I resent the fact that the pain is always with me. I don't always feel like it is my closest possession, but there are many days that I do. I get very angry during these times when even my love that I share with my life partner seems that it cannot compete with the permeation of cancer.

Pain now dictates almost everything for me, including my sense of or awareness of time. On one hand, it does make the specificity of time seem meaningless. On the other hand, it makes five minutes seem like a lifetime. It is wicked that way. And just when you think you can mentally escape the reality of having cancer, the pain is there to remind you of its presence and to remind you that death is looking over your shoulder. It is this control of my senses through pain that has enabled cancer to be my time clock.

My thoughts often feel this consumed—treatments, dosages, pain, metastasis, destruction of tissues, loneliness, loss of functions, medical bills, etc. Sometimes these thoughts all mount up and I find it nearly impossible to think about anything outside of the illness.

I've gotten to the point, now, that pain is the major consumer of my thoughts. It has taken on a more intensive role than I would have thought possible only one year ago. Morphine has undoubtedly become my best friend, something I could not be functioning without. Morphine provides a haze for me to escape into. This is now an invaluable gift. But it is in these times of escape that the paradox of pain is revealed. When I am able to find relief from the pain in morphine injections and pills, I am still inextricably obsessed with the thoughts of pain—and its return. I am never totally free of the pain, but I am able to gain enough distance to allow me to feel "relief." Despite the "relief," my thoughts are still thinking about how much it's going to hurt when the morphine wears off and the pain rears its ugliest of heads. So it is in this manner that the amount of pain no longer can be a measuring stick for the thoughts about pain.

The enormity of having such pain seems to escape most people who have never experienced it. Regardless of their knowledge of how much cancer I have or where the cancer has penetrated, most people cannot seem to conceptualize the inevitable pain that accompanies such cancer. I get so angry with people about this—about forgetting about the energy that this pain consumes and therefore expecting too much. I usually meet these expectations with an angry reminder that I have brain tumors and therefore one hell of a headache. I resent this about people. It feels cruel; or at the very least, it takes the energy that I desperately need for endurance of pain and illness. I know my choice to become angry in response also takes much needed energy, but I can't help but respond in this manner.

It is this aspect of illness that creates in me a desire to withdraw from society. It seems unnecessary, but inescapable—unneeded demands placed on me by people, in addition to the inevitable consequences of cancer. I reach a point when my reactions of anger seem fruitless and too demanding then I retreat to a resignation that most things in life are empty, colorless, and undesirable.

More analytically speaking, cancer, and illness in general, seem to be a litmus test for the place that people are in. In my experience, cancer has provided a test for how much the people in my life are able to give. Consequently, it has provided for me a new set of lenses through which to view relationships with people. For the most part, the results have been undesirable and even sad. I have become disappointed in so many people. On the flip side, I have found depth and sincerity in people who I may have otherwise never appreciated. On most days I can acknowledge that the few people in whom I have found despair I have felt through the inabilities of those who have disappointed me. It is the few that I cherish which I try to focus on. When I do think of others, I feel anger, resentment and judgment, but I feel the deepest part of me holds no grudge. These people just seem not able to give much. I do acknowledge that my needs right now are enormous. The irony is that I seem not to only absolve them of obligations to give, but I additionally take on the burden of giving to them.

I will never be the same for having cancer. Although many events and periods in my life have had tremendous influence on the person that I have become, nothing can be considered analogous to the effect that cancer has had. Even the other events and people in my life that have been influential seem to be placed in a distant sphere. The life I lived before cancer seems uniquely disconnected from the life I now live, and the life I will live in the future.

Impact. Realization. Enormity. Cancer is full of these. Of all the incredulous aspects, the most frightening and even foreign is the enormity of death always being near. This is not to say that I have not had times when I felt like this disease was my ultimate demise. I have had those times. Though I always have tried to have a positive outlook and mindset, and usually truly did have such, there have been times when my realization of my reality came in the form of thinking of myself as a dying person. For instance, driving and listening to my Beatles tapes, and out of the blue hearing in my mind, "My God, I'm dying!" At first, these moments were intense and scary. They would be tempered by the intellectual and rational part of me that placed my intimate feelings in the real of academic speculation about the death experience. This is something I have distantly and academically thought about much in my life.

I feel that my loss of fear came through acknowledging that I wasn't going to succumb to the cancer. I know that there is a chance that I could die. This was my first necessary step of realization. Once I acknowledged this real possibility, I was able to assess the condition of my will to live. Most days, this is strong. It is always strong in relation to the cancer. It is on those days when people and the society make this world seem like an undesirable place to live that I feel like my will to live is insufficient to endure this challenge.

It is on these days when I think that it is probably more realistic to resign myself to inevitable death, considering the great pain and exhaustion I feel and acknowledge when I look inward.

The feelings I have on these days do seem like a contradiction. I've always been passionate, zealous, and the person who always got up, dusted herself off, and continued the fight. But as I feel like not getting up, I do feel ashamed, because I do attribute the lack of desire to feelings of unworthiness. I cannot have my life end on that kind of note. So for me, the sweet amazement is found in this despair being ultimately transformed into renewal. My experience with cancer has provided me with a series of renewals. Once this renewal is found, I am able to appreciate the fighter that I am, and therefore I see myself as a testimony to endurance and human capabilities.

In the cancer experience, maintaining and finding self-worth is incredibly difficult, but imperative. Amidst the processes of tissue destruction, the tissue invasion, and dehumanization through bodily changes, the process of adjustment to this new self as your being is crucial. It's a difficult and continual process of viewing the changing self, and then bonding with it.

I'm not wanting to make this adjustment process sound easy. For me, it has been one of the hardest aspects. At one time I was an athlete with scholarships, who was in scholarship form. I always compare my physical shape and condition to that image of myself in my mind. Now that I am thirty pounds heavier, because of the steroid medications, it causes me great stress to be in the shape I am in. Additionally, I have lost 60 percent of my total hearing and 50 percent of my vision. I've lost almost all of my hair, and most of the time I have enough needle marks on my arms to look like I'm a heroin addict. Because of all this, most days I try not to look in the mirror, so I can still pretend that I look like anything other than a cancer patient. But this coping mechanism, itself, is detrimental. It's a bad place to be in when you don't want to look in the mirror, regardless of the reason. It is at this point that I remember the other component of being an athlete—the psychological mindset.

Survive is what I am going to do. I'll never give up hope. Giving up hope is the worst death of all; it is the most painful death. As in the case of the physical self, cancer does not have to equal spiritual death. I have known cancer survivors who have experienced a spiritual death from having had cancer. Although, in my given place, I cannot imagine ever experiencing spiritual death from this experience, I can understand how it happens. In my experience and in my observations, I think that cancer is like an ocean. The cancer patient is an overboard passenger, treading water and having only two choices—grab the lifesaver or succumb to the enormity of the ocean. I've chosen to grab the lifesaver, because each day I hold on, I am living—I am life.

The insights of this individual are profound as is her anguish. Living in the shadow of terminal illness, dying is her constant companion and source of a multiplicity of sufferings: physical, existential, and social. These sufferings are related not just to the inherent torment and misery of dying. Rather, they are exacerbated by the prevailing ways of life which surround her and which are hostile to the ease of her suffering and the promotion of comfort.

First and perhaps foremost, the dying process wreaks havoc upon the body, precipitating both a corresponding devolution in personhood and an imperative to redefine oneself through a framework of disease, suffering, and death. As this individual contemplates:

... I am thirty pounds heavier ... I have lost 60 percent of my total hearing and 50 percent of my total vision. I've lost almost all of my hair, and most of the time I have enough needle marks on my arms to look like a heroin addict.

Of special significance for her is the consequence that her physical deterioration has for herself as a human being and her self-perception thereof:

Because of all this, most days I try not to look in the mirror, so I can still pretend that I look like anything other than a cancer patient.

Pain is a central component of her physical suffering. It is gnawing, agonizing, unmitigated, unceasing, and became predominate in her life. As she expresses, pain has become an intimate and regular companion—her "closest possession" and the "major consumer of (her) thoughts." In relationship to her disease, there is enormous physical ache and agony. The throbbing and burning of her body may have been temporarily eased by the morphine haze that quickly became her "best friend," but she was never fully emancipated from pain physically or psychologically.

Although technical intervention may have brought oblivion and relief from the pain for a few hours, she remained intensely conscious of it and its place in her life. As part of this consciousness of pain and suffering she began to recognize how undersupported she was as she confronted her disease. She states ever so clearly that those who have not gone through a similar experience—and in this age of death denial and suffering avoidance the number of people is huge—can hardly conceive of the crushing consequences of serious disease upon the body and the spirit:

> The enormity of having such pain seems to escape most people . . . most people cannot seem to conceptualize the inevitable pain that accompanies cancer. I get so angry with people about this—about forgetting about the energy that this pain consumes and therefore expecting too much (of me). I usually meet these expectations with an angry reminder that I have brain tumors and therefore one hell of a headache. I resent this about people. It feels cruel . . .

Cruelty in this case is not just a result of the belligerency of disease; it is directly connected to cultural and social neglect.

A select few persons were capable and willing to provide support. She is deeply grateful to them as they brought relief and comfort to her life. Yet, their support ultimately proves to be inadequate. She finds that her disease overwhelms even her closest, most intimate support systems. And, most discouragingly, she finds that most people lack empathy and compassion for her. When this absence of support merges with the harsh physical realities of coping with cancer and mortality, her tendency is to retreat from the world. In this retreat, however, there is neither peace nor solitude. Rather, emotional chaos and social isolation reign:

> . . . illness creates in me a desire to withdraw from society . . . I retreat to a resignation that most things in life are empty—colorless—undesirable.

If we listen carefully to her voice, she is telling us that her experience with disease and mortality have become all the more cruel because of the absence of systems of meaning and support that could escort and comfort her on each step, and during each moment of her most difficult journey. In this regard, not only is her disease violent in its ravaging of her body, but the broader culture is antagonistic to her by its indifference to her needs. As a result, the natural difficulty that is inherent to coping with disease and mortality is culturally intensified.

In large part, the physical and social suffering that she is enduring establishes the foundation for her existential suffering. Not only does she find herself alienated from the world, she is alienated from herself. As her disease changes her body and transforms her self-concept, she becomes increasingly unknown to herself—a physical and emotional stranger. It is as if her-life, her-body, and her-self are spinning out of control into an alien orbit. She herself recognizes this when she says that she feels like Major Tom—"A Space Oddity."

A yearning for some sense of explanation and of purpose for what is happening to her is implicit and consistent throughout her narrative. Her will to live and her determination seem strong. She recognizes what is centrally required of her as she engages in the battle for life:

> . . . Maintaining and finding self-worth is . . . imperative. Amidst the process of tissue destruction, tissue invasion, and dehumanization through bodily changes, the process of adjustment to this new self . . . is crucial.

However, while her resilience, courage, and strength of character are apparent, existential despair and cultural callousness regularly weaken her resolve:

> . . . when people and the society make this world seem like an undesirable place to live . . . I feel that my will to live is insufficient to endure this challenge. It is on these days that I think it is probably more realistic to resign myself to inevitable death considering the great pain and exhaustion I feel . . .

Truly impressive! This woman's resilience and insight are astonishing. Truly distressing, however, is the unrelieved suffering and the unmistakable ache in her soul for meaning, comfort, and support. For those willing and courageous enough to listen, her experience teaches us important lessons about:

- How contemplating disease and mortality deepens self-awareness
- How facing death makes life compelling and precious
- How suffering, disease, dying, and death transform life and revolutionize its meaning
- How unyielding the yearning for fulfillment is, and how much emptiness there is in the contemporary confrontation with mortality
- How deep the yearning for love is, and how overwhelming the disappointment is at both its incompleteness and the unhelpfulness of others
- How much need there is for improving the ways of life in regard to the relief of suffering in the face of disease, dying, and death.

WHEN THE BODY FAILS:
SUFFERING, DESPAIR, COURAGE, AND GROWTH

The Human Voice of Mortality

I saw both Doctor _____ and Doctor _____ today. They didn't seem too concerned. They decided to run a CT scan on my head, I asked them if it was absolutely necessary. I can see the expense now. The baby needs new shoes and I desperately need to take Scott to the dentist. They both assure me that it is just a precaution and that I shouldn't worry, it is probably nothing. I was told that the results wouldn't be in for several days, that I should go home and try to relax. What a joke! My thoughts keep running through my mind of the possibilities of what it could be and how I will ultimately deal with the news when I find out.

My life and the lives of those around me changed today. Sometimes change is welcomed, however, this time I would like to run and hide. But, that won't make this pain go away. Like my mom always said, I need to deal with the cards that were dealt me.

The doctors that assured me just yesterday not to worry called me today to let me know that I had a brain tumor. You know, I think that it would have been hard to hear this news in person, but to call me on the damn phone and to tell me this news is unreal. The only one here is Justin. He was down for his nap, but I had an urgency to wake him and feel the warmth of another human being. I started crying which caused him to cry as well. Mark came home from work and found us both on the floor in the kitchen bawling our eyes out.

I'm only thirty-four years old! I shouldn't have to deal with this, should I? Death has always seemed natural to me at least as long as it was someone else's. I always knew that I would not live on this earth forever. I can't blame God. God didn't cause it. I've always believed that He is the giver of life. It's funny, though, I know that I shouldn't be angry with Him, but somehow I am. How can He let this happen to a mother that hasn't yet seen her sons grow up to become men? I have so much to do.

I guess that I need to face my future, however bleak it seems at this moment in time. The doctors have given me two weeks to live without an operation. They have also shared this wonderful news with me while they were on the phone earlier! They tell me that I won't live to see the next holiday. Is that supposed to scare the hell out of me? The doctors on one hand give me hope with the operation, but on the other hand they are concerned with my paying for this expensive medical care. Does life come down to that? Nickels and dimes.

If nothing else, I'm a realist. I can't leave my family with so many loose strings hanging. I contacted special services this afternoon to see if anything can be done financially. You want to hear something real funny? They say that we make too much money! I laughed. Be real. They tell me that if indeed I die, they will be able to help the boys. Something must be terribly wrong with this country if we put such little value on a human life. Don't I have more to offer to this world if I live? Can only my death release the resources that are needed? They can't offer much help, red tape and all that stuff, they explain. Perhaps if I sell all my stock, sell my car, and reduce my assets to under $2,200 per month I can apply for Medicaid next month. I can't wait until next month, I will be dead! I tried to explain this to her but she just tells me that she is sorry. So am I.

I saw a specialist today. Mark went with me. As I sat in his waiting room I came to a half-hearted decision. I'm not going through with this operation. Mark and I argue. He thinks that I will. He says that it's only money. But, how can I do this to him and the boys? We don't have much financially . . . but to lose everything!

The doctor is a Neurosurgeon. He has me do tests. He has me walk in a straight line, touch my nose with my arms outstretched. I feel that it's more of a sobriety test that the cops give you if they catch you drinking and driving. I fail miserably. He talks to Mark as if I'm not even in the same room. I would like to scream, Hey, I only have a brain tumor, I'm not stupid! He says that it's a real pity that he will have to mark up my face so. Remove the number 8 nerve that gives me hearing. I can live with being deaf, but not with the facial paralysis that he explains that I will have following this operation. Something to do with the number 7 nerve. It controls the face movement and feelings. Dr. _____ seems excited about being able to use a laser. He promises that he will try to save the number 7 nerve if possible. Okay, now I know that I'm not going to have this operation. I feel empty inside. My life as I know it will change. It's always back to the same thing: change. I shake my head to Mark. No, I mouthed! He schedules me for more extensive tests tomorrow at his _____ office. I leave his office in a daze.

Mark and I really have it out in the car. He wants me to go through with this. Deep down I know I want to somehow go on living, taking a chance with the operation. I will have to learn to live with a pain that seems unreal. We both cried.

I contacted old friends last night. It was so hard to say goodbye, but I'm grateful to have the chance. We cried and laughed. It all seems so unreal at times. They promised to pray for me and were confident that I would survive the operation scheduled for early next week. The hardest ones to call were my mom and brother. In a way it was like I was a little kid that had done something wrong and had to tell my mom. She took it rather well, considering. Both her and Greg will be up in a few days. Families do stick together. I feel guilty laying all this on mom. She has gone through so much, and then having to deal with my illness is almost too much. I guess that we can endure almost anything. When I think back on it she was really ahead of her time. Dad dying while I was only three and her having to raise both Greg and myself. I give her a lot of credit. We never lacked for anything emotionally or physically. I will make sure that I tell her how proud that I am of her accomplishments when she comes this weekend.

I had my Power of Attorney and personal will drawn up today. I feel that these will be needed by Mark soon, I certainly can't leave it all to him. I even picked out my own funeral arrangements. That was so hard! I drove over to the cemetery and took a picture of the type of headstone that I want. They can scrimp on the funeral cost, but I do want a nice headstone! Mark tells me not to worry so about all these things, but I want everything done before I go to the hospital. I have even tried to clean a few drawers out of my dresser this afternoon. I am petrified to think that someone will have to clean out my things and see what a slob I am. I know this is foolish thinking on my part, but I can't help feeling this way. It keeps me busy, and right now that is the most important thing there is.

I think that the hardest part of this whole numbing experience is having to deal with the children. What do you tell them? The truth? Your mom is dying. Chin up, have a good life. I don't have any answers, or at least not the ones I want to hear. I'm not sure exactly how to handle the situation. Justin is only three years old. He doesn't understand what death is. I think that he watches too much TV. He believes that like a cartoon character, I will come back to life. He can't grasp the meaning of a long-term illness, an operation, or hospital for that matter. As for the other boys, they remain quiet and aloof. They don't ask me any direct questions. Maybe that is how they cope with all the changes going on in the family.

It is a complicated situation that I want to ignore. I feel numb at best. Justin asks me questions like, "What is dead?" and "Where do people go when they are dead?" I pray for a simple answer to his questions. It was given to me this morning. A baby bird had fallen from the tree outside the back door. I had him hold the dead bird. He felt that it was cold and stiff, and was not moving or breathing. He seemed to grasp this explanation of touch whereas an explanation of words failed him. I wish that it was this easy to understand death.

I pack my overnight suitcase. It's not that I will be staying just overnight but that I will need little to sustain my stay in the hospital. The last thing that I will pack is a Polaroid picture in a Lucite frame I made today of the boys in the front yard. It may be the last time I will see them. I made a promise to myself that I will not cry.

I went to the hospital today. Mom is staying with the boys and seeing to the running of the house. She really is more efficient at this housewife stuff than I am. Anyway, Mark and Greg are taking me. Somehow I feel like that convict on death row. If I pull out of this thing I will have to rethink my views on capital punishment.

I can't help wondering if I will ever return to the life that I used to know? The doctors want to do the operation tonight. I tell them no. Today is the anniversary of my own dad's death. I don't know if this postponement makes the doctors happy or not, but somehow this helps me somewhat. Yes, I will wait until this day passes. One day, will that make a difference in my living or dying?

I've decided that Dr. _____, my surgeon, doesn't have any bedside manners. I don't care. I want his skill to be with the knife. I really think that Mark believes that I won't go through with it. Deep inside I don't want to. I am like the ostrich, I want to bury my head in the sand the people will go away. I know that I am supposed to be an adult, and I know in my heart I must do this thing to survive. But, it's hard, so damn hard.

We discussed cost with the office at _____ hospital. They are going to write off half for teaching purposes. Dr. _____ has also agreed to reduce his fee. Either way, though, it will financially wipe us out. I've sold our stock. That was so hard to, as it was the only thing that was left me from my grandmother. Next month I will be eligible to receive Medicaid. But that is two weeks away and I can't wait that long for this operation. It's like a Catch 22.

I checked into my room. Scott has even come up to say goodbye. I'm scared. I set the picture of the boys that I have brought with me on the table next to my bed. I put on the hospital issued gown and get into bed. I wait patiently while they take several vials of blood. I'm glad that mom and Greg have donated blood for me. Somehow, it makes me feel close to them. Grandma has sent her minister up to see me. He asks if I've been born again. Hey, I've been baptized twice. First in the Methodist Church and later as a Mormon. I've got it covered! I've always felt a close relationship with God. He prays with me.

I think that the hardest part of saying goodbye was Mark leaving me. I feel alone and cold. I know that I will see him tomorrow but there will be other people around us. This is our time alone. I tell him that I love him. I thank him for sticking by me at a time like this. I ask him to take care of the boys, and to please have patience with my mom and his mom. He laughs. I think it breaks some of the tension that we both feel in the room. I am utterly alone now. It is so quiet, with just my thoughts for company.

At midnight they give me something to sleep. I tell them that I don't want to sleep, I may be sleeping forever after tomorrow. They give me pitying glances. I swallow the damn pill to make them feel better. I've already learned that the hospital does not like you to be different.

Today's the day. I wake early despite that sleeping pill they gave me last night. The hospital is already coming awake. I listen to the various sounds around me. I know that I will not be able to hear them tomorrow morning. Can you believe that they have scheduled yet another pill to give me? They explain that it is to help me relax. I think that the doctors and nurses like to dope you up to keep you quiet. My body is already full of drugs. It doesn't feel like my own anymore. Mark and Greg are here. Downstairs is my friends and family. Waiting. I think they are keeping a vigil of some sorts. That's somehow comforting. They were up earlier, the whole clan. I say goodbye as they gather around my bed. The orderly is here to take me to the operating room. I am scared. Not of dying but living. Things will be different, I will now have a handicapped body. Can I live with that? Am I being vain?

The operating room is so cold! Like death in its final moment. The nurses put warm blankets on me as I lay on the frigid slab. Arms outstretched. I feel like the sacrificial lamb. The neighbor across the street from our house has sent a close friend that is a nurse to be with me. She holds my hand trying to reassure me. Giving me her strength. Will I wake? How different will I be? The anesthesiologist tells me that she is about to put me under. I will taste garlic in my mouth. I ask her why they can't make the anesthesia taste like chocolate. I slowly close my eyes. My last conscious thought was asking God to be with me.

Oh God the pain is so great. To go to sleep and feel normal, then awake with such pain! Why has God deserted me? I want to die. I can't live with this newness. There are so many tubes in my body. Every orifice. My hair is gone, my head a giant bandage. Why can't I just die? I have no energy to do a simple thing like open my eyes. I lie here aware of the movement around me. I can't help but feel that my body is a traitor. Time has a way of disappearing. It's always so light here in the ICU. Hours fade into days, days into weeks. I don't know if it is day or night now. Mark is with me when I become conscious. He wets my mouth with cold ice pops. Does he know how wonderful that feels? I feel like that nursery rhyme, Humpty Dumpty. No one can put me back together again. Sometimes it's easier to just let go, to die, than to go on with living.

I think that the last straw is that I started my period. I overheard a nurse say that is was due to the trauma that I suffered. I have lost all autonomy. I even have a male nurse that changes me! I am angry and embarrassed. Angry because I have lost my privacy. It doesn't seem to make any difference to the staff here. I'm embarrassed from the situation. I am simply a job. Do you think that they think of me as a human being with feelings and emotions? No. I don't think that a person can perform their jobs day after day while letting sentiments get in their way.

I only want to be left alone in my pain and suffering. My hips are numb from the pain medication I receive. I have lost the vision in my right eye, and my hearing is gone as well. There isn't a vein left in this body that hasn't been stuck with needles. I want to give up.

I'm dying. They have sent for a nun to be with me. A sister named Roselee. She is kind and doesn't seem to be in a hurry to be other places as most people do from ICU. She quietly sits with me and holds my hand. We don't talk much but I somehow know that she understands how I feel. Time seems to come to a standstill. I reflect on my past. Have I been blind? Have I been wrong? I only hope that I have made amends with the people in my life. I keep thinking about those damn closets and drawers that haven't yet been cleaned out. So many loose ends. I fall asleep, when I wake she is gone.

It's been almost two weeks now that I have been in the ICU. They come to weigh me with a device that lifts my entire body up. They talk about being careful not to hit my head. I have lost over twenty pounds in two weeks! I think that I might sell this diet to the *Inquirer Magazine*. Do you think that people all over will be trying to get their own brain tumor? Well anyway, I am better somehow. Guess that I am too stubborn to die. The staff yesterday have wheeled me down to perform another CT scan. I guess they were afraid that they didn't get all the tumor.

My family has been visiting nearly every two hours. In ICU they only let two family member in every two hours. There seems to be someone here all the time. Mark talks to Dr. _____ about my condition. I overheard them earlier today. I was too tired to open my eyes. But I knew they were in the room with me. He seems to be pleased with my progress. Ha, is that what you call it?

Yes, I am better. They tell me that if I keep improving they will move me to PCU tomorrow or the next day. I will have a little more privacy there. I don't care anymore. I really don't feel one way or the other. You know, they took away the brain tumor but they also took away my dignity too.

I've come to a decision. It's easy to die. It's hard to live. I ask God to let me die. It would be so easy. At times I feel so guilty. Guilty over the financial burden that I have placed my family in. Guilty in the attention I need. Guilty that I'm not a whole person.

Today's a big day. They have upgraded my condition and will be moving me to PCU. Mom and Joan argue over the fact that I have not had a bowel movement for two weeks. Can you believe it? I feel angry and embarrassed. I'm thirty-four years old, with four kids. I certainly don't need my mother complaining to the staff nurses about my personal body functions! God has failed me. If I would have died on the operating table I would be spared all this and so would my family.

Saw my children today. The Psychiatrist wanted them to visit me while I was in ICU. Somehow I didn't feel right letting them see me with all those tubes coming out of me. I have to admit that I was scared of their reaction when they first saw me. I look so different. They seemed quiet and distant. Justin asked where my hair went. We all had a good laugh. When they left I cried myself to sleep.

My veins have collapsed again! I cry when I hear that damn buzzer go off on the IV pole telling the world that the medicine is not flowing smoothly into my veins. The nurses' station has once again called the special IV unit to start another one. The doctors have talked about an operation to insert a Hickman Catheter that would allow them to hook me up to any medicine. I don't want to think of any more operations. Can't all this just end? I want to go home.

They have moved me into a semi-private room. I actually have a window! It's funny how little things mean so much when you are deprived of them. I watch this house on the street below. It seems so normal. The family has two boys that play in the yard. Around 5 o'clock the father comes home. The mom comes out to greet him. I guess the thing that gets to me the most is that it's so NORMAL. Don't they realize that just across the street at the hospital people are dying? Their lives are changing forever.

The docs did that operation on me this morning. The catheter goes into my upper chest, into my heart, and exits under my left breast. I'm going to have a nice scar there! I don't care anymore.

Mom brought my cards and well wishes today. It's funny that these people that all wish me well won't pick up their phones and call me. Better yet, why don't they come by to see me? They have all deserted me. Mark is here every day, sometimes several times a day. Mom comes, as well as Amos. No one else. I'm lonely.

I feel worse and they don't know why yet. I'm to have another CT, MRI, and bone scan today. Does this sound bad? Why do they keep things from me as if I'm a little kid?

I am leaking spinal fluid out of my nose. At first they believed it to be just a runny nose of sorts but they took a sample to the lab and it came back positive. Great. I had to be rushed down to O.R. earlier. Dr. _____

punctured my eardrum. That really hurt! He said that it would feel like a bee sting. Now how does he know how it feels?

Another operation. They finally figured it out. They ripped the brain sack when they removed the tumor. This time the operation is to repair that sack. I am now leaking spinal fluid out of my ears and nose. I pray that I will die on the operating table and be done with this pain and guilt.

The doc has explained this new operation. He tells me that he is going to remove my ear and take a patch of skin on my stomach to make the necessary repair. I tell him that if he is taking part of my stomach, I would like my hips and rear trimmed up as well. He laughs. Why don't I feel jolly?

I am more physically sick after this operation than with the others. I lost so much spinal fluid that they had to operate at a 90° angle. They were afraid that I would be a paraplegic or something. I am to stay sitting up for nearly three weeks to let this patch in my brain heal. They have put me on morphine but I continue to throw up and be in severe pain. Isn't morphine addictive? Guess that is the least of my worries. I just want this pain to go away. It is so cruel!

I had a doctor bring his troop of medical students today on rounds. Gee, they look so young. They all thought that I had come so far. Shit, why don't they realize that they took away so much? It would have been so easy to die. Sometimes I believe that living is not what it's cracked up to be. Death would be a friend.

Went to therapy today. Now that was a real joke. I can't stand or walk or write with my right hand anymore. I have to start over from the beginning. When I returned to my room and was put in bed, I cried. I think that it was for all the things that I lost. Maybe it was just pity.

The best news today! I am going to take a shower by myself. I can't tell you how happy that makes me. The nurse will have to cover up all my tubes as I still have that Hickman Catheter. I don't care, I'm going to take a shower alone and by myself!

I have to laugh when I think about my shower. Here I am, no hair, lines still on my head from the operation, and wrapped up like a Christmas turkey. But it was glorious. They put a stool in the shower stall for me and the nurse helped me sit down. I was in there so long that they came knocking on the door. It was great.

It felt so strange to be in the car going home. I cried. Mark tried to comfort me. I can't really tell him how I feel. I wished I died. I tried to tell him once and he said that I was being foolish. Why is it when you don't agree with what society believes, you are wrong? Is it really wrong to want to die? Perhaps I've learned all I need to know in this life. Has God forsaken me?

I still have the Hickman and I will have to have home nursing for awhile. This meningitis will take months of antibodies to kill. The medicine I need is $2,000 per week and I will need it for several months. Medicaid will cover it . . . is this all worth it?

Made love last night. It was the first time since the operation for the tumor. I think it was the fact that Mark and I both needed to hold each other. It was kind of comical as I have no hair and still have IV tubes in, but I think the point was that we both needed human touch. Maybe it was a way to become a "normal" family again. I don't know. Mark has been my rock in all this. He has been taught to give me an IV twice a day. He helps me in the tub and washes my head but I still don't have much hair yet! And when I am at my worst, like now, he is still there.

I think that this stage in my life has taught me to embrace life. I have learned that growth is a process and we must accept the good with the bad. I've learned to deal with handicaps, growing from them as a person. I have learned that my family is the most important feature in my existence on this Earth.

I have learned that when faced with adversities you must go on living and learning. Maybe the scar of this time will always be there to remind of the tragedy I had to face. I have learned that life goes on. It is never easy, but then nothing in life that builds and strengthens our character is very easy. Is it?

It is astounding how devastatingly bad news is swiftly and almost super-humanly accommodated into the lives of the seriously sick. It is also amazing how seemingly unendurable news becomes bearable, and how very quickly hope is born from the abyss of disease and mortality. It is almost beyond understanding how some terribly sick and dying persons are able to continue with life in the face of horrifying physical devolution and its corresponding psycho-emotional despair. To my way of thinking, it is almost miraculous how hope seems to spring eternal from the depths of hopelessness, dejection, and the incomprehensibility of mortality.

As I noted in Chapter 1, one of the great ironies is that death cannot be understood until it happens, and when it does happen that which is necessary for human comprehension is destroyed by dying. The understanding of the human impact of physical devolution that stems from disease and dying is similarly elusive. The very first thing we must recognize about the life experience of sick and dying persons is that their physical and personal struggle can never be fully known. It is a universal truth of humanity that each individual must personally suffer their own disease and die their own deaths. However, this personalization of suffering, death, and dying is intensified as modern cultural patterns isolate these human realities from the everyday flow of social life. It is for this reason that the contemporary portrait of suffering and loss is largely foreign and bizarre to most Americans. All the more reason, in order to relieve the suffering of others and enhance our own awareness and caring capacity, to listen to their voices.

The diagnosis of serious disease which brings about the possibility of dying is life-overwhelming and life-altering. Understandably, once again, the onset of serious and terminal illness is met with disbelief and incredulity. Yet, reality forces the suspension of disbelief, and human beings are required to adapt to the alien and unfathomable circumstances of their illness. There can be no doubt that there is an unmistakable ache in this woman's heart when she comments:

> It all seems so unreal . . . It seems like a nightmare that I can't awake from.

Despite the unreality of what was happening to her, physically and emotionally, she continued the struggle to live life and reap meaning. Her struggle was not just existential and personal. It also included an intense reorganization of her social self and its corresponding roles, most notably wife and mother. There is a sense of desperation that appears as she struggles to hold onto a life that is familiar and knowable. As disease and relentless technical procedures dominate her life, she is thrown into a strange world that is not only unlike the world she has known all her life, but is hostile to it. In this new and transforming state she becomes cut off from prevailing and ordinary patterns of living. In addition, she becomes emotionally estranged, not just from the broader culture, but from herself. Her new self, that develops quickly and out of necessity, is not just disconnected from her former self, but is actually set against the way she used to be as a person, wife and mother.

In this process of devolution and transformation she yearns to understand and make sense out of her illness and suffering. Despite feeling close to God and feeling that God is close to her, she feels abandoned by Him:

> I can't blame God. God didn't cause it. I've ironically always believed that He is the giver of life. It's funny though, I know that I shouldn't be angry with Him, but somehow I am. How can He let this happen to a mother that hasn't yet seen her sons grow up to become men?

Her relationship with God, while of enormous importance to her, is inconsistent and insufficient in its capacity to ease her suffering. Her faith has plunged into privacy and isolation, and is notably unsupported by the regular presence of community and religious ritual. In this regard, her faith, apparently indomitable in her previous world, begins to fail her in her new world of redefined normalcy, in which she must personally confront disease and mortality. In this newly constructed and fragile world not only are her belief and faith stressed and fractured, her suffering remains not only uneased but is worsened.

In searching for causes and explanations for what is happening to her, anger is not solely directed at God, but becomes internalized and directed at her own self. She struggles with self blame and guilt:

> . . . how can I do this to (my husband) and the boys? . . . I (also) feel guilty laying all this on my mom.

Her personal and social world is coming apart. Despite the fact that her disease and bodily impairment are beyond her control, she fights feelings of self-blame. In a rather perverse way, self blame locates a source of responsibility and accordingly provides at least some sort of explanation for her. In an age where suffering, dying, and death have become meaningless, the need for explanation and meaning has become intensified. Thus, what may appear irrational on the surface, namely blaming oneself for suffering and disease over which one has no control, may be a modern adaptation to the problem of meaninglessness. In this way, some sense of order is introduced into a personal and physical world of unruly chaos:

> I've come to a decision. It's easy to die. It would be so easy. At times I feel so guilty. Guilty over the financial burden that I have placed my family in. Guilty in the attention I need. Guilty that I'm not a whole person.

Her guilt is especially painful when she reflects upon the impact that her disease and possible death have upon her children:

> I think that the hardest part of this whole numbing experience is having to deal with the children. What do you tell them? The truth? Your mom is dying. Chin up, have a good life. I don't have any answers . . .

I suggest that self blame and guilt make a lot of sense in a world where suffering, disease, and dying make very little sense. Their existence shows how important meaningfulness is to the human experience, and how especially desperate modern individuals become in the face of meaninglessness when they encounter disease and mortality—so desperate that they internalize blame in order to bring some explanation into their lives.

There is great loss in the encounter with mortality. The body is failing as it is systematically cannibalized by disease. Her understanding of herself as a person, mother, and wife is being torn apart. Her faith, so central in her former life, seems troubled and impotent. And, the need to make sense and meaning out of her loss is unfilled. The portrait that emerges is one of anguish, regret, and suffering; all of which are dramatically unrelieved by cultural, medical, personal, or religious sources of support.

In this framework of meaninglessness and suffering, the demolition of self begins with the collapse of the body:

> There are so many tubes in my body. Every orifice. My hair is gone, my head a giant bandage. Why can't I just die? I have no energy to do a simple thing like open my eyes. . . . I can't help but feel that my body is a traitor . . . I feel like that nursery rhyme, Humpty Dumpty. No one can put me back together again.

Not only is the integrity of the body and its functions breaking down, there is enormous physical misery in the very pugilism of her disease:

> I am to stay sitting up for nearly three weeks to let this patch in my head heal. They have put me on morphine but I continue to throw up and be in severe pain . . . I just want this pain to go away. It is so cruel!

Despite the fact that her husband and mother seem wonderfully committed to her, she still suffers in great isolation. Her loneliness becomes especially apparent when her husband is not with her:

> The hardest part . . . was Mark leaving me. I feel alone and cold . . . I am utterly alone now.

She also regrets and bemoans the fact that friends and the broader community remain disconnected from her life.

> Mom brought my cards and well wishes today. It's funny that these people that all wish me well won't pick up their phones and call me. Better yet, why don't they come by to see me? They have all deserted me. Mark is here everyday, sometimes several times a day. Mom comes, as well as Amos. No one else. I'm lonely.

There can be no doubt that technology, technical interaction, and medical providers are central in shaping her life experience. A yearning for empathy from her physicians runs throughout the narrative, an empathy which essentially is not forthcoming. In fact, despite her utter dependence upon her medical caretakers, her suffering is worsened by her perception of the indifference of her physicians and nurses. There is anger and hurt in her voice when she comments:

> I am simply a job (to them) . . .

She is subjected to seemingly relentless procedures in an effort to arrest her widespread disease. Technically competent physicians who are interested in her medical well-being perform these procedures. Yet anguish over the absence of empathy and the legacy of invasive and painful interventions seem to overwhelm her:

> Another operation. They finally figured it out. They ripped the brain sack when they removed the tumor. This time the operation is to repair that sack. I am now leaking spinal fluid out my ears and nose. I pray that I will die on the operating table and be done with this pain and guilt.

Of great importance to her are the activities of omission. While there is technical activity aimed at reducing her pain, there is virtually no concern for relieving her suffering. Her anguish is profound but unexpressed. In the medical context, where technical orientation and activity reign, her personal suffering remains private and invisible, incredibly so. The careful reader will glean from her voice the unfulfilled need for empathy and suffering-support from her healthcare professionals.

This case narrative is far more than a portrait of suffering, disease, and mortality. It is also a study in courage and resilience of the human spirit. As I commented earlier, it is astonishing how quickly human beings adapt to devastating circumstances of loss. Time and time again this woman had hope deflated as she engaged an ongoing battle against disease and bodily destruction. Yet, she continued to desire life. In fact, she thirsts for it. Love, family, warmth, intimacy, and spirituality became her beacons of light, her reasons for living. When she cried out for death she was not renunciating life. Instead she was expressing her desperate need for suffering to be relieved. Her experience is all the more impressive because, despite some temporary moments of comfort, her suffering remained unrelenting and unrelieved. Her adaptation and her struggle continued in the shadow of profuse suffering, and demonstrated a consummate strength and courage that may very well go to the foundation of what human beings are.

As difficult as it is to listen to the agony expressed in her voice, enormous wisdom is contained in her quest for life, and her suffering is of great instruction for those willing to listen. Some of the outstanding lessons her experience teaches are:

- Life is precious and irreplaceable, and facing disease, devolution. and mortality stimulates the desire for life
- How incredibly harsh disease is upon the body
- How privatized and isolated persons are as they encounter and contemplate suffering, disease, and mortality
- The need for meaning is intense—not in a metaphysical or intellectual way but in ways that are concrete

- How deep spiritual longings can run, and how bereft the modern encounter with mortality is of spiritual and religious ritual
- That disease and pain control are not synonymous with suffering control
- How disease militates not just against the body but the whole person
- The importance of empathetic and compassionate medical care, and how it is the exception and not the norm
- How the absence of any systematic effort to provide comfort and relieve suffering is reflective of widespread cultural apathy and selfishness.

JOURNEYING TOWARD DEATH: A STRANGER IN LIFE

The Human Voice of Mortality

. . . I'm not scared of dying . . . If I'm to die I would want it to happen soon. The way I see it, this would be the best way. I figure that all my friends will forget me after a few years. Amy will forget me except for when her kids ask how I died. My mother and father, well I don't know if they would get over it. I suppose that they would live life just the same . . .

I guess my reasons for wanting to die early are selfish. If I'm going to die soon I'd rather it happen sooner than later. I wouldn't want to have to bother living if I were going to die soon. I guess that these feelings stem from feeling alone. I always feel alone. ALONE . . . I was thinking about the last year or so, and I came around to the subject of attitudes. Ever since I first went into the hospital I seem to have built up an attitude.

All my friends have noticed it. Even I know that it's there. I guess that it's one way that I cope with life now. I'm not afraid of dying, but I needed it to get me through. When I was bald from the radiation and ARC I needed something to keep me strong. I formed a holier than Mary attitude. I built up myself so that I had the strength to cope with things. Out of fear I formed a carefree facet of the same attitude. I was worried that my problems would come back. I've never been afraid of anything in my life, until now. I live with the fear that my Leukemia will return. Every time I have a stomachache I get a little worried.

So far I've lost about three pounds, since I talked to the dietitian. I was at about one-fifteen. Now I'm at one-twelve. Hopefully I won't gain any more weight. I think that I can control myself and lose the weight that I need and want to. Tuesday I'm going over to Karen's house and work out with her husband. If I combine moderation in eating with exercise then I should be able to get into shape . . . I'm a lot stronger now than I was about a year ago. My arms and hands are getting into shape. Now I need to trim my stomach . . .

. . . Even though I may do rash things sometimes, I still am in control. Control that's what it's all about, isn't it? I won't lie to myself. Even if I'm afraid of me, I still can't lie to myself. The thoughts of ending it are still there. I guess that I'm just waiting for the one thing that will push me over the breaking point.

Six months ago I would cry every night. Now I just have weird dreams. I kind of like my strange dreams. I need to be protected. The thing is that no one can protect me from me. It's me that has to get a grip. GET A GRIP . . .

Later I'll tell you how I feel about people. For now you have to understand that I feel people are generally stupid. I don't care about people, I don't have a reason to. I feel fear. People ask me, "Are you afraid of dying?" and I can honestly say, No. My greatest fear is of pain. Not mental pain. I don't hold it too close to my thought patterns. I instead fear the threat and reality of physical pain. I've gone through countless spinal taps and bone marrows. I only fear one thing and that is what I've mentioned it is. I'm slowly becoming sick and tired of all of the treatments. I often wish that I could just leave and never look back. I know that I'd die sooner or later, but at least I wouldn't have to go through the pain. The thing that pisses me off the most is that I've gone through all of this but I'm sure that I will be able to make the long haul in the end. Maybe I just wish that I could go through the bone marrow transplant so that people will leave me alone. All I ever wanted was to die in peace. Again I say that I'm not afraid of death, but I do wish that it would hurry.

I was thinking about the last two years or so, and I came to the subject of attitudes. Ever since I first went into the hospital I've built up an attitude. All of my friends and enemies have noticed it. I've slowly become aware of it myself. I guess that I use it so I can cope with everything going on. I'm not afraid of dying, but I need it to get me through. I needed something to keep me strong while I was bald from radiation and ARC. I formed a holier than Mary attitude. I also formed a carefree facet of my attitude so that I didn't have to deal with many things that bothered me.

The biggest problem I have is that I can't pin down the reason I'm so angry. I guess that I'm just fed up with everything. I can't seem to get better medically. And I can't seem to get a girlfriend. I don't know what to do. I sometimes want to talk to people about how I feel, but I don't know what to say.

At this point in time I can only see one way out and I don't want to talk about that. If by some chance I die it would be a relief. Suicide is not me though, but it may be my evil twin. . . .

I realize that I don't want to fight anymore. I never really did anyway, but I know that I would rather die now than go on. I may be somewhat selfish or weak, but I don't care anymore. I can't seem to look my mom in the face anymore. I can't seem to talk to Andy but for a few minutes at a time. Amy is the only one I see in the same light as I always have. I love them all, but I can't stand to live with them anymore. I can't really pin down the problem, though, and that worries me. My anger is building everyday.

I'm not talking about suicide in the actual sense of the word. What I want is to cut out all the doctors and hospitals. Just cut to the shit, if you will. I feel as though I should write a going away letter to everyone. When I try, however, the words don't come out right.

Everyday I feel closer to death. I don't want to die but I still don't have a lot of faith in cures. I don't know if the bone marrow transplant will work or not, but I guess it's my only hope. I always took for granted that I wasn't going to make it, but now the end is in sight and I don't want to die. Still, I'm not afraid of what lies beyond or of the fact that I will stop living. I guess that I'm most afraid of missing out on things that I've wanted to do . . .

Terminal illness is like a madman from a Stephen King novel that relentlessly and without pity smashes everything that is familiar and safe. As unrecognizable as King's madmen and evil icons are to the ordinary and decent folk that they terrorize in his novels, disease and dying not only terrorize but are unfathomable in the scheme of contemporary life. Dying not only overwhelms, it transforms. It brings a destructive sense of aloneness, an intolerable absence of solitude, and renders one a stranger to one's self. Clearly, the young man's struggle is just as much about the decimation of personhood as it is about the devolution of the body. In this transformation, the dying individual becomes a stranger to his self as normal understanding and attachments of the self are destroyed. This self-estrangement, and its associated existential and psychosocial disquiet, occurs as the person is exiled from familiar and secure connections to others. Unlike in the traditional patterns of Western death, there is enormous loneliness and isolation in modern dying. In this regard, it is crucial to recognize that loneliness and isolation can even occur despite the presence of others in the life journey of dying persons. As this individual contemplates his predicament he comes to understand that his desire to die, rather than to continue living in the shadow of death and disease, stems from his social and personal exilement:

I guess that these feelings stem from feeling alone. I always feel alone. ALONE. . . .

In this context of isolation, the need for connection with others is strong, but the cultural excommunication of the dying is severe. There is a lack of norms that show the ways that he might be connected to the modern community and vice versa. We can only imagine the suffering and isolation of his loved ones as they witness his physical devolution as he journeys toward death. In this regard, he speaks not just for the predicament of many dying persons but for their loved ones as well when he says:

> I don't know what to do. I sometimes want to talk to people about how I feel, but I don't know what to say.

Traditionally, dying projected itself visually and concretely into the mainstream of Western life. In this context of public visibility, people knew what was expected of individuals, families, and communities when faced with death. As dying and suffering increasingly became invisible and meaningless in contemporary life, we have correspondingly lost our collective understanding of how to confront mortality. Dying individuals and loved ones are thus typically left feeling confused, strained, and helpless throughout the dying process.

The anger and the helplessness that are "building everyday" for this person are not "abnormal." In fact, the presence of these qualities that overwhelm and decimate one's self and connectedness to others is quite congruent with the dominant styles of death in modern America. The isolation and disempowerment of dying persons generates, for them, a longing to make sense out of what is happening. In addition, they have a strong desire to retain some control over the course of their life. As they struggle against disease and dying the need to stay in control, when all seems to be unraveling, is vital:

> Even though I may do rash things sometimes, I am still in control. Control, that's what it is all about, isn't it? It's me that has to get a grip. GET A GRIP . . .

It is no surprise that in this context of enormous and unrelieved suffering that this person's thoughts turn to suicide. There is tremendous percipience in his words:

> At this point in time I can only see one way out and I don't want to talk about that. If by some chance I die it would be a relief. Suicide is not me though, but it may be my evil twin.

Perceiving death as relief of suffering hovers throughout the narrative. The longing for death, however, is more correctly a longing for peace and serenity. In the throes of disease and unassuaged suffering, death becomes palliative and reflects how deeply unmet human needs are in confrontation with death. It is for this reason that the growing cultural movement toward the right-to-die and physician-assisted-suicide is understandable, and reflective of the cultural worry about intensive and unrelieved suffering.

We can only imagine how massive despair and fear were in this person's encounter with dying. Listening to his words and the emotions they convey once again illuminate some very valuable lessons for those willing to listen:

- There is an overwhelming sense of disquiet and absence of solitude in the contemporary dying experience
- The need for support and empathy is enormous and is often both unexpressed and unaddressed
- Dying persons need to know that they and their suffering matter
- The feeling of aloneness is pervasive and destructive
- There is a troubling inability of loved ones, friends, and the broader community to understand the newly created world that dying persons inhabit.

REFLECTIONS ON DEATH IN LIFE: A SUMMARY

When I was a young boy I had the opportunity to see Michelangelo's *Pietà* on several occasions. Even as a nine-year-old I was struck at how such immense beauty could ruminate from sadness, suffering, betrayal, and death. Like Michelangelo, who was able to sculpt beauty from grief, there is something incredible and special to be found in the lives and words of dying persons. In some ways, life is like the *Pietà* itself, a creation that is full of beauty and possibilities for love and joy, but one that is inescapably tethered to suffering and loss. Voices of dying persons speak to the heart and soul of what it means to be human as poignantly as any great artist. They declare human strength and weakness, reminding us of humanity's great capacity for love and suffering. I have found that unmistakable good can emerge from the lives of terminally ill persons: wisdom, strength, reverence for life, the love of others, and a strengthening of religious faith. There are also some things that are unmistakably heinous about their experience: the betrayal of the body, the inattention of medical professionals to the human side of suffering and dying, meaninglessness, the failure of religious ritual and support to offer solace, and the indifference of the broader culture to their personal anguish. As these narratives highlight, dying persons often live in a state of cultural exile and endure their suffering in social isolation. Simply, they suffer deeply and unnecessarily.

The great cultural emphasis on materialism and success, which was so neatly portrayed by Huxley's character Mr. Stoyle, is of utter insignificance to the lives of seriously sick and dying persons. Not one dying person has ever told me that he or she wished they had a bigger bank account or had achieved greater financial success. Dying persons place greatest value not on material or financial well-being, but on relief of suffering, social support, spiritual fulfillment, and finding meaning. In this regard, to dialogue with dying persons is to enter into a dialogue about living, and on what is truly important in life. Specifically illuminated in their suffering is how the values, organization, and patterns of modem life offer little peace and comfort. Beginning students of classical Greek language will recognize that sympathy means to "suffer with" another person. Clearly, the voices of dying persons bespeak a great absence of sympathy. They illuminate how their experience is warped with loneliness and isolation. In the absence of sympathy and meaningful support systems they must find meaning to their new and unfamiliar lives within themselves. As disease overwhelms and imprisons both body and spirit, dying individuals become strangers to themselves, others, and the culture in which they live. Much of the attempt to reorganize their selves, so as to cope with disease and mortality, is done without the guidance and support of the broader culture.

Friendship and acquaintanceship are relatively easy in daily life because of their shallowness. Disease and dying, however, put friendship to the test. The voices of dying persons, especially their distress over loneliness and disconnectedness, strongly suggest that the test is being failed. While modern friendship may be easy because of its superficiality, support of dying persons is enormously difficult because of the depth and commitment it requires. It requires a willingness to accompany others, one foot in front of the other, step-by-step, as they travel toward the end of their lives. And, as these case narratives illustrate, the journey is messy, complicated, and often time consuming. As a culture, we have typically lost the interest in and capacity for suffering with others. There is no doubt that this decline in sympathy leads to a reduction of the humanity both of dying persons and of individuals in the broader culture generally. Widespread erosion of sympathy produces unnecessary suffering, thereby robbing dying persons of comfort and dignity. It also diminishes the ability of loved ones to cope with suffering, and results in a diminishment of humanizing qualities such as empathy, compassion, patience, loyalty, and the ability to love.

There is a rather stunning notion that seems implicit in the suffering and voices of the above persons: As they are going through the deep and morbid experience of sickness and abandonment they arrive at deeper understandings of life and of well-being. Thus, while disease is painful, degrading, and humiliating, it is also instructive in lessons about life. From the voices of dying persons we learn about the value of certain values and the worthlessness of others. We learn how essential yet fragile love and support are. And, from the suffering and contemplation of mortality we witness a deepening of self-awareness and, above all else, an intensification of the love for life.

Sagan and Céline are absolutely correct that the very idea of death—of our own extinction—is inconceivable and unbearable. Yet, somehow individuals who are confronting mortality, as serious disease attacks their bodies, are able to put one foot in front of the other, and find a way to endure the "inconceivable" and "unbearable." In the throes of awesome bodily destruction, despite absence of support, meaning, peace, and solitude, many dying persons find ways to embrace and continually create and recreate a place for hope in their lives. In this regard, the modern experience with mortality is a profile in both courage and failure; courage in the face of suffering, and failure to relieve that suffering.

REFERENCES

1. F. Sagan, *A Fleeting Sorrow,* Arcade Publishing, New York, 1995.
2. Céline, *Journey to the End of the Night,* New Direction Books, New York, 1983.
3. A. Dumas fils, *Camille,* New American Library, New York, 1984.

CHAPTER 3

The Problem of Meaning:
Dying in an Age of Spiritual Longing

He had just felt death come by again . . . Because, just then, death had come and rested its head on the foot of the cot and he could smell its breath . . . It had moved up on him now but it had no shape any more. It simply occupied space . . . "You've got a hell of a breath," he told it. "You stinking bastard" [1, p. 25].

Ernest Hemingway

And all those who had not made the gestures necessary to live their lives—they were afraid of death because of the sanction it gave to a life in which they had not been involved. They had not lived enough, never having lived at all [2, p. 147].

Albert Camus

The path to joy leads through suffering [3, p. 20].

Fidor Dostoyevsky

Western culture has lost its soul. . . . we have become obsessed with money, convenience, and the illusion of immortality [4, pp. 3-4].

Rose Solari

Dying individuals are ill-at-ease in the modern era. Unlike in traditional patterns of death, where dying was "tamed" by ritual, guiding norms, and a culturally grounded sense of purpose, modern death has become wild and terrifying. It is wild because it has lost its connection to cultural meaning and ritual. It is terrifying because as a result of its wild and meaningless place in our culture, it has become alien, unfamiliar, and consequently frightening. In the hustle and bustle of everyday life, the needs and suffering of dying persons and their loved ones have become invisible and insignificant. As a result of the busy and demanding lifestyles that are characteristic of modern society, death has been pushed to the periphery of daily activity and there is seemingly little time, aptitude, or interest in confronting the complexities and demands of suffering and dying.

Unintentionally, but as a direct consequence of the values and organization of contemporary social life, dying individuals are excluded from full and meaningful participation in the life of the community. As one patient put it:

> I feel as if I have been pushed aside and forgotten about. It's as if I do not matter anymore.

They have become estranged from life's mainstream—socially, emotionally, and existentially. And, as we saw in the preceding chapter, estrangement in the face of serious disease and mortality precipitates great suffering for dying persons. Suffering that is not only unrelieved but exacerbated by prevailing ways of life.

In this context of meaninglessness, dying persons are frequently a source of discomfort to others. Their presence often elicits disquiet and unease, which in turn fuels the cultural tendency to disconnect mortality from daily visibility and social consciousness. Having been disengaged and isolated from dominant patterns of social life dying persons crave comfort, connectedness, and a sense of purpose. While the growth of meaninglessness in dying is directly connected to the development of values and patterns which shape contemporary life, the most persuasive portrait of meaninglessness in life and death was written more than one-hundred years ago. Leo Tolstoy, in his brilliant short story "The Death of Ivan Ilych," explores how the patterns of modern life shape the spirit and the course of the modern dying experience. According to Tolstoy, the life of Ivan Ilych—steeped in affluence, ambition, narcissism, propriety, hedonism, and self-centeredness—had been "most ordinary and therefore most terrible" [5, p. 418]. As Tolstoy describes it, for the most part his life ran its course as he believed life should do: easily, pleasantly, and decorously [5, p. 431]. In all of his success, Ivan Ilych navigated through his life with little self reflection, spiritual enlightenment, or satisfying personal relationships. Ivan lived superficially, and although he enjoyed the pleasures of success, he remained painfully unaware of the deeper meanings and challenges of life.

Unexpectantly, and without warning, sickness entered into his life. At first he denies the seriousness of his illness and deludes himself into believing everything will be fine and return to normal. However, his doctors are unable to arrest the disease or its symptoms, and he is forced to come face-to-face with his own death. And, as he confronts the drama of his impending demise, Ivan is terrified:

> Ivan Ilych saw that he was dying and was in continued despair [5, p. 445].

In his heart he knew he was dying, but because he had lived a shallow and superficial life he could not grasp the idea. Ironically, it took a confrontation with death to jar him out of materialistic complacency and precipitate an active struggle with issues of meaning. As he reflects upon his death, he continues to be tortured and frightened:

"When I am not, what will there be? There will be nothing. Then where shall I be when I am no more? Can this be dying? No, I don't want to!" . . .

Anger choked him and he was agonizingly, unbearably miserable. "It is impossible that all men are *to* suffer this awful horror!" [5, p. 444].

His largely unexamined life never included reflections upon mortality, nor did the endless pleasantries with which he filled his life allow him to have any meaningful encounter with suffering. Heretofore suffering was essentially absent from his life. Now, it is his constant, albeit alien companion.

The dominant response of his friends and family was indifference, coupled with an ever so subtly expressed displeasure at having their lives bothered by his suffering. The superficiality and self-centeredness of these relationships, as they occurred throughout his life, retained their form at the deathbed, becoming a source of isolation and resentment for Ivan:

... during that loneliness in which he found himself . . . a loneliness in the midst of a populous town and surrounded by numerous acquaintances and relatives but yet that could not have been more complete anywhere— either at the bottom of the sea or under the earth . . . [5, pp. 463-464].

For Ivan, the torment of dying was exacerbated by his state of spiritual and interpersonal emptiness, and was relentless:

Whether it was morning or evening, Friday or Sunday, made no difference, it was all just the same: the gnawing, unmitigated, agonizing pain, never ceasing for an instant, the consciousness of life inexorably waning but not yet extinguished, the approach of that ever dreaded and hateful Death which was the only reality . . . [5, p. 453].

If only it would come quicker! If only what would come quicker? Death, darkness? . . . No, no! Anything rather than death! [5, p. 454].

Crisis in dying is crisis in living for Ivan. From the very beginning of his illness he was at a loss, that is to say unable to understand what was happening. Having lived a life of falsity and delusion, having adopted a materialistic and narcissistic way of life, he came to believe that he was invulnerable to serious disease and suffering. In typical fashion of the narcissistic individual, Ivan Ilych became obsessed with his own suffering, and with finding an explanation for his dying. His self- examination became dark and severe, leading to two conclusions that seemed impossible to escape: 1) his dying was truly dreadful and without meaning; and, 2) the way he lived his life led directly to this kind of death:

Then what does it mean? Why? It can't be that life is so senseless and horrible. But if it really has been so horrible and senseless, why must I die and die in agony? There is something wrong!

"Maybe I did not live as I ought to have done" it suddenly occurred to him. "But how could that be, when I did everything properly?"... [5, p. 462].

Ivan continues brooding over his death and life:

"What is it for?"... Why, and for what purpose, is there all this horror? But however much he pondered he found no answer. And whenever the thoughts occurred to him, as it often did, that it all resulted from his not having lived as he ought to have done, he at once recalled the correctness of his whole life, and dismissed so strange an idea [5, p. 462].

In his isolation and loneliness he unceasingly reflects upon his agony. The thoughts which drift into his mind are constant and discomforting:

"What is this? Can it be that it is Death?" And the inner voice answered: "Yes, it is Death." "Why these sufferings?" And the voice answered, "for no reason—they just are so" [5, p. 463].

There is no explanation! Agony, death ... what for? [5, p. 465].

In Tolstoy's brilliant illustration, disease and death reflect the dominant patterns of modern life. Ironically, it is in sickness and dying that life is illuminated. Consistent with the major theme of this book, namely, that the ways of death are both created by and reflective of the ways of life, Tolstoy pinpoints how modern ideas and patterns of living are incompatible with meaningful dying.

The "fiction" of Tolstoy finds itself being played out into lives of dying individuals on a daily basis. Indeed, dying persons commonly agonize over the seemingly unanswerable question:

Why did this have to happen to me?

As Ivan struggled in an abyss of meaninglessness, so do modern individuals. In confronting their own mortality or the death of loved ones, it is not unusual that they experience overwhelming feelings of sorrow, worthlessness, and suffering. These feelings are products of cultural and social ways of life that are diminished in their capacity to provide meaning and comfort to the dying process. This chapter will explore how dominant values and patterns of American life are primarily responsible for the harshness and indignities of modern dying, and will pay particular attention to the role that technology, materialism, and individualism play in shaping the ways of life and death.

TECHNOLOGY AND MEANING

As one surveys the values, institutions, and people of America, it is not difficult to see that science and technology play a prominent part in economic and social life. The combined scientific and technological efforts of the private and public sector are vast. As technology has developed throughout the twentieth century, the seemingly unattainable and miraculous has become pervasive and ordinary. Throughout the country people sit in their living rooms during the evening and watch as new technological achievements are reported. Animals have been cloned, plans to clone humans are proceeding, living stations are being created in outer space, genetic testing and engineering is transforming our views of disease, reproductive technologies have changed the nature of life creation, and scientists are unashamedly talking about halting the aging process and have advanced the idea that death itself may someday be treatable as a disease. Science fantasy of the previous generation has crossed the threshold of science reality. Most people are remarkably unfazed by the forward march of science and technology, and in many ways technological achievement is not just accepted but has come to be expected.

In this regard, technology has become so consistently and deeply a part of everyday life that the American people have fallen rather blindly in love with it [6]. This love affair with technology is perhaps like a relationship with a long-term spouse or lover, namely, that which is loved or embraced in a take-it-for-granted way. As Edward Shils observes, America has fully committed to the scientific and technological way of life, but the value of that way of life has yet to be established:

> . . . readiness to support science rests in part on the belief that science contributes to the material well-being of society. . . . At present, the evidence that fundamental scientific research contributes to material well being is very uneven and not by any means rigorously conclusive. The conclusion is accepted because there is a mood to accept it. . . . But, it is largely a matter of faith . . . and derived from a profound and diffuse "will to believe" in the efficacy of science [7, p. 3].

The idea of progress, as it has evolved during the twentieth century of American life, is anchored by a belief in the efficacy of science and technology. The idea is a very simple one: ensure the advancement of science and technology and "all the rest" will take care if itself. "All the rest" refers to the social, political, moral, and cultural conditions of life. The technological view of progress has become enshrined and embedded in our way of life, and a technocratic mindset has emerged [8]. In this mindset, there are high hopes for the improvement of the human condition and, for the most part, technological developments are favorably and unquestioningly received by Americans. Ironically, this optimism is rooted in feelings, conviction, faith, and belief which emphasize the value of rationality, efficiency, and verification. In this framework, there is a non-rational, unsubstantiated belief in the value of the rational and the technocratic.

The important point to recognize in an examination of technology, meaning, and death is not the dangers of particular technological developments. In fact, any reasonable person will recognize that many positive and humane benefits have emerged from scientific discoveries and advancements in technology. The more important and germane consideration, however, involves the moral and cultural consequences of technological dependence.

The technological developments of the twentieth century have elicited serious sociological and philosophical critique. In their own way and style, writers such as Giedion, Huxley, Spengler, Mumford, Marcuse, and Fromm have explored the dehumanizing consequences of technological growth and development. Arguably, the most far ranging and insightful critique of technical civilization and its degradation of the human spirit is formulated by Jacques Ellul in *The Technological Society*. In this classic work, Ellul examines how modern societies have become technicized. At the heart of his argument is the idea that our civilization is an increasingly technical one. The rule of *technique,* or the intractable value placed upon rational and efficient pursuit of achievement, is the core driving force of the culture. Thus, not only does faith in technique become the consciousness of the modern world, it precipitates a cultural dependency upon the technical ways of life. As Robert Merton interprets:

> By technique . . . he means far more than machine technology. Technique refers to any complex of standardized means for attaining a predetermined result. . . . The Technical Man is fascinated by results, by the immediate consequences of setting standardized devices into motion. He cannot help admiring the spectacular effectiveness of . . . weapons of war.[1] Above all, he is committed to the never-ending search for "the one best way" to achieve any designated objective [9, p. vi].

Technique refers to the attitude, spirit, and consciousness of modern, technological society. It is the way in which cultural values, institutional practices, and daily activities of individuals are organized. In Ellul's language, technique is the totality of methods rationally arrived at and at having absolute efficiency in every field of human activity [10, p. xxv]. Technique extends to every area of life and in doing so increases human dependency on technology. And, as technique has become so pervasive a determinant of cultural life, it is virtually impossible for individuals to disassociate themselves from technical consciousness. As Ellul opines:

---

[1] The public fascination with the technologies of destruction employed during the Gulf War is an example of the cultural love of technology and machines utilized for specific, rational purposes.

> Modern men are so enthusiastic about technique, so assured of its supe-
> riority, so immersed in the technical milieu, that without exception they
> are oriented toward technical progress [10, p. 85].

Thus:

> From the point of view which most interests modern man, that of yield
> (that is to say that of productive achievement), every technical activity is
> superior to every nontechnical activity [10, p. 83].

For Ellul, in the modern world, the most dangerous form of determinism is the technological phenomenon [10, p. xxxiii]. Self-augmenting and autonomous technology shapes the very way in which society is organized and individuals live their lives. The point that he drives home is that technocratic consciousness, not specific technologies, is at the core of technocratic influence in American life. Neil Postman, a critic of technology in the tradition of Ellul, writes about the acquiescence of morality and culture to technocratic ways of life. In his book *Technolopoly* he observes that, in an almost unconscious way, American culture has surrendered itself to technology. And, like Ellul, his critique does not focus on particular technological developments. Rather, it emphasizes the prevalence and dominance of the technological world view:

> Technolopoly is a state of culture. It is also a state of mind. It consists in
> the deification of technology, which means that the culture seeks its
> authorization in technology, finds its satisfactions in technology, and
> takes its orders from technology. This requires the development of a new
> kind of social order, and of necessity leads to the rapid dissolution of
> much that is associated with traditional beliefs. Those who feel more
> comfortable in technology are those who are convinced that technical
> progress is humanity's supreme achievement and the instrument by which
> our most profound dilemmas may be solved [11, p. 76].

Albert Teich makes the essential point even more simply:

> Technology is more than just machines. It is a pervasive, complex system
> whose cultural, social, political, and intellectual elements are manifest in
> virtually every aspect of our lives [12, p. 1].

I raise the issue of technological dominance not to perseverate the debate on the benefits verses the dangers of technology. Instead, I do so in order to amplify the role that technology plays in daily life. There can be no doubt that widespread technicism is a major component of the American way of life and, despite anxieties and frustrations inherent in technological dominance, we are going to continue to live in highly technical ways. Thus, for better or for worse, or perhaps

more correctly, for better *and* for worse, technology and technological consciousness are major players in shaping prevailing ways of life. In this regard, as
technological faith has become a moral standard bearer of modern life it also
becomes a significant force in shaping modern ways of death. Specifically, as we
will see, technicism plays a seminal role in the meaninglessness of the modern
encounter with dying, and in the transformation of dying from a moral, social
experience into a technical one.

There is a close relationship between technological and social change. Some
scholars, however, would have us believe that technology is value-neutral. That is
to say that technological achievements have no vested moral or ethical interest in
social or political agendas. In addition, it is argued that technology does not
possess a self-sustaining life or momentum of its own. Rather, technology created
by free will is either used or not used by humans on the basis of choice. To put it
simply, technological advocates argue that technology is a tool in the hands of
humanity, and humans are in charge of both the means and ends for which it will
be used. These scholars, however, fail to recognize that even if technology is a tool
in the hands of humanity, the presence of the tool itself has an inevitable impact
on the tool-holder. How beautifully this notion was portrayed in the movie *The
Gods Must Be Crazy*. The movie begins with a soda bottle being tossed from an
airplane. It was accidentally found by a couple of indigenous people, whose lives
and community were changed forever by their chance encounter with the bottle.
The bottle and the means by which it was delivered into their lives symbolized the
achievement of technological and consumer society, and transformed the cultural
and social fabric of their lives. Similarly, it is not too difficult to see how
technology affects the nature and experience of our daily lives by its mere
existence. Clearly, humans with television, computers, sophisticated weaponry,
automobiles, etc., experience life differently than those who do not have these
technologies. Thus, there can be no doubt that the existence of technology plays a
major role in molding the social, economic, political, and cultural dimensions
of modern life.

In addition, the way in which technology is perceived and the meanings it
engenders have important consequences. As American culture has increasingly
adopted a philosophy which values "tools" and the "development of new tools,"
this technology-embracing attitude is widely internalized by the American people
and has an intractable impact on their values and activities. In this regard, as
Shils opines, Americans have rather nonreflectively accepted the authority of
technology and have been willing to submit their daily activities to its imperatives. In the same vein, Lewis Mumford writes about:

> . . . the duty to surrender to (technological) novelties unconditionally just
> because they are offered, without respect for their human consequences.
> One may without exaggeration, now speak of technological compulsive-
> ness: a condition under which society . . . submits to new technological

demand and utilizes without question every new product, whether it is an
actual improvement or not . . . [13, p. 186].

Thus, technology claims priority in human affairs: it places the demand
for constant technological change above any considerations of its own
efficiency . . . [13, p. 283].

Although more attention will be devoted later on to this issue, I cannot resist
the urge to note that coinciding with the miraculous technological achievements
of the past two decades is a dramatic increase in spiritual longing, self-help
modalities, and chemical treatment of depression. I'm not suggesting that technology is the cause of the frustration and meaninglessness that prevail in our time.
More precisely, I am emphasizing that these issues have emerged in the culture of
technicism, and perhaps even more importantly, there is little critical discussion of
the connection between technocratic ways of life and their deleterious consequences for the human condition.

In *The Dialectic of Ideology and Technology,* Alvin Gouldner examines the
impact of technology on the conditions of social life. At the forefront of the
historical evolution of technology and science in Western society is the transformation from traditional, ritual-based religious systems of meaning into
secularized systems of thought and activity:

The rise and development of modern ideologies was shaped by the rise
of modern science, by the growing prestige of technology and new modes
of production, and by the development of publics whose favorable judgment of modern science was rooted in the decline of older authority-
referencing discourse. Science became the prestigious and focally visible
paradigm of the new mode of discourse; it was this mode of discourse,
which diffuses the seen-but-unnoticed set of background assumptions, on
which science itself was tacitly grounded [14, p. 7].

Gouldner carefully examines the historical connection between the rational foundation of science and technology, and the value orientation of ideology. The
inescapable paradox of science, with its pretense to value-neutrality, is that it
embraces the values of efficiency, practicability, and rationality in its pursuit of
objectivity. He points out that as Western society modernized, rational secular
thought and efficient application of technology replaced traditional worldviews
that were based on myth, religion, and metaphysics. The modernizing citizenry
increasingly defined itself by the principles of the new social order. Thus, the
character of social life was irretrievably changed by the industrial revolution and
the growth of secularism. Science and technology offered the prospects of a better
life—of life that was longer, cleaner, more prosperous—and societies readily
accepted the assumption that human betterment and achievement would stem
from scientific and technological development. In this way, from its origin,

modern science is not value free. Instead it developed within a cultural framework that prized scientific inquiry, and it was in this way that science and technology became a dominant, value-based ideology of modern society.

The scientific and technological orientation not only affects the values and symbols of culture, it chisels out the contours of the relationship between individuals and the broader society. Gouldner provides an important example. As the influence of traditional, religious-based systems of authority declined they were supplanted by the developing rationalization of thought. One of the central catalysts of the growth of this rational orientation was the development of the technology of printing. The consequences of this technology became profound for the social organization of life and for the human personality. As printing became widespread, it enabled the development of rational thought and discourse. Explanations for human and social life, once exclusively and unquestioningly linked to the sacred, were being challenged by the rational worldview and the associated intellectual clash between competing and often contradictory interpretations of reality. In this age of rationality literacy became imperative, and the technology of printing developed and spread throughout Western society. In turn, a growing supply of pamphlets, newspapers, books, and journals were produced that were both a response to and a stimulus of growing literacy.

The revolution of printing technology was rooted in the developing culture of scientism, and had major implications for the social organization of life. Prior to printing, communication essentially occurred in a social context: people talking face-to-face with others. Communication required direct human interaction and was inherently collectivizing. The printed word, however, initiated a new pattern, namely, the isolation of human communication. As Neil Postman observes, the printed book gave birth to the isolated reader and his private reflections. In this sense, reading and printing technology unintentionally evolved into a conspiracy against human community and social presence [15, p. 27]. Thus, as Gouldner suggests, printing allows for the separation of talk from the talker [14, p. 41]. In addition, it allows for a single individual to speak to a large number of distinct and unrelated individuals, who may or may not share a common social context.

Consistent with the tradition begun by the printing revolution, modern achievements in communication technology have been able to overcome, at least superficially, the restrictions of distance. In doing so, they have also legitimated and created new forms of distance and disconnection between people. It is not too difficult to see how the development of electronic communication technology has enabled the separation of physical proximity from social communication. The isolating impact of television has been extensively documented in the scholarly literature. A more recent society transforming technological achievement is the development of the computer and the information highway. Not only is computer technology changing the pursuit of knowledge and information for better and for worse, it has significantly furthered the connection between communication technology and interpersonal disconnection. In his critique of the information highway, self-described computer nerd Clifford Stoll warns that computer technology cannot provide for a richer, better, more meaningful life. Central to his critique is the argument that for all of the communication taking place on the Internet, little of the information is genuinely useful—in a meaningful way. In addition, he strongly argues that computers and computer networks cheapen the meaning of actual social experience and isolate us from one another:

> Electronic communication is an instantaneous and illusory contact that creates a sense of intimacy without the emotional investment that leads to close friendships . . . (It not only provides for) escape into conversations with distant strangers, (but) . . . network interactions does not pose the same risks as face-to-face conversations do. At the same time, they lack depth, commitment, and ordinary etiquette [16, pp. 23, 26].

Stoll perceptively makes the point that computers are not just a product of the current drift toward alienation, they also have created new and unique forms of alienation:

> Computer networks fragment and isolate us from one another, rather than bring us together. We only need to deal with one side of an individual over the net. And if we don't like what we see, we just pull the plug. Or flame them. There's no need to tolerate the imperfections of people. It's the same intolerance found on the highway, where motorists direct intense anger at one another.

> By logging on to the networks, we lose the ability to enter into spontaneous interactions with real people. Evening time is now spent watching television or a computer terminal—safe havens in which to hide. Sitting around a porch and talking is becoming extinct, as is reading aloud to children [16, p. 58].

In reading Stoll carefully, it becomes apparent that his criticism of computer technology illuminates a broader cultural issue. Although computers are seemingly irrelevant to much of our daily activities, they play a pervasive and inescapable role in shaping the modern world. The virtues of computer technology are extolled by politicians, scientists, businessmen, and intellectuals alike. There is a rush to keep pace with technological advances and to computerize virtually all components of social life. Indeed, the penetration of computers into education, business, dating, friendship, political governance, war, etc., is rooted in a belief that computers solve problems and make life better. In this regard, computer technologies are a specific form of technological achievement that prevails in American life, that is to say, they are a tangible product of the cultural value of technicism. Stoll offers a warning about those enthusiasts who promote technology as the solution to complex social, cultural, and personal problems:

The key ingredient of their silicon snake oil is a technocratic belief that computers and networks will make a better society. Access to information, better communications, and electronic programs can cure social problems.

I don't believe them. There are no simple technological solutions to social problems . . . Access to a universe of information cannot solve our problems . . . [16, p. 50].

Thus, the evolution of technicism and communication technology transformed the culture and organization of social life. It introduced the notions of mass society and public audience. Ironically, however, in the modern conceptualization of public, it is required that people be treated as distinct, isolated, and private persons [14, p. 98]. Communication technology is the lifeblood of mass society, and the massification of the modernizing society was historically predicated on the privatization of the individual and the rise of the value of individualism [17]. Technology and individualism were inherent and central to the social evolution toward modernity. Simply put, the development of modern society has been largely shaped by these forces, and they continue to be prominent in the creation of contemporary ways of life. Technology and individualism are also dominant forces in shaping contemporary ways of death. And, as we saw in the preceding chapter, the modern patterns of technological reliance and cultural individualism are not just major factors that mold the ways of death, they are insufficient in relieving suffering and providing meaning in the modern encounter with mortality.

THE PROBLEM OF MEANING AND SPIRITUAL LONGING

The rise of technological dependency is, in many ways, centered around things, not persons. The driving ideology of technicism suggests that material goods and technology are vital to social progress and improvement of the conditions of human life. As already suggested, there can be no argument that technological achievements have made impressive contributions to the quality of modern life. However, they have also brought unparalleled danger and destructiveness into everyday social experience. Even more important than the tension between the specific benefits and disadvantages of technology is the spirit of the society that is engendered by technicism, and how the spirit of technicism concretely affects the lives of individuals. In many ways, the notion of technocratic consciousness is ethereal and metaphoric. It becomes relevant to the everyday life of ordinary citizens, however, through the value of materialism. It seems that very few people indeed want to be left out of the American adventure in materialism. Thus, ordinary people are influenced not so much by the intrinsic ideology of technicism. Rather, they value technological ways of life because they perceive that personal, material gain will accrue and improve the quality of their life. Thus, it is not technocratic consciousness that promotes loyalty to the system, but concrete technologically-improved gratification, that is to say, "consumerism" [14, p. 262].

Much of the spirit of American society is rooted in materialism and self-gratification. Material consumption and technological control over nature are salient features of social life, as are private property, power, and profit. Acquiring and showing off property is very American, as is the psychoemotional "thrill of acquisition." In many ways, human and social worth is associated with material success, and many persons identify themselves and others by the formula:

ONE IS = WHAT ONE HAS AND WHAT ONE CONSUMES [18, p. 15].

Our society has reached an unparalleled state of achievement in materialism, technological development, and individualism. Yet, despite the triumph and promises of technicism, complaints about unhappiness and meaninglessness abound. I am especially struck by the proliferation of self-help type literature in the past decade. For example, Thomas Moore's book, *Care of the Soul: A Guide for Cultivating Depth and Sacredness in Everyday Life,* spent the better part of a year on many bestseller lists [19]. "Silly," little recipe-type-books on how to live more meaningfully are enormously popular. Books such as *Chicken Soup for the Soul* [20], *How to Survive the Loss of a Love* [21], *Mars and Venus on a Date* [22], *Life's Little Instruction Book* [23], etc., are products of a "new age" emphasis on meaninglessness, soulfulness, and fulfilling patterns of living. Not only is the production of these materials skyrocketing, it reflects the cultural current toward personal discontent and privatization of social problems. Specifically, the new age and self-help movements have grown by leaps and bounds precisely because Americans are hungering for interpersonal and spiritual connectivity. In this regard, we have recently witnessed a resurgence of interest in spiritual rehabilitation in our decidedly materialistic culture. In fact, a small but lucrative "new age" industry has emerged in response to the contemporary longings for a fulfilling and meaningful life. Pop-gurus are flourishing, offering answers to the contemporary malaise of spiritual and existential meaning. Indeed, this recently evolving interest in spiritual awareness may seem at odds with the technocratic vision of life. These spiritual issues, however, have emerged because the purely technocratic worldview fails to provide for nurturance and meaning in the non-material or non-physical spheres of our lives. In addition, as we will see, the contemporary spiritual movement is not hostile to technocratic ways of life. In fact, it has been significantly shaped and molded by the American tradition of materialism and self-achievement and is comfortably at home within this framework.

Perhaps the pivotal question to raise is this: In an age of enormous technological and material attainment, why are so many individuals unhappy and longing for fulfillment? Why, surrounded by the promises of technological and material palliation, is contemporary life so full of tension, strain, and faith-lessness? The answer, I suggest, lies in technocratic ways of life which have paralyzed the meaningful development of spirituality and human well being. As Moore observes:

> The great malady of the twentieth century, implicated in all of our troubles and affecting us individually and socially, is "loss of soul." When soul is neglected, it doesn't just go away; it appears symptomatically in obsessions, addictions, violence, and loss of meaning. Our temptation is to isolate these symptoms or try to eradicate them one by one; but the root problem is that we have lost our wisdom about the soul, or even our interest in it [19, p. xi].

In spite of the dominance of technicism, materialism, and self-focus, enormous personal discontent is part of the everyday cultural landscape. As Moore percep-tively observes, a chill of soullessness hovers over the American landscape and is reflected in the pervasive emotional complaints and disaffections of our time. These include the fact that:

- Depression has become a dominant cultural icon
- Lack of personal fulfillment is a significant part of our cultural conversation
- A longing for spiritual fulfillment simmers beneath the veneer of our materialistic, self-oriented lifestyle
- Complaints of emptiness and meaninglessness persist
- Disillusionment about marriage and intimacy is widespread
- Feelings of personal inadequacy, of feeling diminished in terms of self-worth and self-esteem are pervasive.

These psychosocial-emotional "complaints of our time" have become so commonplace that we take their presence for granted. They are pervasive through-out the culture, disturbing our collective and personal sense of well-being. They are also both reflective of ways of life that create soullessness, and ways of life that are spawned by soullessness:

> All of these symptoms reflect a loss of soul and let us know what the soul craves. We yearn excessively for entertainment, power, intimacy, sexual fulfillment, and material things, and we think we can find these things with the right relationship, or job, the right church or therapy. But without soul, whatever we find will be unsatisfying, for what we truly long for is the soul in each of these areas. Lacking that soulfulness, we attempt to gather these alluring satisfactions to us in great masses, thinking appar-ently that quantity will make up for a lack of quality [19, p. xvi].

The point to be made is that the values of modern, technological society make "soulful life" difficult. Loss of soul and yearning for spiritual fulfillment is therefore inherent to our time and our lives. In the rush to modernize, American society has transformed the problems of the world into technical problems and one of the obsessions of the modern age has become rational control. This obsession is based upon the belief system that all parts of life can be controlled. In this framework we assume that the ability to control everything—from sickness, to the weather, to the economy, to the production of children and life itself—is ultimately for the betterment of humanity [24]. Thus, in the pursuit of the modern ways of life—technological achievement, money and materialism, convenience, self and individualism, we have sacrificed much of our spiritual meaning and interpersonal connectivity. Correspondingly, as we have already seen, we have lost much of our ability to confront and ease the suffering of dying persons. Everything around us in our daily lives tells us we should be mechanically sophisticated, electronically quick, and informational in our dealings with each other. In this age of telecommunications—which, by the way, literally means "distant connections"—we are urged to be efficient [25, p. xvii]. As we become proficient in efficiency and control, however, we lose our capacity to confront experiences which are complicated, elusive, and not rationally manageable. Thus, it is from the conditions of ordinary life that not only enormous spiritual yearnings emerge, but the meaninglessness and horror of dying and suffering as well.

In the midst of our hi-tech, materialistic culture, a resurgence of interest in spirituality is taking place. Spiritual bookstores abound and, as previously indicated, mainstream bookstores are stocking spiritual and new age sections with a deluge of books, magazines, and tapes. All of these materials stem from our great spiritual yearnings and proclaim to be able to transform, illuminate, enhance, and make more meaningful the life of the buyer. It is easy to see how notions of personal growth, self-help, and spiritual transformation have become increasingly a part of the present day cultural conversation. Inspirational speakers and spiritual authority figures are appearing everywhere and have achieved a celebrity-like status [26, p. 14].

Upon first glance, it would appear that the culture is at the threshold of a spiritual revolution that offers to transform the ways of life. The recent renaissance in spirituality, however, is neither revolutionary nor transformational. Rather than offering the possibility of cultural revolution and change, the modern spiritual movement is organized and packaged in ways that make it compatible with prevailing cultural values. Most notably, contemporary spiritualism appeals to the materialistic and narcissistic impulses of our times. As superstar guru Deepak Chopra rather shamelessly puts it, spiritual conversion is the way to make all one's worldly dreams come true:

> Together we will seek self-knowledge and a profound understanding of
> our mind/body/spirit connection to the universe outside of us. With this

understanding we will have infinite power to break through limitations
and create a world where all dreams come true. . . . where our every
desire—emotional, spiritual, and yes, material—is spontaneously fulfilled [27, p. 46].

Not only is the spiritualism of so many of the modern celebrity gurus self-
promotional and self-seeking, it is a fashionable form of capitalistic production
and consumption. It is fashionable and the pop spiritual guru business is flourishing because its message is seductive. In an age where there is so much existential
anxiety and tension, there is enormous comfort in the simplicity of the message
and in the life transforming promises that it contains:

. . . in the modern spiritual marketplace . . . comfort has become more
relevant than truth and, because of this, over time many ideas have
become sacred in order to ensure that no clouds will appear in an otherwise blue sky . . . As the current interest in the spiritual dimension of life
continues to grow, now even beginning to enter the mainstream, simultaneously it seems that the deeper implications of spiritual revelation are
increasingly becoming submerged beneath the prevailing climate of
pleasant feelings, naive expectations *and all-too-often sentimental hopes
and dreams* [26, p. 17].

There is an easy, feel-good aura about the contemporary spiritual movement.
In this fashion, spirituality becomes a means of control and achievement consistent with the broader emphases of modern, technological society. People are
attracted to this new brand of spirituality precisely because it promises escape
from anxiety and meaninglessness:

Gurus often tell us exactly what we want to hear. "There is no death."
That is the primary message of spirituality gurus. Better yet, this relief
from fear of death is easily obtained. The spiritual peace and enlightenment offered by pop gurus doesn't require a lifetime of discipline. It
requires only that you suspend your critical judgement, attend their lec-
tures and workshops, and buy their books or tapes [28, p. 60].

In many ways, material culture is shaping this spiritual movement. Anything
offensive or subversive to the broader values of technology, materialism, and
self-orientation have been removed. The fundamental nature of the technicism,
consumption practices, and self-obsession which prevail in American life has
remained unchanged by the recent cultural interest in spiritual enlightenment. In
reality, the facts of material culture have subsumed the new culture of spirituality
under their rubric, and the new culture of spiritualism is evolving in a way that
preserves and cultivates the identity of material culture. In this way, contemporary
spiritual leaders and activity are packaged so as to honor the ways of hi-tech

capitalism. Spirituality is promoted in a way that resembles the marketing of any other product. It is designed to become easier to propagate by making it more attractive and palatable to the materialistic world-view [29, p. 64].

There is an unmistakable fast food like quality to this brand of spirituality. It is quick, easy, uncomplicated, efficient, profitable, and serves an immediate need. Yet, like fast food itself, which is nutritionally inadequate and satisfies hunger for a scant hour or two, there is strong evidence that modern spiritualism is spiritually inadequate. While offering temporary relief from spiritual hunger, it is essentially vapid and without enduring meaning in facing the complexities of life. And, as we have seen and will continue to see, it is grossly inadequate in addressing the contemporary issues involved in confronting the complex realities of belligerent disease, dying, death, and in relieving associated suffering.

MEANINGLESSNESS IN DYING: A SUMMARY

Ivan Ilych was a product of Tolstoy's imaginative critique of materialistic society, with its proclivity toward meaningless life and meaningless dying. Deluded by feelings of omnipotence and immortality, Ivan embraced ways of life that are characteristic of American technicism: security, comfort, rational control over life and its experiences, self-absorption, success, and materialism. Until his miraculous deathbed conversion, Ivan lived a life bereft of meaningful spirituality, and his impoverished spiritual state was central to his battle with unrelieved suffering and meaninglessness in dying.

Jerome Groopman, an oncologist at Harvard's Beth Israel Deaconess Medical Center, has written a case history of a "real life" Ivan Ilych. In his narrative, he describes how a fifty-five-year-old cancer patient, a Wall Street mogul who, like Ivan, seemingly had it all, was inconsolably terrified by his disease and the imminence of death [30]. During his initial physical examination, the patient described himself with the same sense of shame that haunted Ivan Ilych.

> I'm a bag of water. Even my balls are bathed in this sewage from the cancer [30, p. 65].

This patient had gone to see Dr. Groopman for an opinion of last resort. He was desperate and had been told by physicians at several other medical centers that there was absolutely nothing that could be done for him. He had been diagnosed with kidney cancer. A large malignant mass had been discovered in his right kidney that extended to the liver, major veins, and diaphragm. The kidney was surgically removed, but the cancer had spread to the liver, intestines, and pelvic bones. Upon physical exam, Dr. Groopman found cancerous lumps behind the left ear, a severely distended and swollen abdomen that was full of malignancy, cancerous nodules on his liver, soreness in his pelvic bones that were consistent with tumors revealed by the CAT scan, and grossly swollen legs and ankles that became elephantine from fluid retention. Not only was Kirk Baines seriously sick, he was at death's door. As Dr. Groopman reflects:

> As I examined him, I could feel death in the coolness of his flesh, in the sunken, jaundiced eyes, in the mottled color of his skin and lips [30, p. 65].

Yet, despite the utter seriousness of his condition, Mr. Baines was unable to resign himself to the fact that he was dying. Dr. Groopman felt that he had at most a few weeks to live. He also recognized that Kirk was terrified of death. As Mr. Baines expressed:

> "I didn't expect to be so afraid Jerry." He paused. "I'm not sure why. I rarely feel afraid. Maybe because I know that this is my last chance and I'll probably die, and after death . . . it's just nothingness . . . *nothingness*. No time. No place. No form. I don't ask for heaven. I'd take Hell. Just to be."

> "If you'll help me, I'll undergo anything, the worst side effects. They can't be worse than being dead [30, p. 68].

Kirk's dread of death—its meaninglessness in his very modern and secular world of materialism—drove him to technological dependency and desperation as addiction drives an alcoholic to the bottle of bourbon. He sought treatment after treatment and was essentially told it was time to go home and die.

In response to his fear and desperation, Dr. Groopman agreed to treat him with an innovative, radical, and aggressive regimen of chemotherapy. Astonishingly, and to the surprise of everyone, the treatment seemed to be working and the cancer had begun to yield to the medicines. Miraculously, a once hopeless and clearly terminal Kirk Baines was on his way to remission. The joy and excitement of Dr. Groopman at this turn of events, however, was overshadowed by the despair and despondency of Mr. Baines. Despite all of his medical tests showing that everything was in order, his "piss and vinegar" had disappeared. Painfully he had come to the realization that all the activities that energized him in his previously enviable and "successful" life seemed so unimportant. Like Ivan Ilych, in facing his death he came to recognize that he did not live as he should have. Consequently, Kirk spent his remission gloomy and sad. Rather than joy in the possibility of a full and uncomplicated recovery, there was sorrow in his heart. Indeed, for a man who had feared death so greatly and had struggled so hard against it, this despondency in remission was most perplexing.

Kirk did remarkably well, from a medical standpoint, for three to four months. In the fourth month, however, he developed a persistent, nagging pain in his back. He ignored the pain for several weeks and brought it to Dr. Groopman's attention during a regularly scheduled appointment. It became clear upon physical exam that the cancer had returned. Additional tests showed that it had begun to invade the spinal cord and central nervous system.

Dr. Groopman, who cared so much about and worked so hard on behalf of this patient, had the onerous task of telling him that the cancer had recurred, and that his medical condition was truly hopeless.

> . . . I sat by his bedside, my eyes level with his, and for a long time we were silent, absorbing the indistinct sounds that filtered into the room from the hospital corridor.

> "I'm sorry the magic didn't work longer," I finally offered.
> "It did more than anyone expected, Jerry. But you shouldn't feel sorry. *There was no reason to live anyway*" [30, p. 63].

What happened to Kirk Baines? He lived his life as a "player." He was in the middle of "the action." His success was envied. And above all else, he feared death and wanted to live so desperately. His despondency in remission and his surrender to death was out of character.

It seems that an epiphany of sorts occurred. The confrontation with mortality compelled Mr. Baines to examine his life. And, in examining his life he found that it was not worth living. All the things that were of such urgency to him: the deals, profit, the thrill of acquisition, and power suddenly became lifeless and unimportant. Despair in dying emerged because of his honest self-reflections about the life he had lived. As he says with painful candor, his life was stymied by emptiness and meant little beyond making the next deal:

> "I never really cared about the world's events or its people. Not deep down inside."
> "And when I went into remission . . . my deals and trades seemed pointless because I was a short-term investor. Like I told you, Jerry, I had no patience for the long-term. I had no interest in creating something . . . not a product in business or a partnership with a person. And now I have no equity. No dividends coming in . . ."
> "Jerry, you realize I'm right. . . . the remission meant nothing, *because it was too late to relive my life*. I once asked for Hell. Maybe God made this miracle to have me know what it will feel like" [30, p. 74] (emphasis added).

Dr. Groopman felt the insidious pain and burden of his patient facing death while never having meaningfully lived:

> There is no more awful death than to die with regret, feeling that you have
> lived a wasted life . . . Death delivering this shattering final sentence on
> your empty soul [30, p. 74].

Mr. Baines died on May 8, 1995. Dr. Groopman prayed that his soul had finally found comfort . . . a comfort that it could not find in life.

Ivan Ilych and Kirk Baines lived most ordinarily. Their lives were distinctively modern and reflected a modern consciousness. They were shaped by the interrelated forces of materialism, technological dependency, and self-centeredness. Their cries of anguish and purposelessness at the deathbed were reflections of the lives they had and lived, that is to say, the styles of life that prevail in the broader culture.

In sum, the modern commitment to technological savoir-faire has embraced a fix-it attitude in regard to the material side of life. Predicated upon the values of efficiency, productivity, and rationality, technicism promises efficient and expedient solutions to the problems of modern life. It assumes a panacea-like quality and creates the fantasy that all problems will capitulate to it [14, pp. 260-261]. However, as we see quite clearly, from the metaphorical images of Tolstoy, Duncan, Broch, and Huxley to the more important experiences of actual dying persons, the complexities of dying subvert and render inadequate the "identify and fix the problem" mindset of technicism. In spite of the triumphs of technology, materialism, and individualism, dying persons remain so alone in their deepest sorrows. As a result, self-deception and disillusionment are widespread when individuals and loved ones face death. Unrelieved suffering and terror also prevail.

Lurking beneath the façade of material comfort, technological progress, and self-absorption is an enormous hungering for meaningful life and spiritual fulfillment. The "soulless life" of technicism, materialism, and self-centeredness creates an illusion of problem-free living. It does so, however, by avoiding suffering as much as possible. Despite the fact that suffering can be a great illuminator of life, the everyday forms of modern life strive to promote the illusion of problem-free living, thereby creating widespread patterns of denial and avoidance of suffering. It is no wonder that when suffering, especially the suffering contained in confronting death, comes knocking at our doorsteps we are ill-prepared to respond. Thus, our incapacity to care effectively for dying individuals and ameliorate their suffering is a salient indicator of the type of society we have created and live in.

Yearnings of the deathbed are truly reflections of yearnings in life. Anguish and meaninglessness in dying are mirrored by soullessness and meaninglessness in living. And, as we shall see, the horribleness of modern dying, especially hi-tech dying, is directly produced by the values and organization of American cultural life. We will also see that the technocratic organization of society is evinced by technologically focused patterns of care in the medical system. And we will witness, through the lives of dying patients, that the experience of medicalized death is filled with suffering and is bereft of meaning. In this way, modern dying is technologically sophisticated but lacks a sense of cosmic connection, ritual, and meaning. Individuals, as we saw so poignantly in Chapter 2, are often forced to confront dying in isolation drawing upon private, personal resources. In sum, it may be said that the alienation, stigma, meaninglessness, suffering, turbulence, and normlessness which characterize the life-course of dying persons are created by the life-ways of the society at large.

REFERENCES

1. E. Hemingway, *The Snows of Kilimanjaro,* Macmillan, New York, 1986.
2. A. Camus, *A Happy Death,* Vintage Books, New York, 1973.
3. F. Dostoyevsky, Notes from *Underground,* Universal Press of America, Lanham, Maryland, 1969.
4. R. Solari, *Nourishing the Soul: Discovering the Sacred in Everyday Life,* Harper San Francisco, San Francisco, California, October 1995.
5. L. Tolstoy, *"The Death of Ivan Ilych" in the Short Novels of Tolstoy,* A. Maude (trans.), The Dial Press, New York, 1946.
6. United States Department of Health, Education, and Welfare, *Trends Affecting the United States Health Care System,* DHEW Publication No. HRA-7614503, January 1976.
7. E. Shils, Faith, Utility, and Legitimacy of Science, *Daedalus,* Summer 1974.
8. L. Marx, Does Improved Technology Mean Progress? *Technology Review, 71,* pp. 33-41, January 1987.
9. R. K. Merton, Foreword, in *The Technological Society,* J. Ellul (ed.), Vintage Books, New York, 1964.
10. J. Ellul, *The Technological Society,* Vintage Books, New York, 1964.
11. N. Postman, *Technolopoly,* Alfred Knopf, New York, 1972.
12. A. Teich, Thinking About Technology, in *Technology and the Future,* St. Martin's Press, New York, 1997.
13. L. Mumford, *The Myth of the Machine: The Pentagon of Power,* Harcourt, Brace, Jovanovich, New York, 1970.
14. A. Gouldner, *The Dialectic of Technology and Ideology,* Seabury Press, New York, 1976.
15. N. Postman, *The Disappearance of Childhood,* Delacorte Press, New York, 1983.
16. C. Stall, *Silicon Snake Oil: Second Thoughts on the Information Highway,* Anchor Books, New York, 1995.
17. R. Nisbet, *The Quest for Community,* Oxford University Press, New York, 1981.
18. E. Fromm, *To Have Or To Be?* Bantam Books, New York, 1981.
19. T. Moore, *Care of the Soul: A Guide for Cultivating Depth and Sacredness in Everyday Life,* HarperPerennial, New York, 1994.
20. J. Canfield and M. V. Hansen, *Chicken Soup for the Soul,* Health Communications, Inc., Deerfield Beach, Florida, 1993.
21. P. McWilliams, P. Bloomfield, and H. Harold, *How to Survive the Loss of a Love,* M. Colgrove (ed.), Prelude Press, Los Angeles, California, November 1993.

22. J. Gray, *Mars and Venus on a Date: A Guide for Navigating the 5 Stages of Dating to Create a Loving and Lasting Relationship,* HarperCollins, New York, July 1998.

23. H. J. Brown, Jr., *Life's Little Instruction Book,* Rutledge Hill Press, Nashville, Tennessee, 1991.

24. J. W. Jones, *In the Middle of this Road We Call Our Life,* HarperCollins, New York, pp. 73-78, 1996.

25. T. Moore, *Soul Mates: Honoring the Mysteries of Home and Relationship,* HarperPerennial, New York, 1994.

26. A. Cohen, The Modern Spiritual Predicament: An Inquiry into the Popularization of East-Meets-West Spirituality, in *What is Enlightenment?,* Fall/Winter 1997.

27. S. Bridle, Deepak Chopra: The Man With the Golden Tongue, in *What is Enlightenment?,* S. Bridle, A. Edelstein, and C. Hamilton (eds.), Fall/Winter 1997.

28. W. Kaminer, Why We Love Gurus, *Newsweek,* October 30, 1997.

29. A. Codrescu, The Disappearance of the Outside, in *What is Enlightenment?,* S. Bridle, A. Edelstein, and C. Hamilton (eds.), Fall/Winter, 1997.

30. J. Groopman, The Last Deal, *The New Yorker,* September 8, 1997.

CHAPTER 4

Fear and Denial in the
Modern Context

He who pretends to look on death without fear lies. All men are afraid of dying, this is the great law of sentient beings, without which the entire species would soon be destroyed [1, p. 128].

Jean-Jacques Rousseau

Neither the sun nor death can be looked at steadily [2, p. 17].

La Rochefoucauld

. . . the idea of death, the fear of it haunts the human animal like nothing else; it is a mainspring of human activity—activity designed largely to overcome it by denying in some way that it is the final destiny of man [3, p. IX].

Ernest Becker

And the fears of the people supported the persistent official policy of silence and denial [4, p. 65].

Thomas Mann

I have been exploring what is means to die in an age of technological dependency and individualism. As we have seen, there is much in society that promotes the omnipotence of technology and of the self. Death, however, threatens the faith Americans have placed in these values. Not only is the individual person annihilated by death, death dramatically exposes the shortcomings of technology and reveals that its capacity to fix life's problems is limited. In addition, dying is decidedly more difficult today as prevailing folkways have cast aside many of the myths, rituals, ceremonies, and customs traditionally relied upon to ease the sting of death. The result is that suffering and dying have lost moral meaning and importance, becoming intense sources of fear and anxiety.

In the modern milieu, Americans conspire in many ways to keep death isolated in a deep freeze of silence and avoidance. It is obvious that there is an absence of widespread visibility and engagement with matters of mortality in the daily patterns of cultural life. However, as I indicated in Chapter 1, death and its symbols have not always been so absent from social life. Traditionally, death held an important and visible place in the life of the community. The development of the twentieth century, however, precipitated sweeping and radical changes in humanity's relation to death and dying. Once public, dying has now become concealed—as if it were dirty or indecent. One can glean from the mortality narratives in Chapter 2 the profound sense of shame and humiliation that fills the life experience of persons whose bodies are ravaged by disease. Ariès describes how these feelings are a product of the new world of death that has been established in recent decades.

> Death no longer inspires fear solely because of its absolute negativity; it also turns the stomach, like any nauseating spectacle. It becomes improper, like the biological acts of man, the secretions of the human body. It is indecent to let someone die in public. It is no longer acceptable for strangers to come into a room that smells of urine, sweat, and gangrene, and where the sheets are soiled. Access to this room must be forbidden, except to a few intimates capable of overcoming their disgust, or to those indispensable persons who provide certain services. A new image of death is forming: the ugly and the hidden death, hidden because it is ugly and dirty [5, p. 569].

FOUNDATIONS OF DENIAL

Some years ago when the Supreme Court of the United States was wrestling with the problem of defining community standards of pornography, it commented that something is obscene when it makes an ordinary citizen of the community want to "vomit." It is not stretching too far to suggest that dying has become a form of pornography in the modern cultural context. It has an unsettling, dizzying, and nauseating impact on many lives. Still yet, the parallel between pornography of sex and pornography of death extends even further. As enormous community effort goes into cleaning up areas of pornography, litter, and dirt, such as in the recent transformation of New York City's Times Square area, modern society spends considerable effort on disinfecting the experience of dying. This inclination to hide and exclude death from everyday social activity is supported by the transfer of the place of death from home to the hospital. During the second-half of the twentieth century the burden of care, once assumed by neighbors, friends, and family, was passed onto strangers and medical caretakers. The new sites of death which emerged, most notably the hospital and long-term care facility, enabled the removal of unpleasant and horrifying sights of the dying process from ordinary social and cultural experience. This transformation, whereby death was sequestered and institutionally confined, was attractive to a culture that was increasingly fearful of dying. Ariès succinctly describes this transformation:

The dying man's bedroom has passed from the home to the hospital. For technical and medical reasons, this transformation has been accepted by families, and popularized and facilitated by their complicity. The hospital is the only place where death is sure of escaping a visibility—or what remains of it—that is hereafter regarded as unsuitable and morbid. The hospital has become the place of solitary death [5, p. 571].

In the hospital, dying is removed from the moral and social fabric of the culture. It becomes redefined into a technical process that is professionally and bureaucratically controlled. The horribleness and enormous suffering of dying is banished from public visibility as it is isolated within the professional, technical confines of the hospital. It is also important to note that in this way the experience of dying has become both medicalized and sequestered out-of-the-way. It has been argued that the medicalization and isolation of dying are forms of death denial. Indeed, if we examine the way dying and death are organized in the hospital culture, a clear pattern of closed and obscured death awareness emerges. In their classic studies, Glaser and Strauss have extensively reported on patterns of evasive interaction between physicians, nurses, and patients. In these patterns of avoidance, providers, patients, and loved ones go to great lengths to hide or obscure the realities of death [6]. David Sudnow describes, in his noteworthy study of the social organization of death in the hospital, a wide range of means by which death is symbolically and literally hidden [7]. In the hospital, death is controlled by professionals and its presence is concealed and disguised by bureaucratic routine. Le Shan has found that nurses tend to construct a glass curtain, an impenetrable veil of silence between themselves and very sick, dying patients [8]. Nurses, when performing many specific technological tasks, are at ease and comfortable when taking care of dying persons. However, when free-flowing conversations begin to take place and nurses are nudged out of the protective blanket of professional, technical routine, they tend to become ill-at-ease and impatient. When this occurs, they often scurry to avoid personal interactions with patients and their families as conversations may turn toward matters of suffering, dying, and death. In this process of avoidance, they typically resume their professional posture and direct attention from personal matters of loss and grief by tending to technical tasks—adjusting life support equipment, checking tubular connections, adjusting the bed, etc., before hurrying off to complete paperwork or to see another patient, etc. [9].

As we will see in the following chapter, physicians are notoriously inept at delivering bad news to patients and families. Despite prodding from the courts and a dramatically changing moral climate, physicians remain reluctant to fully share diagnosis and prognosis information. They are even more reticent to engage in meaningful conversation about the human experience of dying. As Jay Katz puts it, the prevailing belief among physicians still seems to be that patients should not be completely informed about dire prognosis. They also seem to believe that expressions of hope and reassurance, which are often unrealistic and exaggerated, are preferable to realistic appraisal of the patients' condition. And, as physicians circumvent meaningful conversations and dispense liberal doses of hope, patients are often left confused and deprived of the opportunity to make informed decisions about the end of their lives. In this context, patients, families, and physicians are complicit in creating a world of avoidance and nonconfrontation. However, as we will see in subsequent chapters, in the prevailing culture of pretense and denial dying patients feel isolated, alone, and abandoned. In this isolation, they tend to cling all the more tenaciously to hopeful reassurances provided by their physicians [10].

In the modern context in which dying has lost its meaningfulness, death is viewed as failure. This fact helps explain the great sense of shame and humiliation that dying persons and their loved ones feel. In addition, many physicians view death as defeat and failure on both a personal and professional level. As long as dying is seen as shameful and death is viewed as failure, open and honest communication will be stymied. Simply, no one likes to talk about their short-comings or failures. These, instead, are remanded to the isolated, invisible realm of our collective human experience. That is to say, they are, in fact, denied.

In the current cultural and medical framework, silence surrounds suffering, dying, and death. These keenly felt human experiences are plunged deep beneath the surface of everyday cultural activities, becoming concealed and privatized. As already indicated, norms and rituals that once helped to sustain and guide persons through the dying process have vanished. It is precisely this devaluation of dying as an important cultural experience that has subsumed the management and control of dying in the technological, medical model. The crucial point to be made is that cultural meaninglessness prompts widespread avoidance and denial, and that the cultural campaign to deny death is waged largely within the strictures of technological medicine [11].

Yet, despite the widespread cultural inclination to avoid open confrontation, there may be reason to believe that death is not actually denied as much as some have claimed. In the first place, death has been a topic of increasing attention in academia and in popular literature. Scholars who have written, during the past two decades, about the American ways of death denial have contributed to a growing body of professional literature. The presence of this literature, some of it even publicly visible on the shelves of bookstores, mitigates denial. Slowly but surely, thanatology courses on college campuses began to emerge. Textbooks began to proliferate during the 1980s. Movies and plays began to tackle the culturally taboo topics of suffering and dying. Self-help and support groups have burgeoned. An entire genre of popular, self-help literature on grief has emerged—some of which, ironically in this age of denial, became best sellers. More recently, newspapers, television, and magazines have catapulted Jack Kevorkian into the mainstream of cultural conversation. National Public Radio has produced an excellent series on end-of-life care. Funeral homes advertise in the Yellow Pages, and more recently have advertised their services on the previously forbidden medium of television. A "dying well," palliative care movement is beginning to take form within the profession of medicine. Death, it seems, is slowly creeping out of the closet and assuming a somewhat visible status in an otherwise death-denying environment.

Thus, it would appear that the American relationship to death and dying is changing. Avoidance and denial seem to coexist with a newly fashioned thrust toward openness. The evolution of this relationship between "avoidance" and "acceptance" requires further contemplation. The key point to consider is whether or not the thanatology movement, with its focus on dignity and openly acknowledging death as a vital part of the human experience, represents a transformation of attitudes or is a recasting of the American framework of denial into a new form.

DENIAL VS. OPENNESS:
TRANSFORMATION OF SUBSTANCE OR STYLE?

The most incisive discussion of the denial of death is offered by Ernest Becker. His observation begin by pointing to the intrinsic vulnerability of humanity to death. I began Chapter 1 by arguing that death transforms the human experience, provides urgency to our lives, and makes our lives meaningful like nothing else can. Similarly, Becker argues that death is an unparalleled force in the human experience. He, however, has a slightly different take on why it has such a significant place. He begins by suggesting that the inevitability of death elicits a fear that is unparalleled, pervasive and all consuming. In his words, of all the things that move humanity, the principal one includes the terror of death, the universality of the fear of death, and the inherent inability to accept what nature and destiny have in store for each of us [3].

Becker's central point is that the need to transcend death is natural and instinctual. Disease and death are principal evils in human life, and humans crave not just life itself but to be prosperous and healthy. Becker argues that disease undermines the ability to enjoy prosperity while one is alive, and death heartlessly eliminates it all together. In this way, the end of life is frightening and is perceived as inherently evil and destructive to human welfare. This fear drives humans, in all times and places, to attempt to transcend death through cultural systems and symbols [3]. In seeking to avoid the realities of death, humans have always relied on cultural folkways to facilitate a transcendence of death. All cultures, in varying forms and styles, create symbols and images that offer an antidote to the horror of death and bodily decay. Or, as in the case of modern society, they develop sophisticated machinery to fight and avert death. In a sense, all societies attempt to provide an escape hatch from death. In other words, they find their own particular way of providing a protective pair of mortality sunglasses that shade the eyes from the horrible glare of death in its naked, most straightforward forms.

In regard to culturally rooted patterns of death transcendence, Becker speaks of hero systems. Heroism, first and foremost, starts from the horror of death and the need to quell its terrifying impact. Society in this regard erects hero systems that are designed to nullify or ease death's impact, foremost of which is to champion the individual who steadfastly looks death in the eye and refuses to quiver in its presence. As Becker puts it:

> We admire most the courage to face death; we give such valor our highest and most constant adoration; it moves us deeply in our hearts because we have doubts about how brave we, ourselves would be. When we see a man bravely facing his own extinction we rehearse the greatest victory we can imagine. And so the hero has been the center of human honor and acclaims since . . . the beginning of . . . human evolution [12, pp. 11-12].

One of the universal facts of all cultures is that they institutionalize heroism in their folkways, symbols, and rituals. Each society, in its own unique and special way, generates styles of heroic transcendence over death, thereby becoming in itself a hero system that promises its citizens a victory over evil and death [3, pp. 11-12]. Frankly, it doesn't matter whether the cultural hero system is magical, religious, and primitive; or secular, modern, and scientific [12, pp. 124-125]. Universally, despite different styles and forms of denial, hero systems create transcendence, triumph, and control over death.

In primitive societies, ritual and ceremony were heavily relied upon to shield individuals and their community from evil and death. These rituals were connected to the ways of life and provided for cosmic meaning to suffering and the end of life:

> . . . primitive life was basically a rich and playful dramatization of life . . . primitive man set up his social life to give himself what he needed and wanted. . . . (He) set up his society as a stage, surrounded himself with actors to play different roles, invented gods to address the performance to, and then ran off one ritual drama after the other, raising himself to the stars and bringing the stars down into the affairs of men. He staged the dance of life, with himself at the center. And to think that when Western man first crashed, uninvited into these spectacular dramas, he was scornful of what he saw . . . Western man was being given a brief glimpse of the creations of human genius, and like a petulant imbecile bully who feels discomfort at what he doesn't understand, he proceeded to smash everything in sight [3, p. 5].

It was the ways of life and the expressions of ritual which secured apotheosis for the vulnerable and technologically inept "primitive." Ritual dramas of life in the face of death enabled personal and collective ascendancy over death. They allowed the living to enter into the world of the dead and the dead to enter into the world of the living. In essence, these grand rituals provided comfort and protection. They paved the way for communities to continue on in the midst of death and destruction, and endowed individual and collective life with an enduring sense of purpose.

The historical account of Ariès is also relevant at this point and provides another point of view. In his discussion of the evolution of Western attitudes toward death, Ariès presents convincing evidence that traditionally individuals were not as terrified of death as modern people are. In fact, Ariès, in contrast to Becker, argues that traditional ways of life were essentially free from fear and denial of death. His point is that while individuals may have been sad about the ending of their lives, their sorrow was slight in terms of both the emotional sensibilities of the time and the contemporary fear of dying. Becker, in responding to Ariès, would argue that the Tame Death, Death of the Self, Remote, and Imminent Death, and the romanticized Death of the Other were not free from fear and denial. Rather, it was the intrinsic fear of death that gave rise to elaborate meaning and rituals consistent with the traditional ways of life. These rituals eased the terror of death, and enabled individuals to confront dying with courage and reassurance throughout the ages. Thus, the seeming absence of fear was in fact a reduction and control of fear by cultural intervention. Traditional rituals and meanings generated an atmosphere of openness that eased the terror of death and offered solace to dying individuals. According to Becker, however, the terror of death would not remain submerged indefinitely. It would return with a fury if traditional rituals and meaning dissipated, as he argues is the case in the contemporary world.

Despite their irreconcilable, interpretive differences, Ariès and Becker agree on an important point. They both recognize the importance of traditional patterns of ritual and ceremony in providing comfort during periods of suffering, loss, and death. For Becker, the richness and palliative power of rituals were emblematic of the genius of traditional ways of life. For Ariès, ritual and ceremony were inherently a product of traditional ways of life and offered enormous solace and comfort to dying and grieving persons. In addition, Ariès and Becker also come to the common conclusion that rituals, once so rich and vibrant as sources of comfort in the shadow of death, have become empty, shallow, and are disappearing altogether. Ariès laments the devolution of meaning and ritualized response: society no longer observes a pause . . . everything . . . goes on as if nobody died anymore [12, p. 15]. Becker, with broader intentions, probes deeper and argues that modern rituals have become hollow and unsatisfying. As a result, modern individuals are deprived of stable, meaningful life rituals, and have become increasingly "confused," "impotent," and "empty" during both their lives and deaths [5, p. 560].

In light of Becker's criticism of the organization of modern life, it is important to pose the following question: What is it that makes humanity empty, confused, and impotent in the contemporary setting? His answer and mine are quite similar. It is because the meanings of life and death in the materialistic, technologically driven society have become shallow, thereby precipitating enormous insecurities and anxieties. As discussed in the preceding chapter, one does not have to look too far to see how complaints of personal unease and worry permeate the culture. And, this widespread base of anxiety in living becomes exacerbated into a deep dread and anguish when individuals are forced to confront the end of life. According to Becker, greed, power, and wealth have become the modern response to vulnerability and insecurity inherent in the human condition. They provide for a base of honor in our materialistic society, and generate an illusion of omnipotence and immorality. Becker takes this argument to its logical extreme, and asserts that the dread of death and emptiness of life in the twentieth century have been responsible for cultivating unprecedented evil through the pursuit of greed, power, and the associated development of destructive capabilities.

Thus, for Becker, the stupidity and inhumanity of humanity lies in the nature of our social arrangements. In the modern context, new patterns of death denial have emerged and have become dangerous and dehumanizing. Up to a point, traditional cultures creatively designed rituals to "deny" death, and these rituals enriched the life of the community. In the absence of meaning systems and rituals, modern society has exploded onto a dangerous and irrational course; shallowness and emptiness have created a crisis of legitimacy. In this regard, the argument of Becker is remarkably similar to Moore and others who have made the case that one of the great afflictions of modern life is spiritual emptiness and soullessness. As discussed in the previous chapter, narcissism, self-seeking materialism, and heroic use of science and technology have become prominent forces that shape daily life. In this environment of self-glorification, material gratification, and extraordinary technological achievement, suffering, dying, and death are pushed to the periphery of cultural experience. Individuals are seduced into believing the illusion that, in this cultural context of denial, the facts of death and suffering are inconsequential to their daily, personal lives.

A significant part of the legitimization crisis of modern society lies in the fact that religion is no longer a far-reaching, culturally valid hero system. Most modern Americans have difficulty in believing what primitive and traditional cultures once held sacred, namely, that death is a cause for celebration and a ritual elevation to a higher form of life or eternal salvation. Fear of death is therefore inherent in our ways of life. So is denial, as a consciousness of death is intolerable in a secular age, and the ways of life in the secular environment are threatened by suffering and death. In this regard, Becker argues that individuals seek to eliminate dying and suffering from their thoughts and daily activities. Escapist, capitalist behaviors that deny vulnerability and mortality are very useful in this regard and are consistent with the collective, modern need to avoid death. Consider, for example, the social organization of sports in modern society. In some respects, star athletes have become contemporary heroes, and enormous numbers of individuals root feverishly for their favorite teams and players. Sports in America have not just evolved into a lucrative industry, they have penetrated deeply into the culture in ways that shape the very essence of our collective character. Conversation about sports that occur throughout the culture—at street corners, at water coolers, and in barrooms—are often passionate and vibrant. These conversations reflect an identification and psychological connection with something that is far greater and more powerful than the individual fan. By identifying with one's favorite team, and investing energy into the success of that team, a vicarious transcendence is achieved. A vulnerable, invisible mortal individual becomes part of something that is triumphant, powerful, and enduring. Thus, a fan immersed in the crowd in a stadium has his energies absorbed by the game. Euphoria-promoting behaviors unify the crowd as one, and excitement and energy swell. Intriguingly, Becker interprets the widespread embracing of the collective sports phenomena as a necessary means of escape in modern life. It is a culturally promoted contrivance that enables individuals to forget their vulnerabilities and impotence, at least temporarily. And, it is precisely because the energizing effect is fleeting that the feelings of euphoria and vitalization must be continually reproduced—by the next game, event, or season. This secures a lucrative financial future for sports and establishes a basis for cultural and individualistic "addiction."

Once again, as we saw in the previous chapter, materialism is a prominent value in American life. Becker makes the argument that the evolution of capitalism as an economic and social system is a modern form of death denial. That is to say, in capitalism it is through the thrill of acquisition and the pursuit of wealth that human frailty is overcome. Power accrues as wealth and possessions amass, and wealth endows immortality as it is passed on to one's heirs [13, p. 247]. Narcissism, another prominent fact of American cultural life, is also related to the denial of death. In an age of individualism, we become hopelessly absorbed with ourselves. Although we know that death is an unavoidable reality, narcissism facilitates the self-delusion that practically everyone else is expendable, except ourselves [13, p. 248]. In this era of individualism, the death of oneself becomes increasingly inconceivable. When one matters more than anything or anyone else, self-absorption does not allow for the possibility that one will no longer exist. In this way, the deeper we plunge into narcissistic, self-admiration and idolization the more we become oblivious to our inevitable fate. As a culture, the more oblivious we become, the more unable we are to face up to the facts of death in our daily activities. Death is accordingly hidden and denied.

Thus, the social organization of modern life precipitates widespread oblivion and denial:

> Modern man is drinking and drugging himself out of awareness, or he spends his time shopping (or admiring and entertaining himself), which is the same thing. As awareness (of our common human condition) calls for types of heroic dedication that his culture no longer provides for him, society continues to help him forget [12, pp. 81-82].

Becker presents a compelling argument. Convincing as his reasoning is, however, he is unable to establish a causal connection between the fear of death and the emergence of scientific, capitalistic, and escapist pursuits of modern society. In fact, it is quite possible that an inverted relationship exists between fear of death and the qualities of life in the modern context. It certainly makes sense to argue that our cultural preoccupation with materialism, narcissism, and technological progress facilitates a fear of death. It is also reasonable to argue that widespread social conditions of diminished community, heightened individualism and secularism lead us to the fear of death. Thus, those very factors which Becker identifies as compensation for our terror of death may instead be what facilitates our fear:

> Becker's fateful assumption is that the fear of death leads to aggression and competition among people, and he never considers that the casual relationship may be the reverse, that the desperate death denying behavior he describes might be altered by a sense of connection and significance to other people that can be provided by genuinely communal relationships [3, p. 2].

There are several factors which make Becker's thesis one-dimensional. He sees death denial as being inherently a product of the biopsychological fear of death. He never fully considers the possibility that cultural values and social structures can cultivate a dread of death. He assumes that the inherent terror of death must inevitably lead to denial. He never contemplates the potential in humanity to find ways to openly reconcile itself to mortality, nor does he allow for the possibility that social structures can be designed to diminish fear and generate meaningful acceptance. In this regard, the failure to fully consider the rich, historical portraits of traditional patterns of death, as described by Ariès, Illich, Stannard and others, leaves Becker's analysis incomplete.

In addition, he typically uses the concept of denial in such sweeping and encompassing ways that at times it becomes overly broad and meaningless. Indeed, he even admits to using the term "unfairly" to encompass every possible explanation for death-related behaviors. Similarly, in the thanatology literature, the concept of denial is often used in overly generalized and indiscriminant ways. It is often poorly defined, and its meaning is too broad for specific application and description [3, p. 284]. There is a difference between fear of dying and fear of death, but the two are generally lumped together in the literature. It may very well be that modern individuals do not fear death as much as they fear dying. In some cases, death may even be seen as a welcome release from intolerable suffering, looked forward to, or actively sought in order to relieve suffering. In a culture where systems of support are fractured and dwindled, individualism is a prized value, and technology is a dominant force, the great cultural fear of death may more precisely be a fear of dying—in isolation, indignity, and meaninglessness. It may be that while death itself does frighten, greater terror resides in the ways of dying that are presently so undignified and dehumanized. The denigration of personhood and dignity, coupled with unrelieved suffering, may be what is most intolerable about death in modern society. Thus, it is not necessarily the ending of life that precipitates the most fear. Rather, it may be the way in which life ends. The patient experiences in Chapter 2, and those that follow, support this view as they reveal that the decimation of personhood and dignity are primary sources of worry and frustration for dying persons. The fear of dying is intensified because dying persons are defiled, stigmatized, and relegated to the role of second class citizens. Thus, on a societal level, fear and denial do not mean the complete avoidance of death, but more correctly refer to the medicalization of death which has redefined the dying process into a low status, technology intensive, and potentially contaminating situation that needs to be contained and sanitized [14, p. 717].

Dying persons create a problem for the culture and the practice of medicine by their lingering, often refectory pressure. This lingering is typically full of chaos and suffering which are inherent to the messy, ugly image of contemporary death. Even the very term lingering, which would have been inapplicable to the life experience of dying persons fifty years ago, carries a negative, frightening connotation. Yet, the term itself offers insight into the nature and course of the dying experience in our technologically dependent culture and medical systems.

Dying persons become a blight upon cultural visions of narcissistic and technological achievement. Leiderman and Grisso's fascinating study of Gomers (Get Out of My Emergency Room) discusses what happens when technological medicine fails to eliminate disease and heal the aging [15]. Gomers, with their irreversible, debilitating illness, have very low status within the broader culture and the medical system. They are most likely to be socially isolated and receive inhumane care in the hospital. The inexorable progress of their disease underscores the inability of modern medicine to avert their deterioration. The Gomer, who is often confused and combative, conveys a distressing image and shatters the narcissistic, cultural dream of invincibility. This image underlines our human fear of illness, physical and intellectual decline, and loss of autonomy. It also dramatizes the fact that modern medicine, which promises to do much, often fails to deliver on its promise [14, p. 717]. Gomers, like dying persons, undermine the faith our culture has invested in technological medicine and our values of materialism and individualism.

The point to be made is that the concept of denial is compelling and useful, but only up to a point and in a loose and approximate way. On a personal level, we have already seen the great tendency for denial in Chapter 2. However, each of the persons I have discussed, either personally or publicly, flirted with open awareness in their confrontation with mortality. Denial for them was neither uniform nor unvarying. It was a significant component of their coming face-to-face with their illness, but it was by no means the only response they had. As we will see in ensuing chapters, denial is a huge part of the dynamics of death in the modern hospital setting. But even the most bureaucratized patterns and culture of care in the hospital are unable to completely avoid and deny the human outpourings of dying persons and loved ones.

In addition, when we think on a societal and institutional level, the concept of death denial is more metaphysical than actual. It expresses a set of cultural, institutional, and structural responses to dying, death, and suffering. In this regard, society engages and confronts death in varying ways. If death were fully denied, there would be no active involvement or relation between humans and mortality. It is for this reason we must revise, slightly, Becker's argument.

Societies, even modern societies, do not entirely deny death. Rather, they organize for it in ways that exert forms of social control. They sanction different kinds of myths, rituals, and strategies that determine the nature of death and set in motion culturally validated processes of conflict, reintegration, and adjustment of roles [16, p. 720]. In the process of organizing for death, modern society seeks to control, manage, and contain the process of dying in ways that least disturb the functioning of the ongoing cultural and social systems. Thus, although I have used and will continue to use the term denial in describing the modern ways of death, I use it in this sociologically qualified way. Death is not, nor ever has it been, produced out of existence. Rather, it is "denied" by social and cultural forces in that it is restrained, managed, and kept under control.

In this regard, when we reconfigure our contemplation of mortality, from the all encompassing concept of denial to the more specific concept of controlling and containing death, the seeming contradiction between America's orientation toward death-denial and the recent movement toward death awareness can be readily reconciled.

The pioneer of the death-awareness movement is Elisabeth Kübler-Ross. With the publication of *On Death and Dying* in 1969, she brought the issue of death out of the closet and into the mainstream of cultural conversation [17]. Ironically, in a culture of "denial" where issues of death and dying received such scant attention, her book received widespread recognition. It begins with a tone of lament in which she criticizes the technological underpinnings of modern death— loneliness, mechanization, dehumanization, and impersonalization. In fairly straightforward language she portrays how gruesome dying could be, and how medical treatment of dying persons is often missing compassion and sensitivity. She contrasted how dying persons may cry out for peace, rest, recognition of their sufferings, and dignity, but receive instead infusions, transfusions, invasive proce-dures, and technologically-driven plans of action. Her contrast struck a cord with the American public, which was becoming increasingly worried about the indig-nities in dying. Throughout her book there is reference to the idea of death-with-dignity. She zealously advocates the proposition that dying need not be some-thing terrible and tragic, but could become a springboard for courage, growth, enrichment and even joy. She offers a rather uncomplicated view of the serenity, acceptance, and personal courage that can be achieved in the stage of acceptance. Her rather simple and facile view of dignity and how it could be obtained was embraced as a source of comfort in a society that was becoming fearful of the indignities of technological death. In many ways, the appeal of her message was directly related to its simplicity and optimism. In short, it offered an uncomplicated solution to a troubling and complicated problem.

In addition to her emphasis on the personal triumph of dignity in dying, Kübler-Ross' subsequent work delved into a more ethereal realm, and probed spiritual and new age meanings of death. According to the latter body of her work, physical life means nothing. All matters of the physical world are mundane and trivial. Physical earthly existence, accordingly, is nothing more than a necessary prelude to "authentic experience," which she characterizes as the spiritual life of the self:

> You have to be in this temporary prison we call physical life, and you stay in this form until you have all of the positive experiences that this experience can afford you. But when you are in an energy pattern, you have access to all knowledge, understanding and unconditional love. You have all the wisdom of the universe [18, pp. 69-106].

The thrust of Kübler-Ross' message is two pronged. It stresses the humanistic feat of achieving dignity throughout dying. It also argues that death is not the cessation of life. Rather, it is the transition of life from earthly existence to unearthly, spiritual life. In either event, however, her message offers comfort. It facilitates control over death: either in its transformation of dying into an opportunity for growth and dignity or in its resurrection of physical death into a spiritual life-eternity.

Both the humanistic and spiritual essence of her manifesto on death and dying have had an enormous impact on shaping the thanatology revolution of the past three decades. The publication of *On Death and Dying,* and the pictorial interview in the November 20, 1969 issue of *LIFE* magazine catapulted Kübler-Ross into fame and national attention. Personal appearances on television, coverage in local and national newspapers and magazines including an interview in *Playboy* [18], coupled with her charismatic personality and outstanding skills as a communicator, quickly established her as the nation's leading authority on the care of the dying. Although she was only minimally involved with hands-on-care of dying patients and the development of hospice programs in America, the name of Kübler-Ross became synonymous with death and dying. In recent history, she has served as the dominant spokesperson for the needs of dying persons, and served as a pioneering advocate for dignified death. It is fair to say that more than anyone else, she has been responsible for the development of the death awareness movement which systematically over the past thirty years has sought to eliminate the long-standing cultural taboo about matters of suffering, dying, and death.

Ironically, despite the fact that America was and remains suffering and death aversive, the culture was ready for "Kübler-Ross' thanatology movement." In an era of individualism, her view of death as a final stage of growth was consistent with the broader cultural value of self-actualization. The human potential movement, with its orientation toward therapeutic intervention and personal transcendence, helped to set the stage for therapeutic management and control of the dying process. It is in this way that hospices, while a direct structural product of the death-awareness movement, are also a structural reflection of the underlying American value of individualism and self-actualization.

Contrary to the life-prolonging focus of medicalized dying, hospices seek palliative, humanistic, and spiritual alternatives. As a philosophy and system of care, they seek to reclaim the solace and support that were provided by the rituals and patterns of traditional ways of death [19]. One of the major everyday, operational foci of hospices is the control of pain and discomfort. In the situation where cure or meaningful life-prolongation are no longer viable, they seek to manage and control the process of dying through amelioration of symptoms. Once pain and other distressing physical symptoms are controlled or minimized, hospices can then turn their attention to the myriad psychological, social, and spiritual concerns of patients and families [20]. In the hospice literature, academic or popular, the themes of comfort, pain control, and quality of life are repeated over and over again. Additionally, facilitating realistic hope for dying persons and loved ones is a central ingredient in the hospice way of death. In this fashion, the ideology of hospice care seeks the "normalization" of life: the facilitation and sustenance of ordinary, everyday styles of living (or as close as possible thereto). For this reason, it can be argued that the death-with-dignity and hospice movements can be seen, within the framework articulated by Becker, as hero systems over death. In the current push toward "dying well" and "good death," the extraordinary and horrible become redefined as ordinary and natural. Sounds of discontent and the howls of suffering are channeled into silent whispers of acceptance. In this way, hospice seeks to defeat the fear of death and seeks penultimate triumph over it. Through its emphasis on maximizing the quality of life in the shadow of death it seeks to protect patients and families from the harsh realities of dying.

The essential point to recognize is twofold. First, the denial of death through relentless technological management of dying individuals is vastly different in its approach, goals, and consequences than the forms of care sought by the death-with-dignity, hospice movement. Second, despite their apparent differences, each of these responses to the problem of death is driven by a desire to control and manage the dying process. It is my contention that technological intervention and the pursuit of dignity have both become new icons and rituals of death control in the modern context. Just as traditional Western society organized to make death palatable through community presence, religious rituals, and cultural ceremonies, modern society seeks to master death through patterns of control and governance that are consistent with broader folkways of life; namely, technological reliance and therapeutic amelioration.

Thus, while there is seemingly no single direction in the thanatology literature, varying and apparently contradictory forces have emerged and converged establishing both a societal and medical program for the control of death. In the remaining chapters, I will examine how the values of modern technocratic society are reflected in the care of dying patients in the hospital setting. In addition, I will illuminate how hero systems of technological faith and individualism are central components in the medical management of death, and play a large role in shaping the end-of-life experience for patients, families, and physicians.

REFERENCES

1. J.-J. Rousseau, *Julie or the New Heloise: Letters of Two Lovers Who Live in a Small Town at the Foot of the Alps,* University Press of New England, Hanover, New Hampshire, p. 128, 1997.
2. La Rochefoucauld, *Maxims,* Press of Braunworth & Co., Brooklyn, New York, 1903.
3. E. Becker, *The Denial of Death,* The Free Press, New York, 1973.
4. T. Mann, *Death in Venice,* Vintage Books, New York, 1954.
5. P. Ariès, Death, Societal Attitudes Toward, *Encyclopedia of Applied Ethics,* Academic Press, San Francisco, p. 569, 1998.
6. B. Glaser and A. Strauss, *Awareness of Dying,* Aldine Press, New York, 1965.
7. D. Sudnow, *Passing On,* Prentice Hall, New Jersey, 1967.
8. L. LeShan, Psychotherapy and the Dying Patient, in *Death and Dying,* L. Persons (ed.), Case Western Reserve University Press, Cleveland, 1969.
9. T. O'Martin, Death Anxiety and Social Deniability Among Nurses, *Omega, 13*:1, pp. 51-58, 1982.
10. J. Katz, *The Silent World of Doctor and Patient,* The Free Press, New York, pp. 216-217, 1984.
11. Moller, *Confronting Death,* Oxford, New York, 1996.
12. E. Becker, *Escape From Evil,* The Free Press, New York, 1975.
13. E. Becker, *The Structure of Evil,* The Free Press, New York, 1968.
14. A. Kellehear, Death and Social Consequences, *Omega, 11*:3, 1980.
15. D. Leiderman and J. Grisso, The Gomer Phenomena, *Journal of Health and Social Behavior,* September 1985.
16. A. Killilea, Death and Social Consciousness, *Omega, 11*:3, 1980.
17. E. Kübler-Ross, *On Death and Dying,* Macmillan, New York, 1969.
18. E. Kübler-Ross, Playboy Interview, *Playboy, 28*:5, pp. 69-106, 1984.
19. Moller Op cit., p. 743, 1988.
20. I. Ayemian and B. Mount, The Adult Patient: Cultural Considerations in Palliative Care, in *Hospice: The Living Idea,* C. Saunders (ed.), WB Saunders Co., Philadelphia, 1981.

Technological Medicine, Technocratic Physicians and Human Dying

Your wound looks lovely!

Surgical resident speaking to breast cancer patient

I almost had a croaker upstairs!

W.L.J., M.D.

She's in deep ca-ca!

*Attending physician speaking about
a patient with metastatic cancer*

Death is not the enemy, Doctor. Inhumanity is.

Male Patient

When a surgery resident told a patient that her wound looked lovely, she was correct from a medical and surgical standpoint. However, the bewildered look on the patient's face when she had heard these words indicated how clueless the physician was about the profound personal meanings of having cancer, and the psychological consequences of breast resection. As the resident removed the stitches and examined the scar, her interest was confined by a technological focus that was, in large part, out of tune with the fears and needs of her patient. Several minutes before, the patient had been informed by the unit secretary that continued treatment was necessary, and that appointments would need to be made with specialists in both radiation oncology and hematology oncology. There can be no doubt that the patient's point of view and her emotional needs were very much different from the clinical focus and language of her physician. She was worried and frightened by the seriousness of the disease, and what that meant in terms of the "big question" of life and death. Whether or not the wound looked lovely was not apropos to her fear and concerns. She was frightened by the possibility that she might suffer greatly and die from her cancer. Additionally, this patient, who was in her early sixties, was devastated emotionally and psychologically by the removal of her breast. A deeply important part not just of her body, but of herself, had been surgically removed. A penetrating sense of loss hovered over her life and she feared greater loss in the future. This personal anguish, however, never entered into the narrow, technically delimited interest of the physician, nor did it become relevant to the physician-patient interaction.

From the restrictive confines of the technological viewpoint this patient was well served. The surgery was completed without complication, and her referrals were appropriate and to physicians who were prominent in their specialty. Yet, the unwillingness and inability of the resident to recognize the piercing, personal suffering, and tailor her interactions and conversation with this patient accordingly, only served to intensify the patient's distress. There was absolutely no malevolence or intention to be abusive on the part of the resident. Nonetheless, the consequences of her well intended words, YOUR WOUND LOOKS LOVELY, were harsh and cruel, and left the patient perplexed, frustrated, and isolated. Just as hard and cruel was the lack of recognition of how difficult the experience was for the woman and her husband. Similarly punishing was the absence of reassurance that her suffering mattered, and that she would be well cared for and supported throughout her treatment as a patient and as a person.

The crucial point illustrated above is that the patient's view of illness is fundamentally divergent from the physician's. Patient experiences and the clinical foci of physicians are often incommensurable. In this way, this particular interaction is typical. At the heart of the matter is the fact that personal issues are quickly redefined into medical categories, and the medical interests of physicians are bereft of interest in the personal meanings and consequences of illness. As Kathryn Hunter observes, the patient's account of illness and the medical version of that account are fundamentally different narratives [1]. Inherently in the doctor-patient relationship there is epistemological variance and conflict. That is to say, what a physician knows about a patient's illness and confrontation with dying is virtually disconnected and often antagonistic to what a patient knows and experiences. In the quest to efficiently treat the patient, personal experience and meaning are translated into a category and typology of disease and re-constructed as a "medical case." In the present system, which stresses technological focus and activity, the patient's experience is brought to the realm of medical understanding and therefore viewed in medical terms [2, p. 96]. Thus, as in the case of the resident who spoke about her patient's "lovely looking wound," eliminating compelling personal issues of the disease or dying experience offers enormous emotional protection for physicians. But, as we will see, it also facilitates unfeeling care, increased patient isolation, and exacerbates the suffering of patients and their loved ones.

The dominance of technological emphasis in the physician-patient relationship diminishes the value of the patient as a person in that relationship. Thus, if a woman with breast cancer is reconstrued as a breast cancer case her personal travails become irrelevant to the medical management of the case. In this clinically focused framework, there is no need to be concerned with such questions as: Is she afraid? Is she dying? Is her self-image decimated by the disease and the physical legacy of treatment? Is she anxious and worried? Is she bewildered by what is happening? Is she painfully isolated? Such questions have little value in the contemporary delivery of medical care, and therefore become eliminated from the frame of reference and professional consciousness of physicians. But, as seen so vividly in Chapter 2, these questions and issues are at the very heart and soul of the dying person's life experience. In short, the central point to be made is sixfold:

- The experience of diagnosis and illness is not encompassed by the pathology of disease
- Dying patients are disoriented, disarmed, and vulnerable
- In their state of vulnerability and chaos, they are profoundly dependent upon their physicians
- Dying patients have a deep need to be cared for as persons and human beings
- Technocratic focus fails to satisfactorily attended to this need
- In order to do well by their patients, physicians must become trusted and caring in ways that extend far beyond technical skill.

The following experience illustrates these points, and shows how desperately important respect for personhood is for very sick patients from the onset of the relationship with their physicians:

> I felt a lump in my left breast. I immediately went to the doctor. I went through all the necessary tests. I was so scared. My mind was filled with images of my grandmother. I had been referred to this specialist by a family friend. His reputation was wonderful. Mom, dad, and I arrived at the doctor's house a few minutes early. We sat in the waiting room for twenty-four minutes. It was filled with blue-haired ladies with thick ankles. Melinda (the nurse) called my name. My mom got up first then I slowly got up. My dad sat there with his head lowered. I put out my hand to him and he grabbed it so tightly and looked up at me and said, "Honey, I love you." I started to cry. We were placed in the doctor's office. We sat in there for sixteen minutes. He came into the room and looked grim. He had a huge stack of paperwork in his hand. He had a big envelope with X-rays. He took the X-rays out and placed them on his lighted table. He showed us the lump in my breast and it looked so big. I couldn't believe something that size could be in there (maybe that's why my boobs were so big). He then blurted out it's malignant. I immediately started to cry. My mom began asking him a lot of questions. My dad's grip on my hand tightened. The doctor got up and left the room. He and Melinda were

outside the door discussing their lunch order for the day—sweet and sour pork or kung pao chicken. He came back into the room and began discussing what my treatment would be. As I began crying even harder my dad put his arm around me. I looked up and saw the doctor staring at me with disgust on his face. He then told me that my crying had no place here and that I was being childish. And to "knock it off now!" I was totally pissed off with that statement. This asshole just told me I had cancer. What was I supposed to do, get up and do cartwheels down the lobby? My father got up and grabbed my hand and looked at the doctor and said, "You were obviously absent that day they taught compassion at medical school. How dare you talk to my daughter that way, you insensitive jerk!" As I was being pulled from the room my dad and I looked at the doctor with tears rolling down my face, and I said "You think because you have all these fancy degrees on the wall that you have the right to take away my hope? Well, you're wrong."

The inability and unwillingness of this physician to recognize the personal meaning of the diagnosis and respond to his patient as a human being only served to bring further chaos and suffering into her life. In addition, despite his impressive technological credentials, this physician did more harm than good. His indifference to the personal, human side of the illness-diagnosis clearly undermined his ability to serve the welfare of his patient. This indifference may be reflective of this individual physician, but more significantly it is inherent in the technocratic orientation of modern medicine. The main purpose of this chapter is to elucidate the tension that exists between technological focus and respect for personhood. In order to unveil this conflict and identify its consequences, I will also describe some of the strategies utilized by physicians to constrain and restrict the emotional, social, and personal presence of dying persons.

TECHNOLOGICAL DOMINANCE

A colleague [2] recently described the effort he and I are making to improve the ways of caring for dying persons in the following way: It is like five locomotives are pulling a train at breakneck speed and we are standing on the tracks wildly waving our hands to get them to stop. Metaphorically speaking, the locomotive represents the force and fury of technology. The essential and most serious point to be made is that the drift of technologically-focused care is so powerful that attempts to humanize the care of dying persons are often overwhelmed by medical and technological priorities. It is important to keep in mind, however, that the source of technological dominance within medicine, and the prominence of technology in managing the dying process, stems from the cultural value of technicism in the broader society. As I have been arguing, the technological focus of medical care is a reflection of the broader technological underpinnings of everyday life. It is precisely for these reasons that it must be emphasized that the dominant orientation and daily activities of the profession of medicine are an extension and reflection of the technological foundation of society. It is in this framework that the profession of medicine becomes an agent of the body social. It encapsulates and denies the personal horrors of dying in a systematic program of technological management that is commensurate with the orientation of the broader culture.

Physicians are shown the power of technique and technological focus to preside over death early on in their training. As first year students, the preeminent, sustained involvement with death occurs in the anatomy lab. The first encounter with the cadaver, and the subsequent year of dissection and trisection of dead bodies, has an inevitable and enormous effect on students. In fact, the anatomy lab experience is a watershed event in the socialization process of student physicians that teaches not just technical knowledge, but the value of emotional detachment in the presence of death as well.

Breathless, cool to the touch, un-human looking, of sickly, ashen pallor and macabre texture, the cadaver is a huge source of anxiety for beginning students:

> In the weeks before they began dissecting cadavers, the students spoke of their anxiety about seeing and cutting the body. They expressed fears that they would become sickened, that they might faint or vomit . . .
> [3, p. 20].

Meeting one's cadaver is a memorable and emotionally significant experience in a physician's training. Ironically, however, the intense emotionalism of anticipating and finally encountering one's cadaver is very quickly obliterated by myriad strategies of detachment, foremost of which are dehumanizing the cadaver and rationalizing one's involvement with it. Students are explicitly warned that they will be overwhelmed by the task of learning everything there is to learn. In other words, they are told that they are expected to get control over whatever emotions and fears they have so they can properly tend to the intellectual and scientific challenges that await them. For all the fear and anxiety that leads up to the first day of anatomy lab, it is astonishing how quickly and pervasively nonchalant behavior emerges among medical students. As one student comments:

> I just could not believe that everyone was so unaffected as they appeared.
> I had never been more terrified in my life.

As students familiarize themselves with their cadaver, an uncanny folkway of emotional control emerges. They recognize that suppression of fear and of one's emotion is a non-negotiable, behavioral requirement of becoming a physician. The cadaver itself is depersonalized: hair is shaved, breasts are smashed, the chest is flattened, and the genitals and face are generally covered. Yet, students are notorious for putting their own imprint of depersonalization onto the experience.

It's not unusual for cadavers to be named, to be arranged into different positions, and become the object of pejorative comments and jokes. As one student commented:

> My cadaver's name is Helen. She's really kind of gross. . . . Had a breast removed. . . . You deal with them very casually. Like eventually one part of her anatomy was removed and placed upon another part, if you know what I mean.

The tumultuous emotional response to the cadaver, its being studied, explored, and dissected is smoothed over and replaced by an attitude of emotional disinterest and detachment. By restraining and containing their emotional responses, students swiftly learn to isolate their attention on technical and scientific matters. In addition to gathering knowledge that is important to becoming a physician, these students learn something more subtly expressed, but yet essential. They are socialized by the anatomy experience into an objective, emotionally neutral, and technologically oriented worldview. In important ways, medical students learn a pattern of relating to future patients through the patterns by which they relate to the cadaver. In some ways the cadaver is an ideal patient. In addition to being a haven for technical and physical exploration, it is emotionally undemanding, passive, acquiescent, and fully cooperative. These qualities which are intrinsic to the cadaver come to be valued as appropriate, expected behavior in future, living patients.

The observations of Renée Fox in her eloquent essay on the autopsy and socialization of second-year medical students are also relevant here. Fox writes that like the anatomy lab experience, the autopsy serves to transmit attitudes and values which are salient to the prevailing definition of a physician's role. More specifically, by providing students with a real workout in objectivity, the experience fertilizes the seeds of emotional detachment that are planted the year before in anatomy lab. This way, as Fox notes, the most potent impact of the autopsy is in the realm of training students for detached concern [5].

Fox begins her account by contrasting the cadaver experience with the psychosocial impact of the autopsy. She observes that the autopsy has a greater link with human life than the cadaver in the anatomy lab. The body is often still warm, is not mummified, will bleed when cut into, and is legally protected by concern for the family and impending funeral. This awareness of the human dimensions of the deceased is articulated by a second year student:

> When you see the initial incision and first bleeding, that's a point at which you are very aware of the whole person. . . . You realize that this is someone who has died, and that what you are going to do is look inside that person . . . [4, p. 58].

Fox makes the point that, because of its greater connection to human life, the autopsy poses more emotional difficulty for the medical student. While correctly pointing to the greater resemblance to human life of the corpse to be autopsied, she, however, tends to minimize the significance of a student's very first professional encounter with the dissection of a dead human body. As I have indicated, the seeds of emotional detachment are sown in the first year of study as students learn the obligation to repress their emotions and to restrict their own personal involvement as human beings in their work. Thus, second-year training in pathology nurtures qualities of objectivity and detachment that have already been firmly established during the first year of study. In this sense, Fox's distinction artificially fragments what needs to be seen as a continuous and comprehensive program of professional socialization throughout the entirety of a medical student's years of study.

There can be no doubt that the autopsy experience plays a central role in shaping technocratic consciousness, of instilling professional values of detachment, objectivity, and rationality. It demands that students give their exclusive attention to the "facts of the case." Personal response is taboo, and students are pressed by peer and teacher expectations to become so "engrossed in the scientific angles that the emotional aspects are obscured":

> Now when I see a lung, for example, I concentrate on its structure . . . I don't picture its being someone who was once living, breathing, talking. . . .

> Most of the fellows are so eager to be good doctors that they force themselves to look at things in a scientific way. . . . Every guy was interested in the facts . . . asking questions and wanting to learn about what had happened [4, p. 63].

In short, the autopsy facilitates the emergence of an attitude of depersonalized regard of the corpse being autopsied in particular, and toward the phenomenon of death in general. Since the focus of the watershed experiences of the anatomy lab and the autopsy is technical, as is the thrust of all years of medical training and socialization, young medical students are taught an important lesson about the centrality of technical activity in relating to patients and to death. Indeed, students throughout most of their training, but most explicitly in anatomy and pathology, learn to redefine the human problem of death into a technical framework. In doing so, they develop the following crucial ingredients of technocratic consciousness:

- To manage the emotional without emotion
- To deal with the cultural taboo of death clinically and rationally
- To routinize death and dull one's own response to it
- To view death merely as a matter of physical, medical fact

- To learn that they have special authority in relationship to death by virtue of their enormous knowledge and exclusive right to cut apart, look inside, and explore a dead body.

As we shall now see, the technical worldview established during the pre-clinical years of training is the standard by which physicians relate to their dying patients in clinical situations.

WALTZING AROUND THE TRUTH

The medical approach to the care of dying patients is distinctly clinical and technological. Despite the fact that there is increasing variation in the style of behaviors which characterize the relationships between doctors and their patients, there is a strong behavioral and attitudinal uniformity in the way physicians relate to each other in the backstage arenas of medicine. I have observed that both formal, inter-physician consultations and informal conversations about dying patients are decidedly detached and sometimes even quite callous. In the absence of a patient's physical presence, physicians are personally and professionally "free" to characterize to the dying patient in ways that are reminiscent of their relationship to the cadaver in anatomy lab. Thus, in some ways, backroom joking about patients, defilement of physical or social selves of patients, and objectifying their human needs frames the care of dying patients into the emotionally detached realm of "cadaver-treatment." Consider the following hallway conversation between a surgeon and an oncologist regarding what they should tell a patient whose leg biopsy had just come back positive, and whose chest x-rays had revealed progression of an already identified tumor:

Surgeon: This is a bad, aggressive disease. We are talking months.
Oncologist: He really can't be irradiated to his chest. His Adriamyacin isn't working. He's on full dosage, and his disease is progressing.
Surgeon: But we have to do something for him.[1]
PAUSE . . .
Surgeon: I'm not impressed with his moral fiber. I don't think he has the moral strength to withstand the news. His family also impresses me as being weak. I don't think they have the strength to cope with the consequences of someone dying. . . . So, what do we tell him?
Oncologist: Well, we have to tell him that his biopsy was positive. But we also need to assure him that we are not going to give up on him.

---

[1] In itself, this is a powerful statement about heroism of the technological management and manipulation and death.

Surgeon: Yes, but you really can't irradiate his chest. He's going to drown from his disease, and you don't want to make it worse for him by his catching radiation fibrosis and drowning from that.

Oncologist: Then, that'll help his drowning. . . .

Surgeon: Okay. We'll tell him that the femur biopsy was positive and that we want to treat it with x-rays.

Oncologist: What about the lung? We have to tell him something.

Surgeon: We'll tell him that we are watching some areas closely . . . that some areas seem to be suspicious.

This backstage-hallway conversation enabled the physicians to develop a protective strategy that would guide them through the tasteless task of delivering bad news to the patient. It is notable, especially in light of the newly devolved emphasis on truth-telling within medical circles, that these physicians decided to *tell the patient the truth—nothing but the truth—but not the whole truth*. As we shall see in greater detail in Chapter 9, focusing on specific symptoms is a useful means of diverting attention away from the harsh, emotional realities of dying to the *more manageable concern of symptom treatment*. In this way, truths are told but the truth about dying is averted. It is precisely this process of "selective truth telling" which enables physicians to salve their conscience in regard to the patient's right to know while simultaneously protecting themselves from having to deal directly with the human face of dying.

This fancy footwork around the truth-of-the-truth is rooted in the patient's best interest, as explained by the surgeon and as accepted by the oncologist. Their concern seems beneficent: Patients have enough to worry about without being confronted with harsh, naked truth which may destroy all semblance of hope. As illustrated in the above scenario, physicians often feel that revealing the whole truth will shatter the lives of patients and their families. In reality, however, avoidance of full disclosure can deleteriously affect the lives of patients. It instills false hope that leads to shattered expectations and serves ultimately the interests of doctors, not their patients.

Let us now return to the hospital floor and listen in on how the patient was actually told "the truth."

The surgeon proceeds from the hallway to the patient's room while the oncologist temporarily goes down to the doctors' lounge to take care of some business. The surgeon enters the room and sits in a chair to the right of the patient's bed, with the tray-stand between him and the patient. After a brief exchange of pleasantries, the surgeon begins:

Surgeon: We got the results of the biopsy back, and there was tumor in it.

Patient: There was?!

Surgeon: Yes.

Patient: But, I thought you said you had gotten it out.

Surgeon:	Yes, but I also said there was a possibility that it may come back. That is why we want to treat it with X-rays.
	PAUSE . . .
Patient:	How effective are the X-rays? . . . Does it work? . . . Will it work for me? What are my chances?
Surgeon:	I really can't say. It varies tremendously. 100 percent from individual to individual. I can't tell you what your chances are. Those who succeed do so 100 percent; those who fail are 100 percent failures. It makes no sense for me to quote you statistics. Either you as an individual will succeed or not.
Patient:	So, therefore, if we succeed, my chances are 100 percent, and if not, then we are somewhere in the middle.
	PAUSE . . . NO RESPONSE FROM THE SURGEON
Patient:	Is the leg the only biopsy which you did?
Surgeon:	Yes, only on the leg.
Patient:	Then I only have cancer in my leg?
Surgeon:	Well, . . . [PAUSE] . . . We did take some x-rays, and we do want to watch your chest closely.
	(ONCOLOGIST COMES IN AND SITS ON THE BEDSIDE)
Patient:	What did the X-rays show?
Surgeon:	There's some areas that seem to be suspicious, and we want to watch them very closely.
Patient:	Will you treat those areas with X-rays?
Surgeon:	No, but that's Dr. _____ 's department (nods to the oncologist).
Oncologist:	We want to get you started on radiation for your leg as soon as possible, and we'll be watching to see if chemotherapy is indicated. If we do opt for chemotherapy, it will be of a milder form than the combination you are now on with Adriamyacin.
Patient:	Will you still continue to give me that?
Oncologist:	No.
Patient:	When will I be getting radiation?
Oncologist:	Well, we have to talk to you about that. About where you are going to get treated, here or at home.
	(CONVERSATION TURNS TO A DISCUSSION OF THE CONVENIENCE OF THE PATIENT'S LOCAL HOSPITAL VS. THE MEDICAL CENTER WHERE HE WAS PRESENTLY ADMITTED)
	. . . PAUSE . . .
Surgeon:	Anything else? . . . Do you have any questions for us?
Patient:	No, it's just that I didn't expect things to go bad so quickly (in deep and somber reflection).
Oncologist:	Yes, but you have been informed that cancer is an aggressive disease that can spread like wildfire—very rapidly. That's why

we want to watch you closely and give you the very latest and
best treatment available.
(FLOW OF CONVERSATION STYMIED) . . . PAUSE . . .

Surgeon: (getting up to leave) Mr. ___, if you have any other questions,
feel free to ask us. We're around. Write them down so you don't
forget.

Ironically, this conversation accomplished precisely the opposite of what
the surgeon intended in his hallway discussion. The patient by his own words
("I just didn't expect things to go bad so quickly") realizes that his condition is
critically serious, despite all of the elaborate jugglery of the surgeon and even the
oncologist in spots. In many ways, the central subject in question revolves around
clarity, ambiguity, and divergent viewpoints in the process of truth telling. In other
words, it is an issue of the various meanings that can be associated with and
emerge from the telling of truth. Physicians by nature of their role definition,
clinical knowledge, and technological focus have a comprehensive picture of
the patient's diagnosis. However, the various strategies employed by doctors in
delivering "bad news" communicate a partially truthful but murky understanding
of their own life-disease situation to patients. In this way, a haunting, worry-filled,
"shadow of awareness" often surrounds the patient. The understanding of his or
her circumstances is often accompanied with, as one patient put it: "anxiety about
what they are not telling me." In addition, a further irony is introduced into the
framework of patient care, namely, that patients who are defined as too weak or
"morally inferior" to face up to the whole truth are presumed to have sufficient
moral fiber and personal strength to wade through the ambiguities associated with
partial truth telling, and cope with the ragings of their own imaginations. It is clear
from the materials we have just considered that while physicians may believe they
are protecting their patients by disguising the telling of truth, their dancing around
the truth-of-the-truth largely reflects their own unease in dealing directly with
dying on a personal level. Perhaps, if it really is in the best interest of patients to
protect them from the whole truth, then they should be wholly protected. The
patient should be told nothing and even lied to if necessary. Of course, however,
deceit in all of its various manifestations is not in the best interests of patients, and
only serves to stir the embers of false and unrealistic hope. In doing so it may
provide some temporary benefit but ultimately worsens the suffering of patients
and loved ones.

Present day realities of truth telling have been influenced by increasing social
pressures from the death-with-dignity movement combined with inadequate
professional training and socialization of doctors in the area of the psychosocial
care of dying patients. In this way, physicians find themselves embodied in a
situation of ambiguity. They feel the societal pressure toward open-death-
awareness, but have not been adequately trained to relate to their patients within
the open-awareness framework. In this context, there is an absence of sanctioned

norms to guide physicians in truth-telling behaviors. As a result, they are often left to their own resources and inclinations in devising ways to tell their patients bad news.

STYLES OF INTERACTION

As repeatedly discussed, technology is the main coordinating force of the medical profession and of medical training. However, this does not mean to imply that physicians relate to their patients in a monolithic, unvarying way. As there are differences in the ways physicians approach truth telling, there are a variety of patterns and ways by which physicians relate to dying patients. These ways are neither fixed nor invariable throughout the career of a physician. In the absence of standardized norms that define how doctors should relate to patients, physicians oscillate among various patterns and even treat one patient differently from another.

One major response of physicians to the process of dying is direct and active technical intervention. This orientation, whereby a physician strives officiously to keep patients alive, has been extensively discussed in the literature. I have found that interns and residents are especially eager to employ and sometimes "overemploy" the skills of their profession, to "save at all costs" a patient with a rapidly progressing terminal condition. Younger physicians are understandably proud and enthusiastic about their achievements, knowledge, and skill. It is not difficult to see how the technical powers they have amassed can lead them toward a zealous utilization of technology. It becomes difficult for many physicians, in light of the societal and medical value of technological activism, the cultural devaluation of dying, and their professional socialization, to simply "stand there and do nothing." Such passivity in the face of death is inconsistent with the flow of modern values and against the grain of physicians' technical consciousness. Hence, when physicians, especially young "unexperienced" doctors, are confronted with the realities of human suffering and dying, they resort to what they are most familiar with in order to help them deal with the experience of dying, namely, technical intervention and activity.

The save-at-all-costs orientation is generally associated with "medical miracles" such as heroics of transplants, connecting patients to life-prolonging machines, surgical triumph, and other dramatic technological interventions. However, the daily unfolding of the save-at-all-costs orientation is not so dramatic as the medical headlines that capture the attention of society at large suggest. Rather, everyday medical practice is driven by the belief that the doctor's job is to treat disease and prolong life through technically aggressive patterns of care. In this way, the save-at-all-costs orientation is ubiquitous.

A second orientation in the care of dying patients is avoidance-neglect. A patient who is dying and not responding to treatment can become a difficult patient. Those physicians who define their role exclusively in terms of treating and curing (as opposed to caring) will naturally tend to spend their time and energy in the treatment of those patients, seriously ill or otherwise, who have a reasonable chance of responding to medical or surgical intervention.

It needs to be stressed that doctors do not make a conscious decision to neglect their patients. Instead, neglect is an unintentional consequence of the doctor's unease in dealing with terminal patients, coupled with a commitment to other patients that are more likely to be medically responsive. Neglect is also a derivation of technological focus and indifference to the emotional, personal side of the illness. One patient tells the story of how she was informed that she had developed cancer in her breast:

> I was in the clinic after being examined, waiting for the doctor to return with my test results. He came in and told me to get dressed. Even when he said, "I have to talk to you," I was not worried. Then he came out and told me I had breast cancer. He was abrupt, real abrupt. He had other patients to see, and he went off to see them. I don't know how I made it. I walked out in tears . . . alone. . . . I was alone for over half an hour, wandering around the hospital. There was no hospital or medical support. The doctor left me, and I found myself facing this myself.

From a technological, medical standpoint this patient had been properly served. Appropriate referrals were made and the diagnosis was clearly explained. However, from the viewpoint of her humanity and psychosocial needs this patient was ill served. If the physician had been sensitive to the needs of his patient as a person, he would have arranged for a more supportive environment and style of delivering such devastating news.

Stories like this abound as patients recount their experiences with the medical profession. Some scenarios are dramatic in terms of neglect, others less so. I have observed doctors leaving patients stranded in hospital beds awaiting various procedures while the doctors have been out of town or otherwise unavailable, doctors refusing to continue seeing particular patients, doctors making every effort to see patients when they were asleep or scheduled for tests so they wouldn't have to interact with patients, as well as doctors paying such minimal attention to the case of a patient that the patient's health was jeopardized. I know the latter because their peers expressed their disapproval about the situation. But, on balance, the common denominator of the spectrum of avoidance-neglect behaviors is the unwillingness of the physician to give the time it takes to adequately care for the needs of dying patients.

Once again, the tension between clinical, technical focus and human need is resolved in favor of a technologically anchored value system. Thus, from the doctor's perspective, what may appear as neglect is really medical prioritizing. As one physician comments:

Yes, it's true that some of these patients receive less care than others. But there are only so many hours in the day, and decisions have to be made on who are going to receive the most beneficial results from our attention. For example, today I've had. . . .

Sudnow's classic study of the social organization of the death in the hospital, more than thirty years ago, pointed to the same phenomenon: physicians exclusively defining their role in terms of activity that would medically benefit patients [6]. It is fascinating to note how much remains the same in prioritizing of physician activity toward the realm of technical activity, and how this narrow focus on technologically-based amelioration of disease jeopardizes the lives of dying patients. Indeed, as Anselm Strauss put it, "I too am amazed at how little the technological base of hospital care has changed over the past twenty-five years" [6].

A third pattern of care of the dying is detached-sympathetic-support. There are physicians who believe that the physical-technical treatment of dying patients needs to be complemented with psychosocial care. The sympathetically oriented physician recognizes and freely speaks of the value of social and psychological support. Detached-sympathetic-support physicians are generally aware of how often the medical and hospital organization of work diminishes the delivery of supportive care. However, most of these physicians do not focus on addressing the cultural or structural underpinnings of inadequate care nor the pervasiveness of insufficient care in the medical system. Instead, they are concerned about the kind of care they provide to their own patients.

It is also important to note that detached-sympathetic-support physicians are typically reluctant to indict other physicians, including interns and residents, for attending inadequately to the psychosocial needs of dying patients. This is not true in the medical or technical arena, however. When medically or technically relevant mistakes or abuses occur, these mistakes elicit responses from physicians, who are correctly seeking to protect the best medical interests of their patients. If mistakes are made by interns and residents, strong corrective sanctioning is used. If abuses or mistakes result from the activity of established colleagues, more informal, softer methods of addressing the issue are generally employed. In any event, medically relevant neglect, abuse, or mistakes are an explicit issue of concern in the professional worldview of physicians. This means that concern over the technical competence is formally built into the professional milieu in which physicians work. Concern for the psychosocial dimensions of patient care is not a structural, institutionalized part of the organization of contemporary medical practice. It exists to the degree that physicians, especially detached-sympathetic-support physicians, make private, individualized statements about the value of psychosocial factors in patient care. In this way, tending to the psychosocial needs of dying patients is not a formally established pattern of physician responsibility. Rather, it occurs on an individualized level of expression, that is to say, it becomes a personal and individualized folkway of care. The point to be made is that the culture and the organization of medical work offers little reward for attending to the personal anguish of dying patients. In this regard, psychosocial care is not a dominant value in contemporary medical practice. It exists primarily as a personalized option of physicians who are themselves caring and compassionate persons.

It is important to recognize that detached-sympathetic-support physicians have not been socialized in a different manner from their colleagues. Their psychosocial support of dying patients is generally not shaped by formal psychosocial training (most physicians never even take a course in death and dying), but rather comes from a personal, informal, and self-expressive effort to bring compassion to their practice of medicine. In this way, the sympathetic physician's approach to the care of patients is consistent with the values of individualism and self-expression already discussed. However, despite the fact that more physicians are becoming aware of the need for psychosocial support of dying patients, sympathetic-support-physicians are still mavericks, and there is little formal, structural training and support for their non-technical activities.

The primary difference I have observed between detached-sympathetic-support physicians and others lies in their willingness to listen to patient complaints, to spend more time in formal professional interaction with patients and loved ones, and to participate in informal conversation with patients. I have witnessed patterns of behavior that include touching patients in non-technical situations (reassuring hand on the arm, shoulder, etc.), consistently and explicitly responding to the comfort needs of patients and to the dignity needs of patients, e.g., privacy, bodily integrity, etc. It is these qualities of patient care which provide a commitment to a broader spectrum of care than that formally taught in medical school and formally sanctioned by peer review and approval.

Still, the central and primary focus of detached-sympathetic-support physicians is technically based. The primary goal is disease and symptom management complemented by the technological amelioration of pain and discomfort. The underlying foundation of care they provide is similar to that of save-at-all-costs and avoidance-neglect physicians. It is the particular forms of care that are quite different. In this way, it may be said that some doctors unrelentingly pursue the cure of their patients, others prioritize their technical efforts toward treating more medically-responsive patients, and the detached-sympathetic-support physician seeks to provide the best technical care possible in a way that is tempered by humane and psychosocial considerations. The unifying dimension of these varying styles of care is technological focus and activity, the purpose of which is to manage, control, and contain the process of dying through the doctor's personalized and varying application of the technological ethos.

Thus, when a patient nears the threshold of death, some doctors seek to forestall death through heroics, others avoid death by turning their attentions elsewhere, while others seek to offer comfort. However, despite the varying styles of interaction, when death is proximate, most physicians uniformly strain to move psychically and physically away from the death setting as quickly as they can. I have noticed a formal and regular rush to move on to the next patient, and on to another floor when doctors are in a situation where death is imminent. Additionally, discussion of the dying patient during the final phase of life becomes increasingly euphemistic, detached, and technically narrow. Consider the following round-robin discussion in the doctors' lounge of a patient with a fourteen-year history of myeloma, who was approaching her death and was lingering at the threshold thereof:

Intern: This could be it.
Oncologist 1:   I don't know what the future holds for her.
                 PAUSE...
Neurologist: Well, my husband is cooking a roast beef tonight. I'm going home and having dinner...
Intern: (speaking to Oncologist 1) What do you think, is Mrs. ____ going to have some platelets for dinner?
Oncologist 1:   (concerned and in brief but deep thought) I don't know what to do for her.
Intern: Well, do you want to say good-bye to her tonight?
Oncologist 1:   She's on autopilot now. Either she makes it or she doesn't. Let's leave her alone.
Intern: Okay.
Oncologist 2:   (speaking to Oncologist 1) I think it's time for her to leave us. The pity of the whole thing though, is that we will not get an autopsy.
Oncologist 1:   Oh, that's something I'm going to insist on!

In summary, with the exception of the unifying technological foundation of physician activity, there is increasing normlessness with respect to how physicians relate to dying patients. The recent thanatology movement, with its emphasis on death-awareness and death-with-dignity, has conflicted with the traditional medical approach of not telling terminally-ill patients about their diagnosis. As a result, physicians today are engaged in a personal and group search to decide how much, and in what fashion, to tell their patients. This search is made difficult because there are no firmly established patterns or norms to direct physicians during the course of interactions with dying persons. The irony of this situation is that as medical technology is becoming more rational, calculable, and definitive, uncertainty and confusion have increased in the relationship between physicians and dying patients.

The professional socialization of physicians is woefully inadequate in teaching effective and supportive care of dying patients as persons. The inadequacy of training often leaves students and physicians on their own in trying to figure out how to cope with the personal side of the dying experience. Some physicians are more effective in offering compassionate care than others. This difference, however, most often stems from the fact that the physician is an outstanding and caring person to begin with. Or, perhaps, she has been deeply influenced by an exemplary teacher. Most student physicians and physicians in practice, however, struggle with their interactions with dying patients and families. The crucial point to be emphasized is that, in large part, this struggle emerges from inadequate psychosocial education and the preeminently technical focus that shapes the culture of care in hi-tech hospital settings. It is no wonder then, as medical training and practice often lack humanizing qualities, that students and physicians are confused, normless, and inept in their dealings with dying persons. It is also understandable, especially is a culture that fears and denies dying, that personal and professional ambiguity will oftentimes result in inconsistent behavior, abrupt bedside manner, and abuse of dignity and personhood.

Despite the confusion and normlessness that hovers over the care of dying patients, the unifying thread of contemporary medical practice is technological worldview and activity. Clearly, technology is the driving force in medical education. Clearly, technological activism is the dominant factor that shapes the professional conscience and daily work practice of physicians. Clearly, technological orientation is the major force which shapes physician interaction with dying patients. Thus, despite the realities of normlessness and differences in the approach of doctors to the treatment of the dying patient, technology is the pre-eminent tool used in the management of the terminally ill. As a result, consistent with the values of technicism in the broader culture, the human problems of dying patients are thereby framed and constrained by technical focus and intervention.

REFERENCES

1. K. Hunter, Patients, Physicians, and Red Parakeets, *Hospital Practice,* May 30, 1992.
2. G. Gramelspacher, Director of Program for Medical Ethics and Health Care Professionalism, Indiana University School of Medicine.
3. D. A. Segal, A Patient So Dead, *American Medical Students and their Cadavers, 61*:1, 1988.
4. R. Fox, The Autopsy: Attitude Learning of Second Year Medical Students, in *Essays in Medical Sociology,* John Wiley and Sons, New York, 1979.
5. D. Sudnow, *Passing On,* Prentice Hall, Englewood Cliffs, 1967.
6. A. Strauss, Personal letter.

CHAPTER
6

Fellowship and Dying:
The Problem of Detachment

Think of what it must be for a dying man, trapped behind hundreds of walls . . . , while the whole population, sitting in cafes or hanging on the telephone, is discussing shipments, bills of lading, discounts! It will then be obvious what discomfort attends death, even modern death when it waylays you under such conditions [1, p. 5].

Albert Camus

. . . it is a reduction of our humanity to hide from pain, our own or others' [2, p. 12].

Wallace Stegner

So she stood unwillingly aloof from ordinary life. My mother hated solitude but solitude was one of the prices this disease exacted from her, the solitude of a misery she could not authentically share, and then the added indignity of physical isolation from the people she loved, who loved her, who wanted to see her, and whose visits she was often obligated to prohibit. She placed as much physical distance between herself and the world as she could; she died in a cocoon of privacy, with only her illness as an intimate [3, p. 93].

Andrew Solomon

Ease his pain . . . Go the distance [4, p. 89].

W. P. Kinsella

Most physicians remain uncomfortable with the subject of death. They lack the training needed to communicate with dying patients and families in an open, supportive, and caring way. Most physicians are educated and work in an environment that restricts emphasis on personhood and makes interpersonal communication difficult. In addition, the technical world of modern hospitals is often antagonistic to personal, human needs of dying patients and loved ones. The social and medical world that directly confronts patients is both unfamiliar and complex. In the modern context of denial, technocratic ways of death have exacted an

105

enormous toll on patients and families. Patients often endure the experience of dying in isolation, feeling helpless and abandoned. They regularly worry about what their physicians are not telling them. They feel worthless and depressed, worry about being a burden to their loved ones, feel physically and emotionally scarred by their illness and the relentless technological invasion of their bodies, and desperately try to make some sense out of all their suffering.

Similarly, loved ones who witness the emotional and physical roller coaster of long-term, terminal illness are overwhelmed by their own personal sense of helplessness, and of not knowing what to do or to say. They navigate with frustration and sometimes anger: the impersonalism of the bureaucracy, the evasiveness and elusiveness of physicians, the parade of strangers who wander in and out of their loved ones' room, the confusing array of specialists, and the ever rotating coterie of interns and residents. They often resent being pushed to the corner of a room as their role as decision makers and caring persons is replaced by the ministrations and expertise of the professionals. Paradoxically, however, despite their need to be actively involved in the caretaking of their dying loved one, they are typically overpowered by a sense of inadequacy, confusion, and inexperience. Often they find the physical and emotional pain of dying unbearable to witness, and they retreat from the deathbed into an isolated world of anguish and loss. This withdrawal not only intensifies their feelings of alienation and suffering, but the feelings of their loved ones' as well.

Thus, modern dying is not only filled with graphic images of medicalization, dehumanization, and meaningfulness. It has become insular, disconnected from shared cultural experience, and lonesome. It is steeped in a sense of isolation that ranges from the inattention and indifference of technology-focused physicians in the face of human need to the disconnection of dying persons from their ordinary social lives and relationships. In the modern organization of death, the natural sorrow that is intrinsic to dying is intensified by detachment and disassociation, that is to say, dying persons and families are increasingly disunited. Their experiences have become more solitary, and their psycho- social-emotional needs remain largely unaddressed. In short, it is for these reasons that their suffering is made worse and the experience of dying becomes all the more difficult to bear.

One of the ironies of modernization is that as America has developed economically and technologically the capacity to care for suffering, dying persons has been diminished. Only the very rich in America can afford what those in lesser developed countries have as a matter of normal course, namely personal attention around the deathbed. In our technocratic society, medical care of the sick and dying has made unprecedented technological advances. However, in our fast-paced, increasingly heterogeneous civilization cultural and social support systems to care for the dying have not kept pace with technological advances. In this way, the modern day deathbed, while technologically sophisticated, is visibly void of cultural ritual, meaningful ceremony, and the presence of human community.

As already noted, dying has become a social evil that is culturally denigrated and extraneous to the dominant meaning-sets of modern society. In this framework of cultural devaluation, the dying process is not supported and sustained through stabilized patterns of ceremony, ritual, and fellowship. In addition, the nature of community and shared concerns at the deathbed is reflective of the nature of community in society at large. The way Americans live—in or out of fellowship, will largely shape and define the way they die—in or out of fellowship. In this chapter, I will explore how the general cultural breakdown of community and fellowship influences the human experience of dying persons and their loved ones.

THE NON-COMMUNAL ENVIRONMENT

One of the most salient features of life in America today is a decline in the spirit of community and a heightening of detached individualism.

As Nisbet observes in *The Sociological Tradition* [5] and *The Quest for Community* [6], the historical development of western society was intimately associated with the rise of political and social individualism. The certainties and unquestioned norms that characterized humanity's traditional ties to religious, kinship, and class structures before the French and Industrial Revolutions have perceptibly disintegrated in the modern Western social setting. More importantly, no new societal patterns have arisen to replace the moral certainty of the traditional folkways and mores. As Nisbet comments:

> The historic triumph of secularism and individualism has presented a set of problems that looms large in contemporary thought. The modern release of the individual from traditional ties of class, religion and kinship has made him free; but on the testimony of innumerable works in our age, this freedom is accompanied not by a sense of creative release but by the sense of **disenchantment and alienation.** The alienation of man from historic moral certitudes has been followed by the sense of man's alienation from fellow man [6, p. 10].

The theme of alienation, as expressed by cultural images of loneliness, isolation, and the shallowness of relationships, is widely articulated in contemporary academic and popular literature. Indeed, serious novelists such as Camus, Kafka, Sartre, Hesse, and Greene on to more popular writers like King, Rossner, Roth, and Irving emphasize the splintering of humanity, the meaninglessness of relationships and the solitariness of modern living. Many recent films made for television and the cinema have also focused attention on turmoil in and disintegration of relationships. Additionally, as one surveys the past two to three decades of scholarly writing it becomes evident that the idea and hypothesis of alienation has assumed a central place in social science thought and research. It is not difficult to see, from these academic and popular sources, that the drift of our times is away from stability in relationships, human fellowship, and communal ties.

In an attempt to study the implications of heightening individualism and alienation, Robert Weiss has delineated four kinds of relationships which are essential to successful adjustment to modern life and to the development of a personal sense of wellness [7]. First, it is important to know people who share our concerns. The function of this relationship is social integration; its absence leads to social isolation. Second, we need to know people whom we can depend upon in a pinch. This relationship fulfills the need for social assistance, without which we feel anxious and vulnerable. Third, we need one or more close friends. Those individuals with whom we can be emotionally intimate, not people who are merely companions or acquaintances. These friendship relationships serve the vital function of fulfilling personal needs for intimacy, without which we would be left emotionally isolated and lonely. Fourth, it is essential to know one or more people who respect our competence. These respectful relationships bolster our self-esteem; their absence leaves us feeling blemished and inadequate.

The point which Weiss makes is that the cultural framework and institutional organization of American society inhibits the regular, ongoing fulfillment of these relationship needs. The detached alienation of our age has promoted the growth of individualism, independence, and an unprecedented sense of *uninvolvement* [6], creating a social environment which makes it difficult to regularly fulfill these needs. In some ways, in these detached and uninvolved times, some forms of activism are on the increase. Most often, however, these are increasingly characterized as ideologically based, self-interest groups, or individuals and groups committed to the promotion of narrowly defined interests. The growing American involvement with narrowly defined, sometimes trivial issues, may be useful in providing individuals with an important sense of personal involvement with issues which are personally important and seem manageable. Involvement with these kinds of issues enables the individual to feel he belongs to something. It also generates a sense of potency for him. However, it needs to be remembered that the forms of this type of involvement are consistent with the ethic of individualism and self-expression. They also point to the generalized lack of involvement in commonweal issues, and to the diminishment of collectively shared concerns among the American citizenry.

Again, as I have been emphasizing, the individual is left to his or her own abilities to carve out a web of satisfying relationships and a sense of purpose to living and dying. The great legacy of social change and modernity is personal liberation and creation of unparalleled opportunities for the expression of human freedom and responsibility. On the flip side of the coin lies the fact that a widespread, stable base of social support is vanishing from the American landscape, exacerbating anxieties and vulnerabilities of modern individuals. As we shall see, this devolution of secure and stable community relations has special and penetrating implications for the life experiences of dying individuals.

DYING AND LOSS OF FELLOWSHIP

The image of a person dying in isolation in a hospital, surrounded by tubes, machines, and professional staff is consistent with the broader American framework of bureaucratization, specialization, technicism, individualism, and alienation. In the modern scenario, as it is not unusual for Americans to live lives that are touched by loneliness and detachment, it is similarly not unusual for Americans to die alone and lonely.

In the first place, physicians who largely shape, define, and dominate the process of dying are generally not capable of or interested in providing support and fellowship for the dying person. The organization and definition of work in the hospital setting emphasizes technical medical-nursing care, and the structure of professional activity of the doctor inhibits the regularized and accountable provision of "comfort work" [8]. The rational, technological framework of medical work often stymies the formation of community and fellowship rituals. Physicians, therefore, are not only restricted by the technological canons of professional training and detachment, they are structurally and psychically constrained from attending to the intimacy and fellowship needs of their dying patients.

Simply, the relief of human suffering is not central to the professional consciousness of physicians. Disease is their interest, not personhood. Thus, as a result of the technical focus of their professional activity, physicians typically offer their patients little in terms of social support, other than referrals to others— social workers, hospice nurses, psychiatric consults, etc.

It is also difficult for family and friends to attend satisfactorily to the human needs of dying loved ones. In light of the absence of a collectively shared meaning-set which makes sense of dying, it becomes understandably difficult for friends, family, and patients to establish a stable and consistent pattern of mutual support. It is also difficult for loved ones, who have lived much of their lives in isolation from death, to empathize fully with the suffering and experiences of dying. Finally, in our age of individualism with its absence of shared concerns, increasingly they bring *their own,* well intentioned definition of the situation to their interaction with dying loved-ones. This absence of a shared set of definitions, understandings, and meanings can contribute to feelings of polarization and disconnection. One patient comments on how differently she and her mother see her situation and how conflict can arise from the divergence of perspective and meaning:

> She has a terrible habit that annoys me. When we meet someone who
> has cancer, she always says: "Oh, your cancer is not as bad as his!" Like

I should be thankful for having this kind of cancer. I know she is saying it for my own good—to make me feel better—but for me, any cancer is lousy, and I'm not able to handle it no matter how good of a . . . quote: "how 'good' of a cancer it may be."

That irritates me. Oh, does that make me angry, and she cannot understand why I hate it when she does this.

This patient and her mother are responding to the problem of cancer and mortality in radically different ways. The implications of the illness are also quite different for each. The patient is losing her self, her life, and her future, while her mother is losing her daughter and part of her motherhood. In the absence of a shared, cultural meaning-set, grieving individuals are left to their own perspectives and adaptive strategies in coping with dying. Such strategies will normatively be defined by one's own personality and particularized role position in relation to the dying experience. In this way, the sharing of concerns and its associated sense of social integration are tenuous and difficult to achieve. Patients and loved ones are often left vulnerable, isolated, and disunited as they try to individually navigate through the unfamiliar world of serious disease and dying.

The incompatibility of concern and interest is even more apparent between physicians and patients. Another patient speaks insightfully and painfully about how the technological orientation conflicts with patient needs, often leaving patients frustrated and feeling like they do not matter as persons:

If I had a classroom of students in front of me, the one message I would tell them is to stay away from medicine. It won't help them in the long run, and it could care less about them as human beings . . .

Why don't they have any compassion for the patient? All they do is continue to put me on new medications which they know won't work. They do this for themselves, not for me. The just don't care.

Three days later the same patient adds:

The hair on my face. That's one thing I'll never forgive him (the oncologist) for. He knew that it was going to do this to my face. But he didn't care. He didn't care what it would mean to me as a person. I won't forgive myself, either, for letting him talk me into taking the medicine.

The irony illustrated above is that advancements in technology and commitment to the use of technology in patient care are placing physicians in an irreconcilable dilemma with an important dimension of the Hippocratic Oath: PRIMUM NON NOCERE—Above all, do no harm. That is to say, what is feasible and desirable from a medical viewpoint may be potentially harmful and damaging to the patient from a personal viewpoint. Furthermore, the management of terminal illness through the application of medical technology may often conflict with the needs, desires, and hopes of patients. This conflict, which is a conflict between the doctor's narrow technical priorities and the patient's broad spectrum of human needs, is a drama that has been popularized by a number of celebrated cases and national media attention (Karen Ann Quinlan, "Whose Life is it Anyway?," etc.). On a less celebrated yet more widespread level, these conflicts regularly unfold in the everyday treatment of dying patients. They represent a clash of competing interests between and among doctors, family members, patients, lawyers, hospital administrators, and even ethicists. In this manner, the modern dying scenario is characterized by an absence of shared concerns. Indeed, it is often replete with unshared, competing concerns and interests. The result aggravates the social isolation of dying patients and establishes a pluralistic dying model in which every death becomes individualized.

The deficiency of integrated patterns of living and shared meanings in the broader culture, coupled with the values of individualism and self-interest, contribute to the isolation and loneliness of the modern dying experience. In a society where dying, death, and suffering have become marginal phenomena excluded from the course of daily social living, it is burdensome for individuals to feel at ease with and become active participants in the dying experience. Simply put, in our age of individualism, materialism, and technological heroism, wherein mortality and suffering are hidden and dwarfed, we have lost our capacity to comfortably accompany others on their pilgrimage to the end of life. In short, as individuals and as society we have lost the ability to "go the distance and ease their pain." One family member speaks of the difficulty in watching and being with her dying husband throughout the course of his sufferings:

> The physical pain, that I can understand. But the hallucinations— the semi-conscious writhing, which is more comfortable for him—is impossible for me. It's incredibly senseless. I can make more sense out of the physical pain than I can out of emotional suffering. Just watching him . . . I get so I can't take it, so I find myself making excuses for staying away. And then the guilt starts . . .

I hasten to emphasize, at this point, that the patient is not the only one isolated from systems of support. Loved ones who are personally involved with the dying person often find themselves in the situation of coping with their grief in isolation, with little assistance beyond their own personal abilities and resources. Indeed, the loving wife who just spoke so painfully about her inability to love and support her dying husband in the way she wished she could, was herself alone and unsupported. Her children, in this mobile society of ours, had moved away and she was almost always alone as she spent time in and out of her husband's room, often wandering the hallways and lounge areas in an isolated daze of grief.

In this context of medicalized dying and absence of shared meanings, family members often become frustrated, helpless, and uninvolved spectators of the dying process. First of all, there is a lack of readily available and culturally approved norms to guide them in their interactions. As such, it is understandable that family members often feel confused and vulnerable in the presence of their dying loved one. One family member, speaking in the presence of and for her father and siblings, questions her mother's physician:

> Should we talk to her? What should we say? What should we do when we are here? We are just so afraid of not doing the right thing.

As patients become visibly sicker, and as sufferings and deterioration become more evident, family feelings of helplessness correspondingly increase. The dying experience of the above patient, whose family expressed concern over how to relate to her, provides a useful illustration. The patient's disease was progressing steadily, and she began to complain:

> I feel so confused. Oh, God. Oh, God! I just feel so confused.

It was believed that this patient's tumor had spread to her brain and that the source of her confusion was related to the progression of her disease. Her sense of confusion continued to the point where, several days after her initial complaints of disorientation, she lost awareness of herself and her situation. When her physician asked her to respond to some basic questions as what the year is, when her birthday is, who the president is, etc., she offered the following answers:

> Today is January 4, 1981.[1] My home is _____ hospital. Today's date? 1974! I was born in 1973. The president? . . . Uh, the president?? Uh . . .

The patient continued to be confused and disoriented, signaling her dissatisfaction and frustration through verbal and physical expressions such as clenched fists, moans, and groans, intensely attempting to concentrate and squirming in her bed. Excerpts from conversations with her physician on the following two days further illuminate her condition:

Doctor:	Do you need anything tonight?
Patient:	Yes. (nodding emphatically)
Doctor:	What can I get for you?
Patient:	I don't know, but something . . .

The physician, who saw that the patient was not requesting something specific but was grasping for some transcendence and control over her condition, offered her

---

[1] It was actually mid-summer of another year.

some words of reassurance and then left her (alone) to proceed on his rounds. The conversation resumed the following day:

Doctor:	How are you doing today, Mrs. _____?
Patient:	Not good.
Doctor:	What's wrong?
Patient:	I don't know. Oh boy . . . oh man, oh man . . . (she squirms in discomfort, but not in pain, and tosses her head side to side on her pillow)

As the patient became sicker during the final phase of her illness and displayed greater signs of distress and unease, her family was less and less present at her bedside. At the beginning of her final admission into the hospital, her husband, son, daughters, and mother-in-law were steadily present during visiting hours. But, as her disease and its physical/behavioral manifestations progressed, family visits became less regular. The pain of watching a loved one suffer without a shared sense of purpose to the suffering, coupled with the inability to alleviate the suffering, is understandably difficult to bear. In this vein, the family's absence from the dying process should not be interpreted as a lack of concern or love. Rather, it should be seen as a consequence of the helplessness, meaninglessness, and absence of social support systems which characterize the contemporary hospital deathbed scenario.

The "case" came to its conclusion at 10:15 one Friday morning. The resident walked into the patient's room to examine her and found her dead (she had died alone). After performing the technical ritual of certifying that she was dead, the resident called the attending physician's office to inform him of the patient's death and said: "Mrs. _____ has just died. What shall we do with the body?" The attending physician responded that the husband would be contacted and that he would then pass on the husband's wishes.[2] The body remained on the same floor, in a semi-private room with the bed curtains drawn, for over three hours while the attending physician tried to reach the patient's husband. The husband, who was finally contacted at his field assignment from work, was told over the phone that his wife had died earlier in the day.

The helplessness of those personally involved with the dying patient often leads to avoidance of contact with the patient or to normless, inconsistent, and anxious moments of interaction.

The isolation and the longing of the dying patient for support leads the patient to look to his or her doctor for comfort and reassurance. In many ways, this is because physicians are prominent in shaping the course of the patient's illness and dying experience. They are the authoritative source of hope upon whom patients are deeply dependent and connected. But, as we have seen, physicians' typical

---

[2] The medical staff had hoped to get an autopsy.

definition of professional obligations excludes them from providing deep and regular support for the psychosocial needs of dying patients. Yet doctors, especially detached-sympathetic support physicians, do engage in some comfort work. The amount and depth of comfort provided, however, is limited by their technical role definition. As a result, patient expectations, needs, and hope often stretch beyond physician willingness and ability to fully comfort. The result is that patients frequently feel neglected and abandoned. As one patient confides:

> I don't have full confidence in Dr. _____. He's a kind man and probably a good physician, but I don't have full confidence in him. I feel that he doesn't listen to me. He's always joking around and telling me what I should be doing, but he never listens to me.

> I can never count on him either. Whenever I really need him, he's never around. He just has this lady doctor see me, and I don't like her. Whenever there is a crisis, he's never around . . . off sailing or on vacation somewhere, but never where I need him.

The patient's doctor had been away at a medical convention when these comments were made. The physician returned from his conference three days later and during the course of his normal rounds entered into the patient's room to examine her. Upon seeing him, the patient perked up and exclaimed:

Patient: You deserted me! I'm sick all this time, and you do nothing to help me.
Doctor: (calmly smiling) What's the matter, don't I love you anymore? (Patient becomes very agitated, disturbed by the doctor's response, sighs, gives the doctor a dissatisfied look, and drops the issue.)

The patient, later in the same day, comments:

> See, what did I tell you? He's always ready with his jokes, so he doesn't have to listen to what I want to say.

Physicians are neither trained to nor believe that they should function to fulfill the social assistance needs of patients. Patients, however, perhaps because of the overwhelming desperation which can arise from dying, look to their physicians as a source of support. Some doctors are markedly more caring than others in the care that they render. But whatever sustained psychosocial support is given is of a self-expressive, informal nature. Because of the way in which doctors' professional role definition is circumscribed by detachment and a technological focus, physicians are not well trained or interested in providing meaningful personal and social support that would assist patients through their dying process.

There are also individuals in our society who die isolated from others largely because their families are dispersed throughout the country or because their family ties have seriously eroded. In addition, there are structural constraints inhibiting fellowship formation even for those dying patients who are connected to a network of people who care about them. The limitations of visiting hours, the restricting of children, the fact that the patient is in the hospital and not home all serve as inhibitors to the formation of fellowship and community at the deathbed. But, perhaps even more important is the fact that life responsibilities of family and friends continue on, unaffected by the circumstances of dying. Ariès was correct when he noted that society does not pause for dying or death. The realities of life with their professional, economic, personal, family, and social obligations limit the role that even the most dedicated of friends and family can play in providing support and comfort to the dying.

In a literal sense, friends and family *visit* a dying person in the hospital, that is to say, they *are outsiders* who temporarily come to offer support. But, they are not an integral presence in the everyday, moment-to-moment life of the terminally ill patient. One patient reflects:

> I realize how much my husband means to me when he is not present. I get to missing him terribly, and I get to feeling sad, feeling loneliness. I know he won't be able to come again till tomorrow . . .

Another adds:

> I don't know what happened to my wife, who was supposed to come and visit. My son was also supposed to come to see me. Neither came, and I didn't know what to do.

In describing their perceptions of support and the absence thereof, despite great variation in their personal circumstances, dying patients commonly and consistently bemoan the loneliness of evenings and of the night, especially sleepless nights.

Regardless of the best efforts exerted by family and friends to be present at the bedside of a dying loved one,[3] believed them to be real. Dying patients often endure loneliness and the psychoemotional void that results from the incomplete fulfillment of "Weiss' needs." A vivid illustration comes to mind. It involves a seventy-year-old patient who had developed a tendency to drift in and out of states of irrationality. Her physicians had feared that her cancer had finally spread to her

---

[3] It is ironic that one family member who was most dedicated to his dying relative (he was present every day during her repeated and sometimes extensive hospitalizations) was informed by his own physician that if he kept up his present regimen of caring for his wife, he himself would be dead in six months. This person was advised by his physician to have his wife placed in a nursing home.

brain and was causing her hallucinations; however, even when the patient was lucid, she had strong remembrances of the torments of her hallucinations and believed them to be real. I walked into her room to see her and found her sitting up in bed, alone, trembling and crying. She had just awakened from "a dream" and was recounting how its images and themes had been coming to haunt her regularly since her hallucinations began a few days earlier:

> ... the funeral velvet—that black draped all over the room. The incredibly kooky stuff that was going on. Behind the mirror, there are performers— dancing. You can't see them, but I can. The nurse, she is with them. I wouldn't take a pill from her. It scares me. It's all so irreligious. I don't believe in that stuff ... I'm so afraid they are going to get my husband ... they're going to make me die. A tall man came in, dressed in black, and told me I'm going to die. And there's a paper menorah in the corner of the room. ...

The patient's vulnerabilities and the suffering, precipitated by her hallucinations, were exacerbated by her aloneness and loneliness. During this particular episode I sat with her for quite a while, holding her hand and just offering some reassurances. (But I myself was out of character[4]. After all, I was present for the purpose of doing research on death and dying, not for providing social support!) The patient was awaiting the arrival of her only regular visitor, her husband, who was expected in several hours. Until that time, and even after he arrived, the patient would have to find ways of surviving her fears and vulnerabilities, in large part, drawing on her own resources and adaptive strategies, in isolation.[5]

At a time when individualism and alienation have become societal norms, there is regrettable absence of culturally sanctioned meanings to the dying process. The sense of helplessness, abandonment, and isolation which surround modern dying is a logical extension of the forces that are dominant in the broader society. The absence and inadequacy of support systems, that is to say, the deficient fulfillment of Weiss' needs, increasingly isolate the dying person in a privatized world of survival and coping. This in turn helps to initiate a self-fulfilling prophecy whereby dying increasingly becomes meaningless and tragic, which makes it all the more difficult to witness, which in turn creates a sense of quarantine, abandonment, and social disconnection for dying patients. The result is that it becomes ever more difficult to establish and sustain the presence of community throughout the dying process. In this way, the experience and

---

[4] For a useful discussion of the spectrum of roles that a fieldwork-researcher typically assumes in the course of medical ethnographies, see: Charles Bosk, The Fieldworker as Watcher and Witness, *Hasting Center Report*, pp. 10-14, June 1985.

[5] Her physicians were reluctant to treat her hallucinations for fear that treatment would mask other symptoms related to her cancer.

sufferings of dying are increasingly privatized, and the privatizing of the dying experience has become a salient means of managing and controlling the death process. Most specifically, it vanquishes the process and its associated horror to the confines of the private world of patients and loved ones. And, in the course of insulating dying from ordinary patterns of social life, feelings of isolation and abandonment intensify the suffering of dying persons.

REFERENCES

1. A. Camus, *The Plague,* Vintage Books, New York, 1972.
2. W. Stegner, *All the Little Live Things,* Penguin Books, London, 1967.
3. A. Solomon, *A Stone Boat,* Penguin Books, New York, 1994.
4. W. P. Kinsella, *Shoeless Joe,* Ballantine Books, New York, 1982.
5. R. Nisbet, *The Sociological Tradition,* Basic Books, New York, 1966.
6. R. Nisbet, *The Quest for Community,* Oxford University Press, New York, 1981.
7. R. Weiss, The Fund of Sociability, *Transaction,* pp. 38-40, July/August 1969.
8. A. Strauss, *Social Organization of Medical Work,* University of Chicago Press, Chicago, 1985.

CHAPTER
7

Impersonalism, Dying, and Social Organization of the Hospital

Poison drips into our veins. Radiation scars our lungs. Bureaucracy diminishes us. Impersonality angers us. We are irritable, wet, cold, seasick, vomiting. We are bad company. Shivering, suffering. Self-centered [1, p. 80].

Christina Middlebrook

The final medical solution to human problems: remove everything from the body that is diseased or protesting, leaving only enough organs which by themselves, or hooked up to appropriate machines—still justify what is left of a person as a "case," and call the procedure humanectomy [2, p. 70].

Thomas Szasz

Since the introduction of modern technology, the hospital has lost its aura of being a place of comfort and has instead become an establishment resembling a factory, where illnesses are taken care of rather than human beings [3, p. 22].

Henry Heinemann

A hospital is a bureaucratically organized social institution. Its major function is to treat and cure disease. Disease is managed technologically in the hospital by an approach that emphasizes rationality and efficiency. Although this orientation often conflicts with the psychosocial needs of patients and families, it is argued that rationalization, standardization of care, and depersonalization of patients are "worth the price" when they medically benefit the patient. In this regard, the underlying premise of the hospital organization of medical care is consistent with the central premise of technological consciousness; namely, that the vital needs of human beings are reducible to technologically definable components. In this framework, the requirements of a patient's humanity must yield to medical intervention. This intervention is carried out by specialists possessing certain impenetrable skills which translate patient needs into a series of management procedures and regimens. According to this philosophy and practice of care, if a problem does not have an objective, somatic base, and a technical solution, then it is not a real problem worthy of real attention. Although deplorable, the widespread indifference to human suffering in the midst of dying is understandable, given the values and concept of care in our culture.

The bureaucratic ethos by which the hospital arranges its daily activities serves an important function in sustaining the technical detachment of physicians from the psychosocial needs of dying patients. As Weber puts it, "the coordinating principles of specialization and rationalization allow for the regular and uninterrupted fulfillment of the duties legislated by the bureaucracy" [4, p. 196]. The bureaucratic environment of the hospital continues to shape the behavior of physicians in a manner consistent with the professional obligations that were spawned in medical school: detachment, emotional neutrality, and objectivity. Thus, the social climate and the culture of care in the hospital are instrumental in maintaining the objective-technical base of the doctor's training throughout the years of professional practice. They also help to eliminate subjectivity, irrationality, and emotionality in daily professional activity. As Berger suggests, "the primary effect of bureaucratic consciousness in technological civilization is the management of emotionality" [5, p. 57]. In this way, when emotions are expressed by patients, family members, etc., they are defined foremost as inappropriate or irrelevant. For this reason, the physician is legitimately able to respond to emotionalism in a manner which ignores those outbreaks and restricts or inhibits further emotional expressions. This process of emotional regulation is illuminated in the following scenario. A doctor, on the course of his daily rounds, was being followed by seven first-year students who had been assigned to him for one afternoon a week, for six weeks, in a program on "perspectives in patient care." While walking down the hallway the doctor encountered, in the hallway, the spouse of a middle-aged woman whose tests had recently come back from the lab with a diagnosis of myeloma in an advanced stage. The spouse wanted to talk to the doctor, who was quite willing to do so. The doctor and his entourage proceeded into a treatment room which would allow some privacy. The physician told the patient's husband the facts of the case: his wife had a serious form of cancer and that her life expectancy was about one to two years. The husband began to cry and continued to cry during the six-seven minutes of conversation with the doctor. The husband was insisting that the doctor lie to his wife about her condition; the doctor refused, saying, "I have to tell her she has cancer, but we don't have to let her know how bad it is." The doctor very calmly, rationally, and without any recognition of or attention to the husband's emotional outpourings convinced him that his wife should be told about the cancer, but that the emphasis in the discussion would be on treatment modalities. This interaction is fascinating and extraordinary but also is fairly typical of the bureaucratic processes which shape doctor-patient interaction. It is extraordinary because what would have been virtually impossible in ordinary social interaction; namely, proceeding as if the emotional expressions of the husband did not exist at all, was fully supported by the bureaucratic organization of patient care. In this way, the emotional turbulence of dying was restricted and kept within the bounds of bureaucratic-technical focus. And, what an introduction to detachment and objectivity these first-year students received!

Specialization is a major component of the modern delivery of health care. The hospital-based system of care is a reflection of and contributor to the growing specialization of the medical profession. Doctors treating only certain types of conditions, others exclusively involved in narrow technical activities (e.g., reading x-rays and CT scans), interns rotating from area to area or patient to patient, nurses increasingly becoming identified with a specified area of care such as pediatrics or oncology, are all reflective of the hierarchical and specialized division of labor that characterizes the system of care in the hospital:

> The trend is clear; increasing numbers of physicians are seeking the personal security and satisfaction of specialization. . . . To be able to deliver what he knows is the best, the doctor today is forced to limit the breadth of his practice—to specialize [6, p. 681].

As specialization has become an institutionalized norm, a vast array of technical and medical experts become necessary in order to staff a modern hospital. The irony of this situation is that comprehensiveness in medical care is defined through an inward spiral of reductionist activity, increasing circumscription of professional roles and competency, and the distancing from breadth. Continuity of care is sought not by an integrated coordinated approach, but by fragmentation and division. In this framework of specialization, the idea of totality becomes operational through the independent functioning of isolated units of technical activity. David Mechanic summarizes the importance of the compartmentalization and specialization of care in the bureaucratic milieu of the hospital:

> Within the technical scientific organization, chief consideration is given to the means to achieve most efficiently a high level of diagnostic work. In this setting, medical assessment is quite specialized, in the assumption that experts in particular fields are more knowledgeable than a general doctor. Moreover, time units are developed which allow adequate evaluation to take place, without sacrificing the efficiency of the doctor's output. . . . The patient thus becomes a unit which is moved from department to department, so that each can exercise its specialized function with dispatch and efficiency. Each department views the patient in terms of its specialized function, giving highest priority to its particular task [7, p. 171].

In direct correlation with the degree to which the patient is narrowly defined and considered, the task of the physician becomes commensurately narrow and standardized. Inherently, therefore, emotional needs of the patient and family are excluded from the specialized, standardized, technical purview of hospital-based medical care. Paradoxically, the movement toward specialization in patient care, while consistent with broader trends toward specialization of work, is occurring in the midst of growing cultural discontent with fragmentation and increased yearning for wholeness and social integration. Additionally, the systematic disregard of emotional expression and needs of dying persons is taking place in a cultural context wherein the value of self and self-expression is being extolled.

The hospice and palliative care movements are seeking to implement a broader, more integrated spectrum of patient care than the compartmentalized care offered in the hospital. Hospice and palliative care, however, are consistent with the modern trend toward specialization. As an alternative to the hospital, hospices are a highly specialized program, which caters to needs of a highly specific population who meet specific guidelines for inclusion. Thus, hospice programs have established new and specialized roles of caring for the dying, namely, hospice medical director, hospice chaplain, hospice nurses, hospice volunteers, etc. In this way, the hospice, while seeking a more comprehensive approach to patient care, is still situated within a broader framework of specialization and compartmentalization of care. Palliative medicine is similarly emerging and developing as a medical specialty.

Given this introduction to the bureaucratic blueprint of hospital-based care, I will now explore the hospital as a system of dehumanization for the medical patient in general and the dying person in particular.

THE HOSPITAL AS TOTAL INSTITUTION:
AMBIENCE FOR DEHUMANIZATION

Every social institution is capable of dominating the time, interests, and activities of the people in it. Some institutions obviously have greater capacity in this regard than others. A total institution involves widespread domination, and is generally characterized by physical separation from and the blocking of continuous social intercourse with the outside world [8]. A hospital, although not completely separational, isolates its patients from the outside world. More importantly, it generally separates the control of patient activity from patient, family, and community. Although the capacity and tendency for domination may not exist unchallenged, the organizational thrust of the hospital is toward standardization, routinization, and objectification—that is to say, toward control and management.

Goffman's classic discussion of total institutions illuminates their efficiency and capacity for control. It depicts the intrinsic potential for dehumanization that resides in their physical and social organization. The main focus of his analysis in *Asylums* is the process by which a person's self is sociologically structured through the total institutional living arrangement. As Goffman observes, the power of the institution is asserted from the moment of arrival. Upon entering a total institution an individual is redefined and restructured by a set of behavioral imperatives that facilitate the bureaucratic operation and flow of work. Although the total institutional features of the hospital are not as fully developed as total institutions such as prisons, concentration camps, or army barracks, entrance into a hospital involves a standardized procedure for processing, identifying, restricting, and redefining personhood. The process of role disengagement, which transforms the incoming person into an admitted patient, is initiated by the interactions that take place between admitting staff and the patient. I have heard patients regularly complain about excessive waiting for admissions procedures to be completed. Waiting is a normal part of the patient experience and is of little concern to those who deliver service in the hospital. In addition, the nature of admissions-interactions is governed by the operational needs of the bureaucracy (insurance information, etc.) and often leaves patients feeling "processed" and alienated. The perceptive patient knows that he is being treated in ways that emphasize objective, standardized business considerations. The less perceptive patient may not be cognitively aware of the meaning of their initial processing, but is nonetheless often angered and frustrated by bureaucratic indifference.

The initial moments of socialization in the hospital further show that the hospital routine and staff are largely interested in individuals only as patients. Although staff normatively "welcome" the patient with pleasant conversation, and do often informally chat with patients whom they know, the stage is being set for starting the operating engines of the bureaucratic patient-management process. Nurses and residents will take extensive case histories and perform preliminary medical exams. At this point, the wheels of the bureaucracy are quickly set in motion: the family is isolated from the care of the patient and the authority of nurses, interns, and residents is firmly established. The attending or admitting physician is generally not present during this period of initiation, but when he or she visits the patient later on, the patient is given a comprehensive physical exam called a "work-up." The work-up includes a hands-on physical exam, some of which has already been performed by the intern or resident, asking a comprehensive set of questions relevant to physical symptomatology and disease management, identifying what tests need to be done, ordering medications to be administered, and establishing and informing the patient of the plan of treatment that is being designed, etc.

Thus, after a mere eight hours or so, if the patient was unaware of or had forgotten about the requirements of the patient role, she learns that deference, obedience, and compliance are required. The patient, even if responded to in the most sensitive and humane patterns of care, is still defined by and through the work requirements of the staff's professional role obligations. As Mr. Smith the person becomes transformed into "Mr. Smith—The Cancer Patient in 402," the uniqueness, feelings, and human expressions of the personal side of the patient become reduced to anecdotal significance.

When patients are admitted to a hospital for the treatment of serious, life-threatening disease their primary concern is with matters of life and death. However, their apprehensions are seen as private and personal. They are quickly immersed within the confines of the technological boundaries of patient care and emotional expressions or worries about dying are circumscribed. Thus, anxiety about the possibility of dying is redefined into less threatening, more manageable categories of patient management. That is to say, the broad issue of dying becomes condensed and packaged into a series of patient management procedures: tests, diagnoses, medical, and surgical interventions, etc. The very human and potentially meaningful expressions of anger, vulnerability, fear, and emotional turbulence which are a natural and personalized response to dying are rendered insignificant and out of place. In this way, the personal and emotional hardship of dying is denied, or more correctly, it is organized and contained by the institutional foci and practices of the hospital.

The objectification of personhood is functional from the point of view of medical efficiency. Thus, patients or family members who fail to accept the institution's definition of appropriate behavior interfere with the felicitous carrying out of work tasks. One woman who was deeply embittered by her husband's grim prognosis became aggressively confrontational with her husband's attending physician. She criticized the care he had been receiving, and complained about the lack of commitment (or her perceptions thereof) to her husband's full recovery. The attending physician, tiring of her attitude, asked her to "please wait in the hallway" so he could begin his work-up of the patient. She refused, saying, "No! John (referring to her husband) doesn't mind me being here." The doctor became quickly irritated with her and authoritatively said that unless she waited outside her husband would not be examined. After an emotionally charged confrontation, the doctor prevailed, and she reluctantly left for the hallway. (The patient meanwhile had been lying on his bed, clad only in his underpants, quietly watching the interaction for the full five minutes it took.) In the hallway, she bitterly spoke about the indifference of the physician to her husband's suffering and prospective dying: THEY JUST DON'T GIVE A SHIT. PUT THAT IN YOUR STUDY! Another illustration involves a patient who had read just about every piece of research in the medical journals that was pertinent to his case. A common piece of backstage humor among his doctors was the statement: "When he dies you can have his money, I'll take his medical library." He questioned his doctors' medical strategies and engaged his physicians in time-consuming discussions about the relative merits of different courses of treatment. (Irritated by the demands made upon their time and by his lack of compliance, his private physicians adopted a policy of doubling the fee they charged him.) The man was remarkably conversant and knowledgeable about the relevant studies in the cancer journals. However, his efforts to design his own plan of treatment were dismissed as "inappropriate and ridiculous" by his physicians. The patient was told by his two doctors that either he comply with their program of treatment or find himself another hospital. (And the latter is precisely what happened.)

It is scenarios such as these in which patients become disruptive to the well-ordered flow of the doctor's work and to the standardized operation of the medical bureaucracy. Expressions of individuality can be tolerated only if they do not interfere with technological routine, focus, and authority. The institutional framework of the hospital redefines the private, emotional concerns of patients, particularly dying patients, into a rational and objective framework. As a result, respect for personhood is systematically undermined and the personal and social self is reduced to a "non-personal medical entity." Goffman eloquently describes this process as:

> The wonderful brand of "non-person" treatment found in the medical world, whereby the patient is greeted with what passes as civility and said farewell to in the same fashion with everything in between going on as if the patient weren't there as a social person at all, but only as a possession that someone has left behind [8, pp. 441-442].

There can be no doubt that the emotional and social suffering of dying patients is exacerbated by institutionally-based disregard for their personal, emotional, and social selves.

The reductionist definition of medical care underlies the neglect of the personal and social needs of patients and sometimes even promotes a callous abuse thereof. One afternoon, for example, I walked into a semi-private room of four patients to see one of the terminally-ill patients in my study. In the bed immediately to the left of the doorway, a man with testicular cancer was undergoing a pre-operative examination by two surgical residents. As the doctors were examining the patient (actually, one examined him while the other sat at the foot of the bed and took notes), it became clear that these young surgeons were interested only in the physical-technical considerations that were relevant to the upcoming operation. The patient was examined without the bed curtains being drawn, and the patient's body was displayed for any passerby to see. His legs were spread and genitals fully exposed. I asked the attending oncologist of the patient I was seeing, who had also witnessed this scene, how he could tolerate such callous disregard for dignity and not have said something to the residents about their behavior? The oncologist replied: "I would have said something if they had been medical residents, not surgical."

The social structure of the hospital is arranged on many of the principles that form a total institution. Its objective, fragmented worldview creates an environment which is conducive to dehumanization. In addition, the idea of specialization and bureaucratization of care enables even perceptive, detached-sympathetic-support physicians to deny responsibility for structurally embedded abuses of patient care. This supports my contention that when caring and compassion occur in the treatment of dying patients, they are far more a result of caring, compassionate individuals than systems of training or professional practice. More to the point, the bureaucratic realities of the social organization of hospital-based care transforms the subjective, personal side of dying into a clinical focus in which dying and disease are technically managed. Thus, in that dying represents a subjective label that is attached to an objective disease state it becomes non-existent as a personal human process. If and when dying is formally addressed in hospitals, it is usually moved out of the mainstream of medical culture—into an associated hospice or palliative care unit. But, more on that later. For now, it is important to recognize that the personal experience of dying is often "denied," that is to say, restricted by bureaucratic routine and technical focus.

PATIENT ALIENATION WITHIN THE HOSPITAL

In recent decades, there has been an impressive outpouring of professional and popular writing about the role of alienation in modern life. The concept, while oftentimes overly philosophical and abstract, is useful in explaining the human condition of dying patients in the hospital setting. For this reason, I will identify some of the specific indicators of alienation as set forth in the social science literature, and explicate their relevance to the life of dying patients.

Alienation is the condition in which individuals are separated from necessary and important qualities of their humanity. It refers to the gap that exists between important human aspirations and actual conditions of a person's life.

Powerlessness, or the belief that something cannot be accomplished, is an indicator of alienation [9]. It refers to the presumption of an individual that she cannot determine or influence a desired goal. It is best expressed by the feeling "there is not much I can do about the important personal and social problems confronting me."

The feeling of powerlessness may be induced by natural or artificial causes. In many circumstances it is in the very nature of being human that one is unable to affect important life issues. Powerlessness in this vein results from the inherent fragility of life and vulnerability of each of us. On the other hand, feelings of personal impotence may be impressed on individuals by the values and institutions of society. In this circumstance, powerlessness is structurally created by culturally specific circumstances. The alienation of dying patients in twentieth-century America is a self-exacerbating blend of naturally and societally occurring powerlessness.

All living things must die, but the certainty of death has special implications for human beings. As pointed out in Chapter 1, human reason and self-consciousness shackle humanity with an awareness of our vulnerabilities in the face of our ultimate fate. As we have already discussed, great societal efforts to reduce the terror of death have been inspired by the inescapable, rational awareness that one day we all must die. In this way then, it is in the nature of being human that one ponders and anticipates the loss of one's life, the loss of one's future, and the loss of important relationships. The anxieties associated with this process of loss and separation form the basis of human anxiety and fear of death [10]. The dying person feels threatened by the inevitable sense of devolution that dying begets. The dying person also anticipates crossing over into the unknowable abyss that is death, and naturally wonders about what death means and brings. It is not unusual, especially in light of the human tenacity for life, that the anticipation of that fleeting moment or second when one takes the final breath, never to breathe again, will elicit not just fear but a sense of powerlessness and helplessness as well.[1]

In addition to natural powerlessness, societally created impotence abounds for dying persons. Inasmuch as life and the body are defined as possessions in the context of our materialistic culture, death becomes perceived as a thief that robs us of our most precious possession. As we have seen, the sufferings of dying are intensified through cultural values and systems of meaning. Dying leaves both dying individuals and loved ones feeling helpless, isolated, and vulnerable. In our cultural environment of diminished community attachment, the death of a loved one is mourned by a shrinking community, and the process of grieving is thereby emotionally intensified. The intensification of grief, coupled with the diminishment of support systems, tends to exacerbate feelings of powerlessness for the dying person and his family. The bottom line is that, despite the promises of technology, human frailty in the presence of death has ultimately changed very little. The faith that Americans place in science and technology, however, has instilled unrealistic expectations of control within the American frame of mind. The result of these expectations is that feelings of powerlessness are made even more acute when death comes knocking at our door and we are forced to face it directly.

There are several forms of powerlessness here. The human needs of the dying person are intensified at a time when support systems of solace and comfort have been diminished. In addition, when dying does arrive at one's personal doorstep, the cultural ideal of life undisturbed by death is destroyed. This disillusionment not only serves to make death and dying more emotionally pungent, but also threatens to unleash a barrage of individual and collective emotions that express the modern anguish of dying. In our age of denial there is a corresponding social impetus to control the intensity and miasma of these emotions, and the technological-bureaucratic management of dying fulfills this function very well. As individuality and emotional expression are repressed, the dying patient

---

[1] It needs to be remembered that while the cultural rituals of traditional death patterns served to mitigate the powerlessness associated with death, the existence of these rituals and dramas of the deathbed, in and of itself, speaks of the natural powerlessness of human beings in the face of death and of the need for humanity to transcend this impotence individually and collectively.

becomes increasingly unable to assert himself. Technical management combines with cultural devaluation of the meaning of dying and isolates the personal dynamics of dying from the clinical focus of medical care. Thus, as disease progresses, powerlessness, like topsy, grows and grows in an environment that is largely indifferent to human suffering.

An important dimension of powerlessness, then, is the social construction of non-person treatment imposed on dying individuals in the hospital. Having so much of their personal identity stripped away and diminished, dying persons become less and less capable of affecting and making decisions about their own fate. The facilitation of medical work demands passivity in the patient role. Otherwise, probing, poking, exploring, injecting medicines, etc., could not be efficiently accomplished. Additionally, it is interesting to observe how many decisions about the life of a patient are made without seriously consulting the patient. Patients often are informed of the treatment they will be receiving in a manner that is more of an afterthought than anything else. As Cornelius Ryan eloquently tells in the autobiographical account of his struggle with cancer, his doctors dismissed the importance of his need to be involved in decision making about his course of treatment:

> "Please tell me exactly what you have found," I said.
>
> "I think, Mr. Ryan, much of the findings are too technical to go into. I would prefer to explain this in my own way." . . .
>
> "Doctor," I began, "the technical findings concern me and my future. I'd very much appreciate your telling me what they are." He did not unbend.
>
> "You are a difficult man, Mr. Ryan, in your persistence in groping for details you could not possibly understand" [11, p. 84].

Goffman argues that the pacification of the patient and the objectification of personhood so completely suppress a patient's personal presence that his or her fate can be openly discussed around the bedside by a variety of experts, without the experts having to feel undue concern. Presumably, a technical vocabulary helps in this regard [8, p. 442]. In the major medical centers, there are many structurally embedded patterns that decimate the humanity of a patient, e.g., medical and surgical rounds, grand rounds, sitting in a wheelchair or lying on a stretcher in a hallway awaiting various diagnostic procedures, etc. I have not observed the complete nullification of personhood of which Goffman speaks. I have witnessed patients and families express anger and discontent, thereby bringing the personal presence of the patient to the fore. Nevertheless, regular and sustained strategies designed to contain disruptive and emotionally turbulent expressions of dying patients are largely present. In addition, the fact that physicians do separate backstage behavior from front stage interactions with patients, indicates that physicians are aware of the presence of the personal self of their patients and, by default, give recognition to the value of personhood.

The powerlessness of personhood is demeaning for any medical patient, but as Mechanic pointed out, there may at least be some medical use-value associated with the objectification of the patient. The terminal patient by definition, however, cannot be expected to get well again. Thus, the dying patient is faced with suffering through the indignities imposed by the "total institutional" hospital while simultaneously not being able to receive the full benefits of modern medical technology, i.e., cure and recovery. Dying patients thus become subjected to double jeopardy: the technical failure and inability of modern medicine to effect a cure along with a structurally-rooted neglect of their personal and social needs.

The experience of powerlessness can have a curious affect on the doctor-patient relationship. Ironically, the more the bureaucratic system of care neglects and dehumanizes the patient, the more the patient is likely to become grateful to the agents of dehumanization. The more the patients are defined as an object to be managed through technical activities, the scarcer and hence more precious personal attention from nurses, physicians, and others becomes. In the presence of scarcity of concern, especially at a time when the emotional and social needs of patients are heightened by the vulnerability of the dying experience, patients tend to become increasingly indebted to the medical staff for the routine and standardized version of care they provide. In this way, the more individual personhood is neglected, the more the neglected person becomes appreciative of *any* source of attention to his or her individual needs. In short, indifference and neglect breed expression of thankfulness and gratitude, despite the existence of deep-seated resentment.

The similarities with Orwell's view of powerlessness and totalitarianism in *1984* are evident and alarming. In terms of metaphor, moral values, and social principles, the impotence and indignity that typified daily life in Oceania is indicative of the dehumanization and powerlessness faced by dying patients. Indeed, the similarities are striking. The citizenry of Oceania were controlled through rational, efficient, technical means. Dying individuals in contemporary America are defined and dominated by technological worldview and activity. The inner party, the experts of social control, was in charge of Orwell's fictitious society. The inner party, the experts of medical control, is in charge of managing dying people in the hospital setting. The power of the experts in Oceania was total; Winston and Julia's revolt was doomed from the very beginning. The power of the hospital system is not as encompassing as that found in Oceania, but the technical, bureaucratic rules, standards, and norms are the guiding principles that shape and dominate the experience of death in the modern hospital.

In the "Afterword" to *1984*, Erich Fromm relates Simone Weil's definition of power to Orwell's discussion of power and power relations in Oceania. Power, according to Weil, is the capacity to transform a person into a corpse, that is to say, into a thing [12]. The central point that Fromm makes is that the rise and abuse of this form of power is widespread in American economic, social, and political life. More specifically relevant to the plight of dying patients is the transformation from person to "corpse" that takes place in the dehumanizing context of bureaucratically organized care. The non-person treatment of the dying, the "cadaver orientation" of patient care, the bureaucratic organization of the hospital, and the restriction of the social presence of the patient for the benefit of technical activity all reduce the humanity of dying patients. The final consequence and means of dehumanization in *1984* was the systematic implantation of a sense of gratitude for the workings of the party and the system. It is difficult to forget the closing scene wherein Winston, sipping his Victory Gin, contentedly reflects on how everything was right with the world: He Loved Big Brother. Although the hospital system of patient care cannot effect the total domination of consciousness which we see in *1984*, there is an unwritten yet stringently enforced expectation that patients be grateful to and compliant with the directives of the "benevolent inner party" [13].

In short, institutionally-supported diminishment of personhood in the dying process is a salient way of controlling the emotional anguish and social disturbance that dying elicits. And, the specific forms that dehumanization assume are reflective of the values of both the profession of medicine and of the broader cultural and social systems.

Two other indicators of alienation are revealed by the above discussion: meaninglessness and social isolation.

Meaninglessness refers to an individual's understanding of the events in which he is engaged [9, p. 786]. It refers to a culturally bound feeling of confusion or frustration—"the sense that for some reason things have become so complicated that I really don't understand what is going on" [14]. As we have already seen, modern death is unmitigated by rituals of support and culturally rooted meanings. The cultural labeling of dying as evil, exacerbated by medical neglect of sociohuman needs, makes dying patients increasingly reliant and dependent upon technological-curative intervention. However, perhaps for the first time in their lives, dying patients find that science and technology are failing to live up to their promises. The generalized faith which Americans place in science and technology, as discussed in Chapter 3, becomes shaken at this point. The dying person understandably becomes dismayed and confused by a startling awareness of the limitations of the technological way of life. We have also seen that the interactional normlessness which surrounds the dying patient contributes an overriding sense of confusion to the dying process, as both patients and loved ones extensively struggle in confusion and discomposure.

I have regularly observed and heard patients express dismay and exasperation over "why this had to happen to me." The bureaucratic realities of the hospital work and the broader cultural meaning-sets which shape the realities of modern dying fail to adequately explain and relieve the patient's quandary. This only serves to drive the senselessness of dying deeper into the life perceptions and experiences of dying patients. This senselessness has major implications for psychosocial identity, and will be more fully explored in the next chapter.

Social isolation is another measure of the condition of alienation and is apparent in the life of dying patients. It refers to the "feeling of being lonely" [14, p. 22] or the unfulfilled yearning for "Weiss' relationships." As already emphasized, the social isolation of dying patients is reflective of the individualism and diminishment of community in American life. The transfer of the place of death to the hospital, however, with its bureaucratic patterns of patient management, further exasperates the isolation and the loneliness of the dying patient. In a very straightforward way, the "total institutional" structure of hospital care of dying patients de-emphasizes the priority of social integration and insists on following a course of treatment that is technical and efficient. The value of social support becomes reduced to a superfluous afterthought, if it even emerges at all.

The crucial issue is control. Dying patients, due to culturally and socially inspired alienation, are increasingly faced with uncertainty and normlessness. The question of what should be done, when, where, and how it should be done is generally decided by physicians motivated by their technocratic consciousness. Patients, for both legitimate and illegitimate reasons, are disempowered. Although patients are formally and legally in control of their own dying, physicians in reality are substantively in charge. By virtue of their medical authority, coupled with the patient's own dependence upon that knowledge and skill, physicians are the dominant actors that shape the process of dying. In addition, despite the presence of ethical and legal statutes that protect patient autonomy and self-determination, physicians are often reluctant to honor patient wishes, especially if those wishes conflict with their professional judgement of what is best. Ironically, despite technological and medical governance over patterns of care, patients are increasingly responsible for establishing their own individualized sense of meaning and patterns of coping. In this way, another paradox is created by the bureaucratic, technological management of the dying process: At a time when patients are individually responsible for their own dying, alienation and disaffection are at their high point. It seems inconsistent that individual obligations should increase at a time of heightened personal incapacity. Nonetheless, this conflicting pattern is reflective of the social forces of technology and self-expression which prevail in the broader culture, and which underlie the widespread yearning for empowerment, connection, and meaning in American life today.

INSTITUTIONAL DEHUMANIZATION:
A SUMMARY

Meaninglessness and normlessness have led to confusion and groping on the part of patients, families, and physicians. All are seeking answers to difficult questions—but in a disunited, non-communal way. In itself, this very divergence of interests and concerns creates a situation that is ripe for detachment, alienation, and avoidance to flourish. Bureaucratic organization of care promotes further disconnection, and gives rise to subtle, yet sophisticated patterns of care that objectify death and impersonalize personhood. Rationality, efficiency, and technicism are at the "heart and soul" of this process and loom large as sources of dehumanization.

The following scenario effectively highlights the point.

A middle-aged woman with seriously advanced cancer was quickly approaching the moment of her death. She was in a private room with an oxygen tent hook-up to provide some help for her laborious breathing. She was in tremendous pain and discomfort, and was becoming increasingly weak. Nonetheless, in a strange way, despite her technological surroundings and physical debility, she looked very pretty. Her physician walked into her room during the course of his rounds and found her husband quietly sitting by her side. After an exchange of amenities, the physician sprang into a flurry of technical activity, listening to the woman's chest, probing her abdominal areas, checking the swelling in her lymph nodes, etc. During the course of this physical examination, he informed the patient and her husband that he was going to give her some medication for the pain.

The doctor left the room, indicating that he wanted to give the medication by injection so that it would take effect more quickly. He promptly returned with the syringe and medicine and began to prepare the patient for the injection, only to find that her veins had collapsed. He searched fruitlessly for four to five minutes for a vein that would tolerate the injection. Frustrated by failure, he told the patient that a nurse would come down and administer the medicine by mouth. Assuring the patient that he would make every effort to keep her as comfortable as possible, the doctor took his leave. The patient's husband followed, about fifteen feet behind, out into the hallway and called to the doctor when both were fully out of the room and the door had swung closed.

There is no effective way to describe the husband's facial expressions except to say that he was lost, aching, lonely, confused, and desperate. During the course of a very brief conversation, tears welled in his eyes and he struggled to hold them back. He asked the doctor how his wife was doing and what could be expected. The physician very calmly responded: "I doubt she'll make it through the night." The husband, pleading and hoping with every ounce of faith he could muster, asked if there was anything else that could be tried. The physician again calmly responded and said that "there was nothing that could be done for her except to try to make her as comfortable as possible."

The conversation lasted for approximately two minutes, during which time there was no explicit mention of death, nor did the physician make any attempt to recognize or comfort the husband's suffering. Indeed, I did observe a noticeable straining to exit from this death scene as quickly as possible. As I have already discussed, the tendency to flee from death typifies physician responses to the nearing of death. As one doctor expressed it, "the roller skates are put on," namely, one gets as quickly away from the death setting as possible. As the physician bade farewell to the husband and turned to leave, I did the same. Upon glancing at the husband, who was returning back to the room on the brink of tears, the meaning of alienation became so apparent. Sensing the powerlessness and loss of the husband, and thinking of his wife struggling for breath, awaiting his return to the bedside, I saw so clearly how deep their needs were and how miserably they remained unaddressed. To this day, I do not forgive myself for failing to eschew my own professional role definition and the obligations I had for the remainder of the day, in order to stay with the patient and her husband during the final hours of her life.

Many of the ironies of dying in modern society are made evident by this situation. All too often, dying patients and isolated pockets of loved ones are left to their own resources and strengths at a time when they are highly vulnerable and their personal and social selves have been reduced to a point of insignificance. In this sense, patient powerlessness is exacerbated at a time when the strength of personhood is most essential. Although it is only implicit in the above scenario, the cultural and social meaninglessness of dying heightens feelings of vulnerability and impotence. Thus, the experience of dying, in the bureaucratic social system that is the modern hospital, is superabundant with the self-exacerbating, culturally promoted conditions of dehumanization and alienation. In no small part, the profound suffering of dying patients and their loved ones is tethered to this fact.

REFERENCES

1. C. Middlebrook, *Seeing the Crab,* Basic Books, New York, 1996.
2. T. Szasz, *The Second Sin,* Anchor Books, New York, 1974.
3. H. Heinemann, Human Values in the Care of the Terminally Ill, in *Psychosocial Aspects of Terminal Care,* B. Schoenberg et al. (eds.), Columbia University Press, New York, 1972.
4. M. Weber, Bureaucracy, in *From Max Weber,* H. Gerth and C. W. Mills (trans.), Oxford University Press, New York, 1958.
5. P. Berger et al., *The Homeless Mind: Modernization and Consciousness,* Random House, New York, 1973.
6. C. Code, Determinants of Medical Care: A Plan for the Future, *The New England Journal of Medicine, 283*:13, 1979.
7. D. Mechanic, *Medical Sociology,* The Free Press, New York, 1980.
8. E. Goffman, *Asylums,* Chapter One, Doubleday, New York, 1969.
9. M. Seeman, On the Meaning of Alienation, *American Sociological Review, 24*:6, pp. 784-785, 1959.
10. E. Fromm, *The Art of Loving,* Chapter One, Harper and Row, New York, 1956.
11. C. Ryan and K. M. Ryan, *A Private Battle,* Simon and Schuster, New York, 1979.

12. E. Fromm, Afterword, in *1984*, G. Orwell, Harcourt Brace Jovanovich, Inc., New York, p. 263, 1949.
13. E. Shelp, Courage: A Neglected Virtue in the Patient-Physician Relationship, *Social Science and Medicine, 18*:4, p. 352, 1984.
14. G. Zito, Marx, Durkheim and Alienation, *Social Theory and Practice,* pp. 223-242, 1975.

CHAPTER
8

The Stigma of Dying

Sickness had entered Marceline, henceforth inhabited her, marked her, soiled her. She was a tainted thing [1, p. 116].

André Gide

How the tumor was spreading! Seen though the eyes of a complete stranger it would be frightening enough, but seen through his own . . . ! No, this thing could not be real. No one else around him had anything like it. In all his forty-five years Pavel Nikolayevich had never seen such a deformity . . . [2, p. 18].

"If only it would stop growing!" said Pavel Nikolayevich, as though begging it to stop. His voice was tearful. "If only it would stop! If it goes on growing like this for another week, Goodness only knows . . ." No, he couldn't say it, he couldn't gaze into the black abyss. How miserable he felt—it was all touch-and-go. "The next injection's tomorrow, then one on Wednesday. But what if it doesn't do any good? What will I do?" [2, p. 176].

Alexander Solzhenitsyn

Am I ever going to get relief from this thing?

Dying Patient

She has a perfectly healed wound!
Surgeon, speaking about a breast cancer patient

In many ways the popular ruling idea of modern society is the idea of the self. While present day American individualism has served as a liberating force creating opportunities for individual expression, development, and leverage, the individualism of our age is also excessive in that it entails a movement away from shared notions of societal responsibility. In fact, contemporary individualism is different from the value of individualism upon which this country was founded. Traditionally, individualism emphasized the reciprocal relationship between rights of the individual and responsibilities of the individual to the common good. In this fashion the historic value of American individualism not only affirmed the individual as distinct and unique, it also created mutual responsibilities between people and attached individuals to the social commonweal. Contemporary individualism is not predicated upon notions of social connection. Rather, it is rooted in social isolation and detached egoism [2]. The widespread appeal of pop-psychology, with its gospel of self-affection, assertiveness, and personal fulfillment, emphasizes that productive living is the result of self-actualization and satisfaction of the needs of the individual self.

The development of self and human potential does not necessarily require detachment from others. In fact, self-actualization, as Maslow envisioned it [3], does not nullify the value of shared concerns and sociability. Rather, his concep-tionalization stresses that the fulfillment of the "lower needs" for affection and self-respect must take place within a context of interconnection and mutual concern. However, the drift of our times is away from shared common concerns and mutuality. The present-day quest for self-fulfillment and actualization fre-quently undermines the ability to form enduring and sustainable relationships. In this framework, relationships become a means to an end not an end in and of themselves. Accordingly, exaltation of self becomes preeminent, and concern for others becomes fleeting, superficial, and diminished.

One indicator of the narcissistic impulse of our times is the widespread infatuation with fame and celebrities among the American people. This love affair with the rich and famous is reflective of our cultural embrace with self-veneration, an important feature of which is glorification and promotion of physical attractive-ness. This ethos of "believing in me" has cultivated widespread attraction to diets, exercise, health consciousness, commitment to the latest fashions, and an ongoing concern with physical image. The glorification of physical beauty is not a new phenomenon, or one that is uniquely American. But, as we soon shall see, the widespread societal commitment to physicality is a salient factor in stigmatizing dying people.

Another major vehicle for satisfying the needs of the self is the pursuit and accumulation of material goods. Technological-capitalist society, as discussed earlier, has socialized its citizenry to believe that commodity accumulation is an extension and reflection of self-worth. The American commitment to physical beauty and to materialistic consumption is also complemented by the growing American obsession with social and personal improvement: the honing of the skills and qualities that elicit a sense of admiration for the personal and social presence of the self. The development of personality skills, business techniques, and a sense of cultural sophistication have become important to the modern form of self-development. Fromm takes this process of self-absorption to its logical extreme when he writes:

> Modern man has transformed himself into a commodity; he experiences
> his life energy as an investment with which he should make the highest
> profit, considering his position on the personality market. He is alienated

from himself, his fellow man and nature. His main aim is profitable exchange of his skills, knowledge and of himself, of "his personality package," with others who are equally intent on a fair and profitable exchange [4, p. 88].

Like the Greek youth who looked into a pool of water and fell hopelessly in love with himself, Americans have established self-absorption as a dominant cultural value. The notions of self-expression and beautification, pleasure seeking and fulfillment, grabbing for all the gusto, "getting better all the time," and surrounding one's self with the finest things and the "finest people" are continually celebrated by American culture. It is not difficult to see how widespread these values and activities are in our daily lives. In fact, they surround us all of the time—in advertising, tabloids, talk shows, television shows, the messages of self-help gurus, etc. In this framework, preoccupation with self—its desires and needs—is a striking and noticeable part of American cultural life.

IDENTITY PROBLEMS:
BEYOND THE LOOKING GLASS

Women and men are social beings. Our passions, anxieties, moral beliefs, values, desires, all of these are cultural products. Our behaviors are distinct from those of our non-human animal counterparts in that they are largely defined and shaped by cultural and social forces. Not only is the formation of identity largely a social process, but the definition of the successes and triumphs, along with the failures and tragedies of the self, is in many ways also a construct of social forces.

Charles Horton Cooley explores how the dimensions of the self emerge from interaction and association with others. In his classic formulation of the looking glass self, Cooley suggests that an individual is socially defined through one's own perceptions of another's evaluation of her [5]. This is a process which has three principal elements: the imagination of our appearance to the other person, our imagination of the other's judgment of the qualities of our self, and feeling and acting according to how one thinks others are judging these qualities. The relevant point to be drawn from Cooley is that feeling good or not good about oneself does not emanate from within an individual. Rather, it emerges from social interaction processes. Thus, within his framework, an identity problem is something that is associated with unsatisfactory feedback from others, or more exactly, one's perception of the disapproval of others. Orrin Klapp's well-known study of identity crises defines an identity problem as any serious dissatisfaction with one's self, that is to say, the feeling of being blemished, the feeling that "there is something wrong with me" [6]. These feelings of self-inadequacy are characterized by symptoms of self-hatred, being overly and excessively sensitive, time weighing heavily on one's hands, desiring to be someone else, and excessive concern over one's appearance [6]. Identity problems have emerged as a serious issue of study in the contemporary setting, as the existence of an identity problem reflects personal failure and undermines the cultural value of self-actualization. And, as I have already suggested, the proliferation of self-help therapies, self-improvement gurus, self-help books, etc. reflect how widespread feelings of personal inadequacy are in contemporary life. These self help modalities are also consistent with the underlying principle of technicism as discussed in Chapter 2, namely, that the self can be repaired and improved.

While Klapp, Cooley, and traditional role theorists see the self in terms of face-to-face interaction with others, more recent scholarly efforts have shown that the electronic media, particularly television, have been responsible for bringing images into the American home which shape and define the perceptions and identities of the viewing audience [7]. The electronic media, in their own unique way, have provided direct access to social information, social interaction, social values, and social situations without requiring the direct presence of others. In this way, television, through its special means of communicating, interplays with human senses and perceptions in ways that influence individual definitions of social reality. The messages delivered by the electronic cultural media clearly and strongly reinforce the values of individualism, materialism, physical beauty, and vitality of the body. The media also forcefully promote images of what it means to be successful and desirable in this culture. Thus, through the impact of their collective, representative images, the media identify personal qualities and traits that are culturally valued. The degree to which the lives of television watchers are touched by this electronic medium, a foundation is laid for individual viewers to compare, contrast, and evaluate themselves in relation to the standards which emanate from the screen. In this manner, feelings of satisfaction, self-esteem, and success can be promoted in ways that do not require direct face-to-face interaction with others. Likewise, feelings of inadequacy, diminished self-esteem, and stigma can be promoted through an individual's negative evaluation of himself or herself in relation to the images that flourish in the symbols and representations of the electronic media. Hence, an identity crisis can be spawned or exacerbated.

The notion of a socially rooted identity problem is basic to understanding the human plight of dying people, but the concept does not go far enough. Consider the following illustration. A young obese woman who is fifty pounds overweight begins to feel dissatisfied with herself as she perceives signs of disapproval from others and as feelings of unhappiness with herself are fostered by the media. In an era of self-improvement, it is possible for this person to commit herself to a rigorous weight loss and exercise program in the pursuit of a new body and self-image. If she achieves her goal, positive feedback from others and less dissatisfaction in her self-comparison to media images will mitigate her feelings of inadequacy. In relation to the problem of obesity, she is journeying toward a positive self-image, free from many of the negative implications that are associated with the condition of being an overweight female.

It is important to recognize that many sources of dissatisfaction with one's self are potentially reversible. The conditions and causes of dying, however, are neither temporary nor reversible. Thus, while the concept of identity problems is useful to study the predicament of dying people, the potential for transience and reversibility makes it only partially explanatory of the personal suffering of dying patients.

The intrinsic fear and difficulty of confronting death is accelerated by generalized devaluation of the dying experience by American culture. There is little culturally supported relief from suffering because the problems are fixed by and entrenched in the cultural definition of dying as a social evil. This problem of meaninglessness is constant and almost universal within American culture. It is for this reason that a less temporal concept is necessary in order to portray effectively the horrors of modern dying. This is where the notion of escalator-social-stigma becomes useful.

The term stigma refers to the disgrace of a person. It signifies something unusual, immoral, or bad about an individual [7]. Every society sets forth a range of qualities and behaviors which it prescribes as being desirable, and an additional complex of attributes and behaviors which it proscribes as undesirable. Individuals who fall within the range of acceptable qualities and behaviors are said to be normal. Those who live in the range of undesirable activities and attributes are labeled as abnormal. In any given society, those who, in the perception of the normals, are bad, dangerous, or immoral will find that their identity is systematically tarnished and discredited. In this way, the existence of stigma represents not just a denigration of the different and deviant, but a defensive response by the collective normal citizenry to what is defined as threatening and denigrating to their lifestyle.

Goffman's theory on social stigma emphasizes that discrediting personal attributes are the essence of stigma. He describes how qualities discredited within a given cultural milieu lead to the stigmatization of personhood for any individual who possesses such qualities. Thus, as Goffman indicates, to be blind, crippled, mentally ill, or obese is to be discredited. These persons, in the societal framework of stigmatization, are largely defined in terms of their discredited quality, the result of which promotes a generalized, stigmatized identity.

It is the presence of discreditable qualities and the process of discrediting which distinguishes social stigma from an identity problem. A person who is shy, for example, may find it difficult to integrate easily into social gatherings and may feel blemished and inadequate as a result. However, in all likelihood the consequences of the shyness could be contained and would not lead to the person's identity being publicly discredited. Generally speaking, identity problems are less total in their impact on the ability of an individual to proceed through life. Social stigma is a qualitatively more potent, life defining condition. It refers to those factors which disqualify and disengage a person from social acceptance and normalcy.

The strength of Goffman's thesis lies in his description and perceptive understanding of the injustices of social stigma. He correctly associates stigma with the devaluation of personhood and its corresponding feelings of anxiety, uncertainty, and inadequacy. The weakness of his discussion lies in his failure to distinguish between the degree and extent of the social unacceptability of varying and undesirable attributes. To be sure, some qualities carry greater potential for stigma than for others. In addition, the degree and intensity with which a quality is discredited is a significant factor which shapes the individual's reaction to and perception of stigma. This qualification becomes especially important in considering the issues of death and dying.

In the literature on courtship and dating, Willard Waller discusses the processes involved in dating and how these processes lead to an escalation of intensity and commitment between partners. In his conceptualization, every step in the courtship process has a customary meaning and constitutes a powerful pressure toward taking the next step [8]. In this process of a continuing and progressive commitment toward greater intimacy, the couple is in fact journeying on a one-way-dating escalator. The more the escalator advances the more difficult it becomes to reverse direction and escape the drift toward the final commitment: marriage.

The dying individual is also on an escalator. As terminal disease progresses, physical well-being regresses. The dying individual is swept along a downward path of pain, suffering, and deterioration. For all reasonable considerations, this downward journey is not reversible. Thus, unlike the obese person who can lose weight and look forward to a fat-free, positively reinforced future life, the dying person is irreversibly encompassed by an essentially unchangeable fate. For this reason, the stigma of dying is a very special and unique stigma. In an age of self-actualization, it may very well be that dying is the ultimate source of stigma and identity diminishment.

Escalator-social-stigma, then, can be defined as the unilateral movement toward a totally encompassing, discredited state. Escalator-social-stigma is dying.

A salient exacerbating factor of the escalator-journey-of-dying is an individual's negative evaluation of himself—in isolation and/or in association with others. A revision of Cooley is useful here. The concept of looking glass self implies an element of freedom in interpreting or imagining the perception of others. However, the scope of this freedom is seriously restrained by the technological and narcissistic underpinnings of society. The increasing American emphasis on self and self-expression and the way in which the valuing of the self is grounded in the technocratic consciousness has already been established. As such, the social forces of individuality and technicism become internalized, that is to say, they penetrate beneath the surface of the skin. They are infused into and become a part of the consciousness of the individual. As a consequence of a lifetime of continuous socialization into prevailing values, dying persons are likely to judge themselves as being inadequate—failures in light of the American value complex. They correspondingly will draw strong, negative conclusions about their self-worth and the way others are perceiving them.

As themes of hedonism, personal wellness, beauty, sexiness, and success are pounded home in daily cultural life, a narcissistic worldview is created and influences the way we imagine others are judging and seeing us. Within this framework, dying persons facing the prospects of futurelessness—often feeling weak, looking thin and pale, and otherwise physically diminished are likely to make negative assessments of their worth and other's judgment of them. Coupled with the probability that significant others are acting in a confused and often helpless way, it is not difficult to envision the feelings of stigma that invade the dying person. It is in this way that the broader framework of technological society defines the parameters in which "looking glass" assessments of the dying self take place. More precisely, it is in this manner that the forces of individualism and technocracy become dominant forces in discrediting the identity of dying persons and in shaping their feelings of inadequacy.

THE STIGMA OF DYING:
SCENARIOS OF PERSONAL TERROR

Dying people are invalidated and stigmatized in several ways. A very common concern of the dying patient is: "I don't want my husband (or wife) to see me this way." This negative judgment about one's self and the perceptions of others is typical, and reflects the often bleak, fatalistic self-perception of the terminally ill patient. The process of dying, as it is shaped and experienced in the modern context, elicits enormous suffering and self-antagonism in the lives of patients. Uncomforted pain, hopelessness, anxiety, feelings of ugliness, and worthlessness wreak havoc on their personal and social identity.

Pain is a quality or experience that is normally devalued in everyday life. Most individuals go to great lengths to avoid pain and its associated sufferings [9]. When pain and suffering cannot be controlled or contained, the individual person is left to her own personal resources, often in an isolated private world, to cope [10].

Pain is a major source of worry and anguish for dying persons.[1] It becomes all the more frightening because in the prevailing context of dying, pain and suffering are endured largely in isolation and meaninglessness. The deep anguish expressed by patients dying with pain makes the point:

---

[1] Not every patient in my study suffered through the extremities of serious pain, but pain was a salient force in the dying experience in that it dominated many of the life concerns of about half of all the patients in the study. It is also something that patients who were pain free were concerned about.

> Pain, pain, pain . . . Sometimes it's so hard to describe the pain. It's a pain
> like . . . well, the way I feel when pain gets over me . . . It's like . . .
> EATING AWAY AT MY BONES.

Another patient, frustrated and disgruntled over the growth of his head tumor,
comments:

> The pain is excruciating. It goes from my shoulder, up through my neck,
> and into my head, sometimes shooting right across my ears.

An additional patient adds:

> If you were to measure it on a scale of one to ten, the pain would measure
> fifteen. Simply a severe, severe back pain that inhibits mobility and
> inhibits appetite. With pain, you are not hungry. . . .

> The pain, it stops me from doing things I would normally do. Just moving
> is difficult enough, never mind raking leaves or going sailing. It's really
> the worst thing that can happen, the worst feeling that there is.

The typical response to pain in everyday life, in the hospital, in the hospice,
etc., is flight. Pain killers are regularly prescribed by physicians, aspirins are
downed by the ton to alleviate hangovers, tension headaches, and the like, and
drug companies have been able to exploit the American intolerance of pain to
very good financial advantage. Running away from pain, in a curious sense, has
become a national pastime. Unless, in logical consistency with the American
value of individualism, the pain is the result of something that is self-initiated and
meaningful, an exercise regimen for example, pain is seen as meaningless and
intolerable. For the dying cancer patient, however, the pain is not self-originated,
and there often is little escape from it. Nor is there a justifying frame of reference
or legitimizing slogan to provide purpose to pain. The idea of "no pain no gain" is
a catch phrase relevant to a particular experience with pain that is connected to
self-improvement and narcissism. It is wholly irrelevant in the life context of
dying individuals. Pain, thus, is an uninvited, unwelcome, and an ever present
worry for many dying persons:

> The pain is always there. Even when it goes away, it's there. I know it will
> be back. I expect it.

Given the constancy of the pain experience in a culture that devalues pain
and seeks its avoidance, it is only natural to expect that feelings of frustration and
even hostility will arise in dying patients whose bodies are being unmercifully
ravaged by the disease:

When the pain starts, I wish I could get something to get rid of it right away. When I wake up and I'm not due for medication, I think: Oh God, what am I going to do?

It makes me shaky and nervous. It's an incredible kind of tension. When I get that pain, I sometimes become angry and nasty. I get so desperate that I act in ways I shouldn't act. When I'm going through it, I just get so desperate.

The desperation that underlies the experience of pain results from two societal "failures." First, the forces of technology are failing the dying patient by their inability to fix and relieve "the worst feeling there is." During earlier phases of their lives, the needs of many dying patients were well served by technology. Their comfort, luxury, and ideas of success were intimately linked with the pursuit and accumulation of material goods. Now at a vital time in their lives, perhaps at a time when it has never been so desperately needed, technology fails to deliver on its promise to provide a transcendence of the human condition, and a remedy for suffering.

In conjunction with the failure of technology, the American cultural complex also lets dying patients down because it is unable to provide a blanket of support, solace, and meaning to their pain and suffering ridden lives. It may be useful at this point to reflect back upon the experience of Kirk Baines and Ivan Ilych as they suffered their pain without cultural support and mitigation.

Unrelieved pain often becomes so intense and severe that it utterly encompasses the life of the dying patient. As one patient observes, relieving pain and "again enjoying the pleasure of not being in pain" becomes everything she hopes for. Another expresses how dominating the pain experience is in the worldview of the terminal patient:

Do you really think the pain will continue? That's all I'm really concerned about. Relief from the pain. . . .

Another patient comments:

Going on and on for months and months in pain all of the time . . . that scares me. Deteriorating! Sometimes it gets so bad that I wish I could go just like that (snap of fingers) instead of suffering, and that's what you do with cancer. You just go down and down. Deteriorating, being in pain. Yes, that worries me very much.

Yet another adds:

I don't think I could tolerate the pain getting worse. If that comes, I don't know what I would do. If I had just one wish, it would be to be pain free.

Yes, pain free. I'd be the happiest person in the world if I could get up and find myself without pain. Oh God, I don't know what I'd do. Go crazy . . . If that ever comes, oh God.

As depressing as it may sound, it needs to be recognized that the horrific experience of pain is accentuated, even expectable, within the cultural and social realities of technocratic society. Thus, meaninglessness of pain in dying becomes an additional source of stress with which the terminal patient must cope. One patient voices his dismay at the senselessness of it all:

Purpose, meaning to the pain? No, no, no, no, no. I just keep asking myself: Oh my God, what did I do in my youth to be paid back with this kind of bullshit?

Another patient, in a profound and insightful moment of reflection adds:

The pain is evil. It's destructive, bad and even demonic. The cancer makes me nervous, anxious, obsessive. The pain and suffering is so bad that it must be evil.

I often ask, what did I do to deserve this? I can't see any reason for pain. I can't see any reason for suffering. I can't see any reason, I really can't. If I had an explanation, it would set my mind at ease. Without it, there is just confusion; helplessness sometimes. I just can't be sure that there is a God. It's disturbing and uncomforting. Really, there is no meaning to the pain. Pain like this has to come from the devil. At certain times, I feel that the pain is punishing me. But for what? That I just can't see.

How vividly the fictional words of Tolstoy on the meaninglessness of dying leap to life. The four words: "There is no explanation!" may very well serve as the epitaph of dying as we begin the twenty-first century. In a society which values both the here and now of hedonism and the future orientation of success, it is not hard to see why the suffering and pain of dying is a feared and discredited part of the human condition. Pain, by overwhelming the sensories with anguish and distress, violates the pleasure principle upon which much of social living is based. It also can become so pungent that it dominates the life of the dying patient. In this way, the metaphor of pain as an insidious evil, a meaningless monster to be conquered and avoided at all cost, becomes a reality.

In addition to physical pain, the dying person is beleaguered by feelings of helplessness. A form of powerlessness, helplessness refers to the inability to accomplish the things that one expects one should normally be able to accomplish. It is characterized by feelings of impotence and insignificance, and may lead to feelings of worthlessness. As one patient summarized his dying life, "I really am no good at all."

The importance of individualism to the American way of life has been a central theme of my observations. It is this value which establishes the moral obligation of self-responsibility. Successful living is very much defined on the basis of whether or not one is self-sufficient and capable of looking after one's significant others. In this regard, the cultural drift toward detached individualism promotes socially based feelings of inadequacy in dying persons. Specifically, helplessness and feelings of inadequacy are intensified as disease progresses and terminally-ill patients become increasingly dependent on others. This enforced dependency in an age of individualism and self-sufficiency leaves them feeling distressed and burdensome.

Dying people regularly complain about helplessness. They bemoan not being able to do the things they typically would do if they were not so sick. One patient, in moderate to severe pain, contrasts her present predicament with lasting remembrances of the past. As she speaks, tears fill her eyes and flow down her cheeks:

> I used to be so active. I had a good youth. . . . Did so much and enjoyed life. I get to feeling so sad when I think about the things I used to do and how I can't do them anymore.

Another expresses the frustration of unrelieved helplessness:

> I've had a good life. Now I'm shot though. This tumor . . . or cancer . . . or whatever . . . Well, let's just say I'm three-quarters shot. I just feel so sluggish. Oh, to have the appetite. To be able to do the things I used to do.

Longing to do the simple things normally done in everyday life, and taken for granted by so many people, blossoms into feelings of inadequacy as the downward escalator journey of dying progresses:

> I just hate this helplessness. The feeling of wasting away. I used to be able to do things for myself. To be able to take the train into the city for my treatment. That was good. Now, I'm so weak I can't even walk. I have trouble going to the bathroom without help. It's just all so scary.

Another patient tearfully voices her comments:

> I'm no good to anybody. Why am I living? Why doesn't God just let me die? I feel so useless, and I'm a burden to everyone. This is no way to live. The pain, oh why? I'm just no good.

Perhaps it does not take many words to capture the essential meaning of helplessness to the dying patient:

> I'm useless! I'm of absolutely no use to anyone.

The physical deterioration of the self eventuates in increased reliance on others. This dependence often facilitates guilt when personal feelings of inadequacy combine with feelings of becoming a burden to others:

> I worry about my husband. He works, you know. And he comes to see me every evening. When I go home, he cares for me all the time. It's just not fair to him, for me to do this to him.

Another patient says:

> I feel guilty even when talking to my mother. She has enough to worry about without hearing all of my complaints.

This same patient voices her feelings about becoming a burden directly to her mother, after being informed by her doctor that there were no immediate plans for her release from the hospital:

> Mom, I want you to go home and take care of Daddy. I'm going to be here for a long period of time, and I don't want you stuck with me.

The burden of helplessness that dying patients struggle with becomes severe in our age of individualism wherein dependency on others is devalued. The situation is also exacerbated by the social forces of detachment and alienation which generate feelings of vulnerability. Often socially isolated, many of their emotional and social needs are inadequately met. A further complicating factor resides in the fact that the more some of the needs of dying individuals may be attended to, the more obligated and dependent they become. Ironically, when social support needs are being met, patients can experience feelings of shame and disgrace. Despite being urgently needed, the process of care and support places an intrusive responsibility on the lives of loved ones and becomes fodder for guilt among dying persons. This nullifies the ability to be self-sufficient and, in turn, fosters feelings of self-blame and guilt. In a curious way, then, either neglect or attention to the needs of dying patients may result in increased feelings of helplessness. Simply, this is how enormously complicated the modern experience of dying has become.

SEXUALITY AND DYING:
FERTILE GROUND FOR STIGMA

Ideals of beauty and models of sexual attractiveness are extensively promoted in American society. Consider the following, not too facetious, description of the modern ideals of sexual physicality,

The "modern American woman" is sexy. Her slender stature allows for her firmly toned yet silky soft flesh to highlight her look. Her body may very well be at its best when enticingly tanned. The fashion which she adorns generates mystery but hides nothing. Snug-fitting pants accentuate her legs and derriere. Her high heels alluringly add sensuality, which is furthered by the properly seductive gloss of polish which graces her nails. Her blouse is finely designed, loosely fitting but highly suggestive of her breasts that lie within. Her lips are red and full and add to the luster and depth of her eyes. Her posture is one of independence; she's charming, vibrant, cultured, and sensual. Indeed, the modern American woman has come a long way!? This is an image that is exalted everywhere: at the checkout counter in supermarkets, in advertising, television, nightclubs, movies, and so forth. And, this picture of feminine beauty is deeply, perhaps inescapably, a part of our materialistic-narcissistic ways of life.

The male counterpart is differently but equally attractive. Tall, slightly muscular, well groomed, handsome, and appropriately affluent, he too is a desirable commodity. His strength, intelligence, and success combined with perhaps a newly-developed-modicum of sensitivity create an ideal yearned for in American society. Consider then, the erotic encounter which emerges when the American male and the American female unite in sexual interplay. Such a scenario would be so compelling that Webster's would offer its description as the primary definition of perfection. And, in many ways, the fictitious creation of the sexual and physical ideal is not the least of the attractions of popular romance novels and films. In fact, physical beauty is not just a romantic ideal. It is a highly prized and sought-after cultural value.

These descriptions not only provide for a moment of diversion. They illuminate one expression of the extreme American commitment to physicality and bodily image. They also provide at least one standard to which dying people compare and judge their physical selves. It is at this point that the injustice of America's obsession with sexuality and ideals of physical attractiveness becomes apparent, namely, in the dehumanization, devaluing, and stigmatization of those who lack the qualities and necessary features to fit into the prevailing definitions of sexy, attractive, and desirable. Indeed, it is not difficult to see how the obese, the disabled, the debilitated, and, of course, the dying are rejects of the American sexual model.

The more social and personal identity is defined in terms of sexual and physical well-being, the more the physical predicament of the terminally ill becomes a source for stigma. Self-perception is radically altered by physical devolution. As one patient remarks:

> I used to be so happy. Really, I was a happy person and have been able and ready to go out and have fun. I've always felt good about myself and was always active socially and at home . . .

I've always thought of myself as having a nice shape. Not being perfect, but having a nice body. Now, all of this has changed.

Another patient comments:

I used to be strong as a bull. I could hold my own with the toughest of them . . . don't you worry about that. But all I do now is lose weight. I'm not the same guy I used to be. I've lost so much weight that I don't even know myself. Look at me. I try to eat as much as I can. I love to eat, you know, but I don't have any taste anymore, and I get weaker and weaker as I lose this weight. If I could only get this stabilized. You know I used to weigh 220 pounds.[2]

A third patient speaks carefully about the impact of physical blemishment on her perceptions of self:

I'm not myself, anymore. Oh, the way I used to be. I can't even stand to look in the mirror anymore (tears begin to stream from her eyes).

Another patient expresses how her sexuality and self-concept have been tarnished and stigmatized by her radical mastectomy:

I don't feel the same way as I did before because of that breast not being there. I don't see myself as being sexy as before . . .

It's a big difference having one breast on one side and the other side partially flat and scarred. To me, not having that breast there means that I'm not sexy anymore . . .

When I see other girls in low cut dresses or in a sexy bathing suit, I think to myself: Oh, I used to be like that, and I can't anymore.

Another patient expresses his feelings of sexual inadequacy and embarrassment over his colostomy:

As far as sex goes, I can't worry about that anymore. I just have to accept the fact that I can't do the things I used to do . . .

This goddamn bag, though, is one thing that I can't stand. It smells, and it . . . ugh . . .

---

[2] The patient weighed 147 pounds at the time this statement was made.

Well, what am I going to do if I'm at a dinner party, and it breaks? Then everybody would know, and that would be too embarrassing to take.

It is important to note that stigma penetrates deeply into the private, personal world of patients. It is a central, life-defining experience for dying persons. It is, however, not of prominent interest to physicians, who often trivialize and dismiss its importance. In fact, when the above colostomy patient tells his oncologist that he is worried about his bag breaking, the physician ignored him and went on to discuss other matters. The physician commented later on about this patient, in a hallway conversation with the patient's radiologist:

He's too much. He's worried about his bag breaking at a dinner party. Doesn't he realize that he's dying and won't be at any dinner party for the bag to break?

Another situation involves a patient who had developed a secondary cancer in her breast and was terrified of the impending mastectomy. She expressed her fears and anxieties by asking an inordinate number of questions, many of which were repetitive, of her physicians. Although she was never confrontational or disrespectful, her physicians became irritated with her lack of composure and uneasiness, and they quickly tired of having to repeat answers to questions already asked. The patient, deeply frightened and isolated in her fears, became quickly labeled as inappropriate and a problem. Indeed, her surgeon returned from a post-operative examination and totally nullified any regard for her suffering and exclaimed to all present in the doctor's lounge:

I don't see what she has to be angry about. She has a perfectly healed wound!

It may seem ironic in terms of America's obsession with sexual physicality that the sexual-stigma concerns of dying patients are systematically ignored and denigrated. But, when considered in terms of the general devaluing of dying, the transformation of dying into a low status position in American society, the attachment of a label of social death prior to biological death, it is not difficult to see why the sexual concerns and self-images of dying patients are of minimal interest in the medical management of the dying process. The central point to be made is that physical and sexual stigma in dying has implications that affect overall self-image and personhood. As one patient thoroughly and honestly explains:

I feel very self-conscious about losing my hair. Really, I'm scared to start a relationship with anybody. I gained a lot of weight on my first chemotherapy, and that didn't help my image any. I felt lousy about my self-image and didn't like the way I looked . . .

No, I'm not thin, mysterious, nor have gorgeous hair. Since the start of this cancer, I don't feel like a temptress at all. To think of myself as being pretty now, that's ridiculous. (She begins to laugh nervously.)

I don't even feel a desire for sex, but I feel strange not having sex. I think you should have some kind of sexual drive, some kind of sex life. This I don't have, and it makes me feel inadequate and shy.

This feeling of sexual inadequacy makes me avoid meeting people or beginning a relationship.

The same patient continues:

I used to feel pretty confident . . . have a lot of confidence and be pretty outgoing. Now I feel shy and ugly . . . trying not to be noticed too much. I sort of withdraw and don't really like to go out too often.

To a certain extent, I feel so much less adequate than before. I'm so very self-conscious. I feel like I don't know how to communicate anymore. You know, make conversation, small talk . . . So I avoid people very often.

It seems that everything keeps going back to this cancer. It makes me feel so ugly, and it's just so depressing.

A particularly memorable incident occurred one evening when this patient was convinced to go out with some friends. Despite her initial reluctance to go and the anxiety she felt when they arrived at the nightclub, she was having a reasonably good time until someone bumped into her. She had been standing by the bar of the somewhat crowded club, and a man accidentally brushed against her head with his hand. He instantly recoiled and said: IS THAT A WIG? She answered: YES. We can only imagine the horror and shame she felt when he then said: WHAT, ARE YOU BALD OR SOMETHING? She was so scarred and humiliated by the interaction that she said that she would never again go out socially.

The ideals of sexual attractiveness which dying patients violate are deeply entrenched in the American psyche, especially among women. Even supportive outreaching from one's sexual partners or spouse often cannot ease the pain of physical and sexual stigma. The following patient benefited from continuing support from her husband, who was genuinely concerned for her well-being and recovery. Yet despite his warmth, acceptance, and love, her sexual stigma and inadequate self-image haunted their relationship.

As far as sex life is concerned, we have been drawn apart . . . and all because of me. I know, I know, because of me.

I feel funny. I just don't feel like myself, having that breast removed. I just don't feel 100 percent like myself.

My husband told me it didn't matter. And I really believed him, but it was never the same. Me/myself felt different. Once again, we come back to that word "sexy."

Although my husband continually told me that it was unimportant and that he loved me the way I am, I always felt that I am not good enough for him. That made me get out of sex by making excuses. I was always thinking about my missing breast.

The same patient continues:

There was always something I was holding back. In my mind, I was always thinking: No, I'm not the same. Not the same. Even though he kept telling me it didn't make any difference. But to me, it's not the same.

All the while I was making love, I would be thinking of how inadequate I was because of my missing breast. You better believe that this feeling made me want to avoid sexual relationships. I always had an excuse. I wasn't feeling well. . . .

And after having made love, the feeling of not having that breast remained.

The insecurity of this patient does not stem from physical disfigurement. Instead, it evolves out of her negative judgment of herself in connection to her physical and sexual deformation. This is precisely the point where my revised version of the looking glass self applies. Having internalized the American values of narcissism and sexual physicality, it becomes difficult for physically blemished, dying people to imagine a positive presentation of self to others. It also becomes difficult to imagine that others are judging them favorably, even when others are doing exactly that. In this way the technological and narcissistic strictures of the broader society, brimming with images of sexual and physical ideals, become a standard source of reference which precipitates negative self-image and judgment in dying persons. In other words, the imprint of sweeping technological and narcissistic forces penetrate into the experience of dying and is felt deeply, privately, and painfully, by dying persons.

AS THE NEW SELF EMERGES

During the dying process, the dying person undergoes an identity transformation and endures the emergence of a new self that is beleaguered by debility,
doubt, and feelings of inadequacy. The newly emerging self possesses many
qualities that are disvalued and discredited by prevailing American values. As
one patient put it:

> If I could just go back to the way I was . . . used to be . . . then I'd be ready
> to die.

The negative self-image that emerges during the process of dying entails both role
transitions and the devolution of personhood. The self of the dying person is
infused with a variety of discredited cultural traits that become a permanent part
of their newly formed identity. This means that the self is not only ripped apart,
but also that dying threatens to irrevocably impair one's self concept and the roles
that an individual will play for the remainder of his life.

One of the tragedies of modern life is that the role transitions of dying patients
are not eased by cultural legitimations and support systems. As we have seen, the
technical system of care is incapable of supporting the needs of the emerging self
of the dying patient. This was so clearly evident in the patient narratives in
Chapter 2. Dying persons, thus, are often left to experience grief and confront
mortality in cultural and social isolation. The absurdity of this situation is that
patients are pressured and expected to die uncomplainingly and with dignity at a
time when they are weak and vulnerable. This is precisely what sets dying apart
from other forms of cultural evil and social stigma: having to face the terror of
personal extinction while personhood and identity are systematically debased
and decimated. The irony is that individuals are expected to engage (with dignity)
the problems of dying through their own personal resources at a time in their
lives when they are disempowered and vulnerable.

Dying persons typically are forced to fight a battle for meaning and legitimation without the necessary personal and social tools to do so. In this age of
self-growth and expressiveness, however, some heroic individuals are able to
successfully carve out dignity and purpose to their dying. Curiously, in this era of
death denial, there has been a recent outgushing of personal narratives, written
by dying individuals and interested professionals that portray meaningful and
inspiring death experiences [11]. This literature seeks to craft an image of "good
death" that is reminiscent of the traditional patterns of dying. Almost to a universal fault, however, the feel good tone of these efforts skims over the deeply
embedded cultural and institutional factors which make "good death" exceedingly
difficult and rare. They also assume that in the real world every death can and
should have a happy ending [12]. This image, however, as selective and mis-
representative as it is, is consistent with zeitgeist of our times. It is indicative of the

value of individualism, the gravitation toward new age philosophies, and the therapeutic inclinations of the technocratic world view. This new wave of literature focuses on heroic, personal triumph and intentionally ignores the cultural and social forces elaborated upon in this book. Thus, while the contemporary movement toward "dying well" may reflect and influence the ability of some individuals to die with grace and dignity, it fails to examine how meaninglessness, isolation, stigma, and neglect of the psychosocial needs of dying patients are embedded in the cultural and institutional arrangements of modern life.

In this regard, a salient method of organizing human death is the "psychologizing of death," that is to say, treating it as a predicament that is either resolved or unresolved on the level of private troubles. Ironically, this approach is emblematic of the broader cultural tendency to avoid death, in that dying with its attendant problems is defined as a clinical-psychological issue. Society is, therefore, freed from the encumbrance of having to address dying and death in its everyday social and cultural organization. In many ways, the therapeutic model of intervention and the psychologizing of death serves to privatize the experience and contributes to its cultural invisibility.

Additionally, I must emphasize the point alluded to above. Images of the good death, while appealing and comforting, are out of tune with the real experience of most dying persons. In fact, there was not one patient in my study who expressed the feeling that his or her dying offered life enhancing possibilities for creativity and growth. Indeed, every single patient was mired in suffering and viewed their situation as frightening and regrettable.

The point to be made is that there are many patients who are not able to make the psychological adjustment that is necessary to effectively cope with dying in "positive" and "creative" ways. Often they may not have the resources to die gracefully or uncomplainingly and will employ a variety of psychically adaptive defense mechanisms to sustain their sanity. These include denial, avoidance of death-related conversation, living with the fight against terminal disease one day at a time, withdrawal and purposeful isolation from others, reliance upon the faith invested in technology, and the widespread use of metaphors to describe their battle with cancer. Despite many variations in their attempt to cope with terminal illness, the image of their disease and dying as enemies is pervasive. One patient who was completely rational and appropriate until she was asked questions that touched on the issues of cancer and death illustrates how fearful patients can become of the enemy that is cancer/dying, and how overwhelming the fear can be:

There is this guy who is persecuting me. He comes into my house and takes my food. I had ziti in the refrigerator, covered with sauce and ricotta cheese, and he took off the sauce and the ricotta. He keeps taking my food. Tomatoes, which I also had. I guess the only way to get rid of him is to die. Everything new and nice which I have, he destroys. I can't have anything new and nice because of him. I have a nylon summer dress, and he shortened the length of it, and along the hemline, he made cuts. He cut it. I also washed and shined my kitchen floor, and he came and put black splotches all over it . . .

He just destroys everything I have.

During another conversation, the same patient adds:

He comes in during the middle of the night, and he steals everything I have. My pills (she was referring to the chemotherapy she was taking at home), he took them, one-half of them. I had a glass of water on my nightstand, and he took half of that.

I can't keep food in the refrigerator, because he keeps stealing it. I've tried changing the locks, but that doesn't work. He picks the new locks, and once he does that getting in is easy. I can't keep him out. I just don't know what to do.

Every time the patient was asked how she was feeling, the question would elicit a similar outpouring of bizarre metaphors. Her interactional skills were normal in every other observable situation, and her doctors merely attributed her strange response to her inability to face up to dying. Although it is beyond the scope of this work to delve into the psychological factors at work here, the fear and threat that this patient perceived, and for the most part privately endured, is representative of the emotional anguish experienced by dying persons. It is especially interesting to note how "this guy" was taking away many of her life-sustaining sources: food, water, and medicine. Also, he either stole, shortened, or blemished everything he touched.

Additionally, we have seen that patients commonly place tremendous trust in the curative powers of medical technology. Since comfort during the dying process is inhibited by many of the social factors already discussed, identification with the healing powers of technology provides some relief from the vulnerability and stigma of dying. One patient expresses her relief over the starting of a new regimen of chemotherapy:

I'm so glad it's started. That he's back (referring to the attending physician who was on vacation) and decided to put me on the medication. I was so afraid, and now things are going to be okay.

Another patient seeks to negotiate a bargain:

Doctor, you remember the cars we talked about? The MG? Well, you cure me, and it's yours. I'm not kidding. If what you are doing works, it's yours.

For these patients, and for many like them, hope flows from technological intervention. In this regard, technology may provide a curious but temporary sense of relief and psychosocial comfort. In that hope is absolutely vital to dying persons, technological intervention, despite all the criticism put forth in this book, may be of some important psychosocial benefit to dying persons. However, as we will see in greater detail in the next chapter, when unrealistic hope is engendered by technological intervention and dependence, the result can be deeply injurious.

The point to be made is that myriad coping mechanisms are employed by dying patients to support themselves throughout the dying process. These individualized patterns of adjustment, however, emanate from a self that is enfeebled by the downward escalator journey of dying. Dying persons confront and live with a mixture of gnawing anxiety and acute fear. They suffer stigma, helplessness, and smashing of their self-image, in isolation and disconnection from needed support systems. Hence, their personal misery is aggravated by cultural values and social organization. Their misery unfolds daily in hospitals all across America. Their plight is real and the conditions of their lives often harsh. All of which is too frequently hidden behind a veil of avoidance, silence, and indifference.

Trapped in a diseased and protesting body and existing in a social order that has virtually no use for them, dying persons are diminished by a variety of external and internal forces. In many ways, dying people are the dregs of society. They are personally and socially insignificant, and dying often results in a cruel and painful transformation into non-being and social death. In a nutshell, internalized fears, anxieties, and frustration merge with culturally established patterns of meaninglessness, and submerge the dying person in a world of stigma and suffering. The reflections of a dying patient best illuminate the point:

Everything seems to lead me back to my cancer. Cancer, cancer, that's it! That's all there is. I'm just wasting my life away. There's absolutely nothing positive happening. It's (having cancer) all just so time consuming. It doesn't make me feel well . . . feel good or happy. It's boring and painful. Physically and emotionally, it's confusing and depressing. There's nothing positive! All it does is hurt. Everybody!

The words are self-expressive.

REFERENCES

1. A. Gide, *The Immortalist,* Alfred A. Knopf, New York, 1970.
2. A. Solzhenitsyn, *Cancer Ward,* Bantam Books, New York, 1969.
3. A. Maslow, *Toward a Psychology of Being,* Van Nostrand, New York, 1968.
4. E. Fromm, *The Art of Loving,* Harper and Row, New York, 1956.
5. C. H. Cooley, *Human Nature and the Social Order,* Scribner's, New York, 1922.
6. O. Klapp, *Collective Search for Identity,* Chapter One, Holt, Rinehart and Winston, New York, 1969.
7. E. Goffman, *Stigma: Notes on the Management of Spoiled Identity,* Prentice-Hall, New Jersey, pp. 1-4, 1963.
8. W. Waller, The Rating and Dating Complex, *American Sociological Review, 2,* pp. 727-734, 1937.
9. I. Illich, *Medical Nemesis* (see especially Chapter Six), Pantheon, New York, 1976.
10. D. W. Moller, On the Value of Suffering in the Shadow of Death, *Loss Grief and Care: A Journal of Professional Practice, 1,* pp. 127-136, 1986.
11. I. Byock, *Dying Well: The Prospect for Growth at the End of Life,* Riverhead Books, New York, 1997.
12. M. Webb, *The Good Death,* Bantam Books, New York, 1997.

CHAPTER 9

Approaching Omega:
The Roller Coaster of Dying

Each society is a hero system which promises victory over evil and death [1, p. 124].

Ernest Becker

I'm afraid we got him too late in his disease process to be of any help to him.

Oncologist, speaking to doctors and nurses in the staff lounge, after informing a patient that he would soon be starting a new course of chemotherapy

Hospitalization removes dying people from the hub of everyday social intercourse and helps organize and control the problems associated with the dying process. In many ways, the sequestering of dying patients protects ordinary people from the terrorizing issue of death. In the hospital, medical professionals will sometimes find their lives directly touched by death. Their involvement with dying, however, is clearly deliminited by technological focus and their emotional response is chilled by bureaucratic routine. This technological coordination of dying serves to submerge, "deny," and organize the dying process into professionally restricted categories which restrain the expression of personal pinings and fears for both providers and patients. As discussed in Chapters 2 and 3, the idea of dying-with-dignity has merged with technocratic strategies of control to create a broad societal base for the arrest of potentially turbulent and disconcerting behaviors of dying persons.

We have also seen how the values and priorities of the death-with-dignity movement have affected the consciousness and behaviors of the profession of medicine. In effect, many healthcare personnel have uncritically adopted the credo of Elisabeth Kübler-Ross and have become travel agents for the dying. Physicians, interns, residents, and even nurses often act to discourage expression of the more hostile and emotionally charged "early stages of dying," and have defined the proper role of dying patient behavior as facing up to dying with courage and patience, i.e., dignity.

The unwillingness of medical professionals to accept dying patient behavior which is publicly undignified is based on an assumption that dignity in modern dying is possible and desirable for all patients. In addition, there is an underlying assumption that predetermined, essentially linear stages of dying exist. Consequently, if a patient is angry or difficult to interact with, he or she just needs to be transported to the acceptance stage. The purpose of this chapter is to examine the impact of technological management on the life course of the dying patient, paying particular attention to the idea of dying-with-dignity and harmonious adjustment of the dying patient's self to the terminal process.

Dying-with-dignity has become an enormously utilized concept during the past decades. There have been, however, despite widespread use of the phrase, few successful attempts to define or operationalize the concept. Dignity in dying, as it appears in the sociomedical, psychological, and thanatology literature, refers to a non-specific, generic dying process. As one surveys the relevant literature, one finds the following themes associated with the idea: courage, natural death, pain control, tranquility, support systems, peace, spiritual meaning, and acceptance. There can be, of course, no particular equation which defines the concept of dying-with-dignity. Rather, dying-with-dignity refers to an attitude and philosophy of dying that seeks to mitigate the undesirable aspects of medicalized death. At the same time, dying-with-dignity seeks to recapture some of the sentiments and mores that are associated with traditional death patterns. In this way, dying-with-dignity is a broad concept and tends to become clinically useless. Nevertheless, it is useful in articulating a set of values regarding the meaning of human dying experiences and in unveiling societal reactions to technocratic death patterns. It is also important to note that dignity, as an overly general concept, has become part of the contemporary history, language, and metaphors of dying. In both a general and specific sense, dying-with-dignity has become a significant frame of reference which defines the American cultural framework of death and dying.

When one looks carefully at the human realities of dying-with-dignity, two distinct types of dignity emerge. One has social meaning and prescribes for dying patients a restricted and inhibited course of behavioral and emotional expression. This type of dying-with-dignity is related to the social organization of contemporary death patterns and leads to a therapeutically appropriate death. The second type of dying-with-dignity has personal, existential meaning. This type of dying-with-dignity is related to the effectiveness of a person's private coping patterns and leads to an individually meaningful death.

Personal dignity in dying is individually achieved. Therapeutic assistance, such as psychotherapy, participation in self-help groups or involvement in a hospice program, can help facilitate an individual's personal achievement of dying-with-dignity. The individual, as we have already seen, is the primary basis of "successful" and "unsuccessful" dying. Coping capacity, in this way, means far more than enduring physically the process of dying. It implies coping that has existential significance in terms of the search for meaning, the maintenance of personal morale, and coming to terms with death [1]. Achieving personal dignity in the course of dying may be, in Becker's theoretical framework, interpreted as a triumph over death. On the level of personal human existence, however, authenticity, purpose, and meaning are its consequences. Coping well and achieving personal dignity may be one of the most dramatic existential statements an individual can make during his or her lifetime. Because physical survival alone has little significance for the human being, the pursuit of meaning becomes an essential challenge for humanity. If a person's quest for meaning in life is successful, that is good for the individual. If an individual succeeds in the quest for meaning at one of the darkest times of human life, dying, the achievement is all the more dramatic and uplifting.

Social dignity, unlike the existential meaning of personal dignity, has purely interactional significance. One of its main dimensions is that dying patients should behaviorally respond to the process of dying with poise and restraint. The significance of the social framing of dying-with-dignity is that the process of human dying does not burden, disconcert, or disrupt the activities of healthcare professionals at work. The primary interactional significance of social dying-with-dignity is the facilitation of medical work for physicians and nurses. Dying patients achieve social dying-with-dignity when they adapt their behavior and expressions to fit the requirements of medicalized death. In this way, social dignity leads to a therapeutically acceptable death process, which essentially means that a patient's behavior is acceptable within the framework of medical and technological management of the dying process.

In the social dimension of dignity there is little need or regard for personal dignity. Private feelings of dejection, disillusionment, despair, defeat, or even private suicidal inclinations are of little consequence to the management of dying patients. As long as correct patient behavior is maintained—as long as poise and courage do not give way to cantankerousness—the absence of private dying-with-dignity is of little concern to physicians. However, when private feelings of disillusionment, despair, and anger are unleashed into the public arena, they become relevant to the physician-patient relationship. Patients' or families' expression of private, negative feelings is disturbing to others and stymies the smooth flow of medical work. Thus, personal dying-with-dignity becomes an issue for patient management when a patient's inability to successfully cope with dying rages into the public arena and jeopardizes the tranquility of social dying-with-dignity. In order to facilitate technical control and management of the dying process, the private issue of dignity in coping must be sublimated to the social dimensions of dying-with-dignity. If this is accomplished, the frightening unleashed, and troubling qualities of dying are reeled in and once again contained.

The distinction between private and social dying-with-dignity is essential to the psychosocial and sociological dynamics of the modern dying process. Clearly, social dignity is a significant part of modern, technical modalities of death control.

Personal dignity has tangential, peripheral relevance for the medical management and control of dying patients. It becomes relevant when it leads to transgressions of social dignity, that is to say, when it leads to patients becoming uncooperative and difficult to deal with. This does not mean that the personal dimensions of dignity are insignificant. Clearly, they have significance for the private, psychological lives of dying individuals. Personal dimensions of dying-with-dignity are also relevant inasmuch as they reflect the penetration of the human potential movement into the arena of human dying and death. In fact, the evolving cultural embrace of idea of the notion "a good death" is predicated upon the possibilities of growth and transformation that emerge from personal dignity. Thus, "dying well" in many ways is the ability to muster the personal resources necessary to die-with-dignity. Additionally, the personal dimensions of dignity are potentially relevant to the success of social dying-with-dignity. To the degree to which patients are successful in achieving personal dignity in dying, their personal victory is the foundation for social dignity. In this way, perhaps the ideal realization of social dignity is based on successful personal adjustment to the dying process. However, if personal success in coping with dying has not been achieved, various management strategies will then be employed to render "privately non-dignity patients" socially dignified in their dying.

THE COURSE OF DYING AND SOCIETAL FORCES

While Becker may be right in arguing that fear of death is a universal human trait, the ways which people seek to cope with the fears of mortality and seek comfort during the dying process are defined by the sociocultural sensibilities of the time and place in which they live and die. Historically, as I have already indicated, humanity lived in greater harmony with the idea of death, and the traditional deathbed was typically characterized by acceptance, fellowship, and meaningful cultural rituals:

> Naturally [in the traditional pattern of death] the dying man feels sad about the loss of his life, the things he has possessed, and the people he has loved. But his regret never goes beyond a level of intensity that is slight in terms of the emotional climate of this age . . .
> Thus, regret for life goes hand in hand with a simple acceptance of imminent death. It bespeaks a familiarity with death [2, p. 15].

As one chronicles the artistic and literary sources of traditional European and American societies, the theme of simple acceptance of death is paramount. For example, La Fontaine's portrait of the death of a peasant portrays the harmony that existed between living and dying. The dying peasant recognizes for himself that he is dying. He is able to know that death is approaching because he has lived in an intimate familiarity with death for much of his life. Once he understands that death is imminent, he gathers his children around his deathbed for final instructions and farewells:

> My dear children, he says, I am going to our fathers. Goodbye, promise me that you will live like brothers. He takes each one by the hand, and dies [2, p. 15].

As the historians of Western death have shown, the traditional orientation toward death began around the fifth century and lasted, despite variations in form, until the nineteenth century. The nineteenth century brought some changes in that it was an era whereby familiar simplicity was replaced by romantic, sentimental, and overly inflated expressions of grief. It was also a time where fellowship at the deathbed was reduced from broad communal presence to a circle of intimate friends and relatives. Yet the peaceful sense of harmony between dying people and their process of dying stills remained a salient feature of the Victorian deathbed. Bram Stoker's novel, *Dracula,* classically portrays love and fellowship conflicting with evil and power, and offers scenes which memorably capture the harmony and intimacy of the deathbed that were typical of the era. Lucy Westerna had been violated by Stoker's *Prince of Darkness* and had succumbed to his powers. Lying on her deathbed, surrounded by a concerned and intimate circle of friends:

> For fully five minutes Van Helsing stood looking at her, with his face at its sternest. Then he turned to me and said calmly: "She is dying. It will not be long now . . . Wake that poor boy, and let him come and see the last; he trusts us and we have promised him" [3, p. 161].

As Lucy's fiancé, Arthur, is awakened, the fellowship returns to her bedside:

> "Arthur! Oh my love, I am so glad you have come!" He was stooping to kiss her when Van Helsing motioned him back. "No," he whispered, "not yet!" "Hold her hand; it will comfort her more."

> So Arthur took her hand and knelt beside her, and she looked her best, with all the soft lines matching the angelic beauty of her eyes. Then gradually her eyes closed, and she sank to sleep. For a little bit her breast heaved softly and her breath came and went like a tired child's [4, p. 168].

As the scene progresses, Lucy again awakes:

> Very shortly after she opened her eyes in all their softness, and putting out her poor pale, thin hand, took Van Helsing's great brown one; drawing it to her, she kissed it. "My true friend," she said in a faint voice, but with

untellable pathos, "My true friend, and his! Oh, guard him and give me peace."

"I swear it!" he said solemnly, kneeling beside her and holding up his hand, as one who registers an oath. Then he turned to Arthur and said to him: "Come my child, take her hand in yours, and kiss her on the forehead, and only once."

Their eyes met instead of their lips; and so they parted.

Lucy's eyes closed; and Van Helsing who had been watching closely, took Arthur's arm, and drew him away. And then Lucy's breathing became stertorous again, and all at once it ceased.

"It is all over," said Van Helsing. "She is dead" [4, p. 168].

Social support and community involvement in the traditional rituals of death offered comfort and a sense of well-being to dying individuals. Additionally, the active social presence of others at the deathbed reflected the harmonious integration of life with death and assisted in promoting simplicity and acceptance in the shadow of life's ending.

The powerful imagery in the foregoing passage is rooted in the mutually supportive interactions of the fellowship with the dying Lucy Westerna. Not only did the support of community participation in the dying rituals of the past provide for a sense of comfort and well-being to those who were dying, it was both a reflection of and partly a source of the simple, tranquil, and harmonious acceptance of death. Death was tranquil because, even under the most extraordinary circumstances, dying was a familiar, ordinary, and natural process.

As the twentieth century emerged, the images of tranquility and harmony that characterized traditional death were replaced by a new model of death: death as a social evil. As dying became shameful, ugly, and dirty, it became perceived to be ordinary only under extraordinary circumstances. For that reason, the horribleness of dying must be denied in order to be organized in the least disturbing way possible. Modern dying lacks the simple acceptance of traditional death. Typically it is uneven, turbid, and turbulent. It is characterized not just by the hideous, stigmatizing qualities discussed in the previous chapter, but an ambivalent and twisting course that involves a non-rhythmic amalgamation of false hope and despair.

One of the inherent consequences of the medicalization of dying is the prolongation of the dying process. As disease progresses, medical-technological efforts to combat the disease and postpone death are intensified. In this way, the "natural progression" of disease is deterred by medical and surgical treatments which offer the dying person reassurance, optimism, and hope. Despite its constant evolving nature, hope emanates from the promise of technological victory over disease and is reflective of the faith Americans hold in science and technology. However, during the course of terminal illness, improvements in physical states are often transient and temporary. The resurgence of disease elicits feelings of dejection and deflated hope. Renewed medical efforts may seek to moderate the progress of the disease, and the degree to which these efforts succeed dejection is replaced by a rekindled flicker of hope. In this zigzagging process of dying, hope can be successfully used as a management mechanism to divert attention away from the more encompassing and disturbing issue of dying and death.

Let us consider this emotional roller coaster ride of heightening hope and plummeting despair as illustrated by the following case. A patient with a relatively unsuccessful medical history of lymphosarcoma was admitted into the hospital with a severe swelling and pain in her abdomen. Her physician discusses some test results with her:

Doctor:	The preliminary results of your CT scan show a growth of nodes, which are causing an obstruction. You have been urinating today—losing some weight—which is the first time you've done that since coming in. If that continues, we'll continue you on Lasix to get the swelling down. If not, I'll ask Dr. _____ to radiate your belly (he points to the spot where radiation would occur) to see if we can't get the nodes to reduce. Then we can get you started on chemotherapy.
Patient:	What will the medicine be?
Doctor:	Some VMF, Methotrexate, some . . .
Patient:	Could you write that down for me?
Doctor:	When it comes time to start treatment, I'll go over the whole thing with you. Don't worry, you'll have plenty of advance warning.
Patient:	For how long will I be getting the chemo?
Doctor:	I'm not exactly sure what the protocol[1] calls for. I have to check it out. It'll be something I give you every three or four weeks.
Patient:	Oh, so then we are talking about something overnight?
Doctor:	Yes . . . , or I can give it to you in the office or clinic.

It is important to note how the patient selectively overlooked the initial concerns discussed by her physician and focused her attention on the details of the

---

[1] Protocol refers to a combination of drugs and/or procedures that have not yet been approved by the FDA for regular use but have been approved for use in experimental studies. The patient was being started on a protocol because she had already been placed on all the regularly prescribed regimens for her type of cancer, and each of those had ultimately proved ineffective.

chemotherapy regimen, placing hope in the curative potential of the protocol drugs. The same interactional pattern occurs the following day after a physical examination and a review of specific symptoms and test results. The patient begins:

Patient: Doctor, so this isn't serious? (pointing to her severely swollen stomach)

Doctor: Serious?? (he hesitates) Well, your disease is serious. You do have extensive nodes (he points to her shoulder), and your swelling is probably due to node growth . . .

Patient: (interrupting) But it won't require surgery . . . ?

Doctor: No, that I can tell you for sure.
. . . PAUSE . . .

Doctor: The critical thing is your swelling. We want to get that down with medication and/or radiation. That is the really important thing for now. Then we can begin to start you on some chemotherapy which will have a chance to work.

Patient: (focusing on the last phrase and showing visible relief) Okay, Doctor, good. That'll be fine. Thank you.

The patient is focusing on her hopes for the future. She is placing her faith in technology and relying on her belief in the benefits to be derived from the anticipated chemotherapy treatments. She is, however, "naively unaware of how serious her condition is," as one doctor put it. There can be no doubt that communication between patient and physician left the patient with a poor understanding of her prognosis. Clearly, her doctors have been unsuccessful in communicating the nature of her diagnosis to her, and/or she has been selectively screening out indicators of bad news. In any event, this naiveté on the part of the patient was not very well understood by her attending doctors. Her primary oncologist, shaking his head in disbelief, commented to her radiologist in a hallway conversation: "She really thinks she is going to get well." And, the radiologist responded: "Do you mean she hasn't caught on?"

Up to this point, chemotherapy had been discussed as a possibility. As a result of miscommunication between her attending physician, the house staff doctors, and herself, the patient had come to believe that the start of treatment was imminent. As it turned out, the resident and intern assigned to her case had wrongly informed the patient that she was to start chemotherapy. The attending physician, upon hearing this, reversed the order, citing two reasons. Foremost was his concern that at this stage of the patient's dying, the best way he could serve her was to make her as pain free and comfortable as possible. The resident and interns aggressively argued with the attending physician on this point, emphasizing that they had an obligation to "try everything to save her." The physician was getting nowhere with the argument that treating her pain and other symptoms of discomfort was all that should be done. He raised a second point, that one of the requirements of the protocol was that the patient could not be edematous. Since the patient had severe abdominal swelling she was not eligible for the protocol for medical reasons. It was this technical requirement of the protocol that prevailed upon the house staff doctors. At this point, they defined their professional obligations in terms of reducing the patient's swelling so active treatment could begin. Her oncologist and radiologist had a similar goal, but had a different end in mind. For the physicians still in training, the objective was to prepare the patient for entrance in the protocol regimen of treatment. Her attending physicians were interested in palliation and ease of physical suffering. Again, from the conflicting perspectives of the doctors involved in the care of this patient, we see how normlessness prevails in the meaning and goals of medical management. Yet, we also see the centrality of technology despite the divergence and conflict in the forms of management.

The following conversation, initiated at the request of the patient's parents, between the patient and a staff associate in the cancer center where she was being treated, illustrates that (for whatever the reason) the patient had not fully accepted the realities of her condition:

Patient:	I'm just so relieved that they are going to start chemotherapy tonight.
Associate:	You seem very enthusiastic about starting treatment.
Patient:	Yes, (with a deep sigh of relief). I just want to get better.
Associate:	That is the hope of many people, but you should realize that being placed on the protocol does not mean an automatic, miracle cure.
Patient:	What do you mean?
Associate:	Dr. _____ told you of the seriousness of your condition two nights ago. Your disease is extensive, and he said it is spreading. It's important for you to recognize that the treatment will not make you well again, overnight.
Patient:	It won't?!? (disbelief)
Associate:	You've been on other combinations of medicine before, and you know that they work slowly, not rapidly. I hesitate even to discuss this with you, except that your doctors and I do not want you to be hooked onto expectations that are unrealistic and be shattered because of it.
Patient:	Yeah.
Associate:	If the treatment will have any positive effect, it will be only with you fighting along with it. The treatment will not instantaneously make you well.
Patient:	Oh.
Associate:	Have you thought about the seriousness of your condition at all?
Patient:	No. I thought he said that I'd get well. . . .

Over the course of the next couple of days the swelling in the patient's stomach worsened. The attending physician decided to begin radiation treatment in order to reduce the nodes that were obstructing her kidneys, inhibiting the passing of fluids and thereby causing her swelling. The early stages of radiation treatment brought some modest success. She was losing some fluid weight, but she was feeling increasingly weak and was in intense pain. At this point, as her swelling was being diminished, her doctors looked again toward the protocol. It was discovered, however, that an additional requirement of the protocol was that the drugs could not be administered if radiation treatment had been received within the last thirty days. Her attending physician, recognizing that chemotherapy could not begin for at least a month, told the patient that he planned to finish up her radiation treatment and discharge her at the end of the week.

In recognizing that the hoped for and "promised" start of chemotherapy was not going to take place, the patient became increasingly depressed over the seriousness of her condition. A brief conversation with her mother expresses the re-emergence of a sense of despair and its superceding of the hope which had been previously, yet falsely, alive and well:

Patient: I'm just so tired and feel so terrible.

Family Member: But Dr. _____ said this wasn't serious.

Patient: I know I'm going to get better, but I just feel so lousy. Feeling this bad, I just don't know. I'm scared about this new protocol. That it may not work. I'm just so frightened.

The faith which previously had been placed in the new chemotherapy regimen had now been shaken, and the fear of not getting well became the dominant expressive and behavioral concern of the patient.

The patient was released from the hospital at the week's end, as there was nothing more medically that could be done for her. She was, however, readmitted after several days. She was later having difficulty breathing, was visibly weak and in extensive discomfort and pain, and her abdominal swelling had again increased.

She was perceptibly nervous and disturbed by her worsening physical condition. This increased worry over her illness became explicitly expressed as an acute sense of fear:

... When will I be going home again? It's just taking so much longer than I thought. I just want to go home so bad. Do you think I'm ever going to feel well again?

I can't even describe the fear. There are no words ... It's too frightening for me to be able to describe. I'm just so afraid.

During the first two days of this readmission, it seemed that death was a likely possibility. Specific symptoms and key indicators were not encouraging. Her physician, at this point, was resigned to trying to make her as comfortable as possible and hoping for the best. Her fears during this period grew and her sense of despair heightened:

> I'm afraid of dying. It really scares me. When I told you a month ago that I wasn't scared to die, I guess I was just denying it. Now I'm so anxious, nervous, depressed. I don't know how much more of this I can take.

On the third day of this admission her symptoms showed improvement. She had lost some fluid, her white blood count was up, creatinine clearance was improving, and her pain was easing a bit. She was generally feeling better, but it needs to be stressed that her cancer remained very widespread. She had obvious and visible growths of tumor on her forehead, around the armpit area, and on her vagina. Also, there was massive growth of internal nodes. In short, she was very, very sick.

Her physical symptoms continued to improve over the next several days, and she and her physician seized upon these particular improvements. Her physician, who never even expected her to live this long, expresses his optimism over these improvements:

Doctor:	I think you are doing incredibly well. Your lungs and your belly have responded tremendously to the radiation we gave you. Certainly better than anyone ever expected you to.
Patient:	When am I ever going to start chemotherapy and go home?
Doctor:	We can't start chemotherapy until your creatinine clearance improves.
Patient:	Cre . . . ? Creatinine?
Doctor:	Creatinine is a waste product that is cleared by the kidneys into the blood. Right now, your kidneys are not operating sufficiently to clear the creatinine as rapidly as should be. As soon as we can correct that, we'll get you on chemotherapy.
Patient:	And that will help?
Doctor:	Oh, yes. It'll help you get rid of your lumps here and there (he gently points to the patient's kidneys and shoulder).
Patient:	These medicines work? You've used them before?
Doctor:	Yes, they are excellent medicines. No magic. They are just good medicines, and when used in combination, we hope to get beneficial results from them.
Patient:	When can I get started?
Doctor:	We want to get your belly flat first.
Patient:	I think it's flat now.

Doctor:	No, you've got another five pounds of fluid left, plus something over here (he probes her stomach). We'll get that out, monitor the creatinine carefully, and then get you started.
Patient:	So by next Monday you'll be treating me?
Doctor:	I hope so.[2]
Patient:	Okay, Doctor. Thank you. Thank you very much.
Doctor:	(preparing to leave) You're doing incredibly well. Your lumps in your belly are rapidly diminishing. Your legs are doing well, and your belly has been really flattened by the radiotherapy. You are doing spectacularly. Again, far better than anyone thought you would.

From the perspective of symptom management the use of words spectacular and incredible may have been accurate, but in terms of the more penetrating matter of life and death, the words were clearly inappropriate and misleading. At this point the despair, which the patient brought to the hospital and felt deeply early on during her readmission, has been replaced by a rekindling of the fires of hope.

The patient, however, died three weeks later, never having been placed on the much-hoped-for chemotherapy regimen. Her attending physician was on vacation at the time. After so much turbulence and suffering, it is almost staggering how abruptly the lingering, roller coaster journey of dying can come to a halt.

The emotional roller coaster journey of the patient from hope to despair back to hope again is largely a consequence of peaks and valleys in the progression of physical disease and the patient's perception of the disease. The uneasy, commingled ebb and flow of hope and despair is a product of the modern, technocratic approach to death, and occurs largely in a context of denial and hidden truth.

Hope is the last refuge from total psychosocial annihilation by the horrors of dying. Hope, especially false hope, enables both physicians and patients to avoid open, honest confrontation with mortality. And, it is precisely the technological focus of medicalized dying which facilitates avoidance and denial. Through technical intervention, specific symptoms can be treated and ameliorated during the final months, weeks, and days of life. By concentrating attention on particular symptomatic improvements, the physician is able to avoid confronting the distasteful issue of dying. Converging attention on improving symptoms also offers patients a haven of hope by facilitating a worldview that is subjectively more optimistic than could be legitimately defined from their objective disease state. When the disease progresses and symptoms correspondingly worsen, physicians can still comfortably dodge the issue of dying and death by isolating their

---

[2] The patient had become so sick that the attending physician, with the full support of the intern and resident, was considering giving her chemotherapy treatment despite not fully meeting the requirements for the protocol.

attention on the exacerbation of disease symptoms and their treatment. Patients, however, cannot remain on such an even keel, as the worsening of symptoms clouds hope and injects pessimism into their view of the future.

The roller coaster journey of dying is a pilgrimage defined by the management of dying patients through technology. It is distinctive from the ritual and fellowship which promoted a sense of harmony between the dying person and her own mortality during the eras of the tame and traditional ways of death. It is important to note that the roller coaster of dying, as generated by the medical manipulation of the symptoms of the dying process, is functional for the medical staff and the hospital system. In this framework, physicians can restrict their attention and activities to biomedical intervention into the disease process. Focus is diverted away from the haunting question of living versus dying, to the more manageable issue of treatment of bodily symptoms and processes. If physicians were unable to find a way to restrict and organize dying within a technological framework, they would be forced to directly encounter the personal, human side of the dying experience. But, as we have already seen, physicians are not only ill-prepared to confront the personal, psychological, and social facts of human dying, they are notoriously unenthusiastic about doing so.

The process of medicalization makes the extraordinary ordinary. It normalizes and gives social credibility to the culturally defined evil that is dying. Specifically, the technical molding of the dying process, with the sharp twists and turns of the roller coaster, serves to maintain the dying patient within the strictures of the sick role. This focuses physician and patient attention on specific bodily parts or physical symptoms. The result sets the stage for the dying patient to be treated within the institutionalized expectations and corresponding set of sentiments and sanctions that are applied to any other medical patient. According to Parsons' well known formulation, the deviancy of illness is legitimized through the creation of the sick role. A person becomes excused for one's illness, that is to say illness is legitimated and made socially acceptable, as long as the individual adheres to societal expectations set forth for him while he is sick. These behavioral definitional role expectations have four major dimensions. The sick person is not responsible for the illness condition and hence must be cared for. In addition, the sick person is exempted from normal social responsibilities; work, school, etc. The third dimension of the sick role is the obligation placed on the patient to want to get well. The final requirement is that the sick person seeks competent professional-medical help and cooperate with that help in order to be well again [4].

The traditional use of the sick role is based on the assumption that the condition is not permanent. Hence, dying, or more precisely the dying patient, would not seem to be legitimately included within its parameters. The discussion of the downward escalator journey of the process of dying indicated how dying progresses without realistic opportunity for reversal. However, as indicated in this chapter, the (unchangeable) course of dying is often ignored by physicians and patients as specific symptoms and the medical treatment thereof become the center of doctor-patient interaction. The degree to which this occurs, the dying person is treated like any other patient, and the sick role becomes an "illegitimately legitimate" category for classifying the dying patient. It is illegitimate because of the diversion of attention from the core issue of dying to the management of symptoms. It is also illegitimate because of the creation of false hope and the corresponding illusion of optimism. This combination enables the relatively unfamiliar world of dying patients to be redefined into rather ordinary patterns of medical management. Since physicians narrowly focus attention on specific physical conditions, and patients frequently mis-interpret improving symptomology as an indicator of generalized improvement of health-disease status, the dying experience is framed by normative expectations of the sick role. Thus, in a curious way, because of technical intervention, a technocratic definition of reality, and the resulting roller coaster ride, dying patients and doctors relate to each other through the specificity of sick role performances, thereby avoiding unpleasant conversations and interactions about dying.

An important point to be noted is that "peaks of well-being" during the dying process are largely doctor defined and technically induced. Thus, the techno-logical organization of dying introduces periods of peaks and valleys to the generalized downward trotting of the escalator journey of dying. This up and down movement between hope and despair is not at variance with escalator dying, but rather is one variable form of the process of physical, emotional, and social deterioration that is part of the daily life struggle of dying persons. In a sense, the climb toward renewed hope does not necessarily divert the escalator from its downward journey but rather serves to delude the patient about where she is journeying, thereby creating false hopes and unrealistic expectations. The infor-mation that "today your symptoms are not doing well" deflates hope and brings concerns about death to the fore. Tomorrow's message that "your symptoms are improving" reinstates hope and relegates fears about dying to the private recesses of patient consciousness. In this way, the dying process in American society is characterized by emotional turbulence and focus on technical manipulation of physical symptoms, the unavoidable consequence of which is vacillating patient hopes and expectations for the future. It is precisely this turmoil and disorder which is a characteristic part of the downward escalator movement of the dying process.

As the sick role is applied to dying people, patients are socialized by the medical staff to focus their attention on the treatment of specific, often isolated, physical symptoms. Patients are socialized into an understanding that physicians are mostly disinterested in the human, personal meanings of dying. In this way, the emphasis on physical symptoms and disease processes not only encourages unrealistic patient expectations, but functions to restrain patient emotional expressions. The imposition of the sick role becomes then an effective vehicle for controlling the disturbing and distasteful psychosocial outpourings of dying patients. Of course, this is of use to physicians and hospital systems as the efficient carrying out of medical work is not jeopardized by emotional turbulence.

The ambivalence and the emotional jockeying of the roller coaster of dying diverts attention away from considerations of death and dying and individualizes the grieving process. As attention is focused on disease, symptoms, and treatment options frontstage expressions of grief by patients or loved ones become inappropriate and negatively sanctioned. Appropriate death, after all, is death with social dignity and this requires emotional restraint. Thus, the roller coaster, sick role treatment of dying patients facilitates the privatization of grief and suffering, as expressions of emotion related directly to dying are defined as inappropriate to the technological management of death.

In addition to helping to assure that grief does not spill forth into the public realm of doctor-patient interaction, the stress upon treatment of symptoms and the application of the sick role to dying patients serves to de-emphasize the specialness or uniqueness of dying. Dying, in this way, is transformed into something ordinary. And, as dying becomes ordinary, it becomes organized into the thread of everyday life in ways that are neither dramatic nor disturbing. Making death, which is alien and threatening to modern sensitivities, ordinary serves to ensconce the process of dying neatly into the everyday, standardized, bureaucratic routine of the hospital. Thus, dying is stripped of the public expression of many of its disturbing and perturbing factors. In this way, the horror of dying and the rage of dying patients are contained or, to borrow from the language of Ariès, death itself is tamed.

In short, the ambivalence created by the roller coaster of dying is one form and consequence of doctors dancing around the truth-of-the truth; of avoiding the harsh socio-human realities of dying. As we have seen in this chapter, there are at least two ways of not thinking about death: the way of our technological civilization which finds ways of refusing to talk openly and honestly about death, and the way of traditional civilizations which is not so much a denial of death but a recognition of the impossibility of dwelling on death for very long. The traditional patterns hence emphasize the comforting functions of fellowship, ritual, and ceremony. The roller coaster of dying with its emphasis on the applicability of the sick role to the dying patient is a manifestation of the American attempt to organize and control human death. It is a means of encouraging silence, social dignity, and even false optimism on the part of dying patient behaviors which, in effect, become powerful mechanisms of death management and dying "denial."

REFERENCES

1. E. Becker, *Escape from Evil,* The Free Press, New York, 1975.
2. A. Weisman, *The Coping Capacity: On the Nature of Being Mortal,* Human Sciences Press, New York, 1986.
3. B. Stoker, *Dracula,* Ballantine Books, New York, 1959.
4. T. Parsons, *The Social System,* The Free Press, New York, 1964.

CHAPTER 10

A Concluding Statement: Technicism, Social Isolation, Medicalization, and Remedicalization of Dying

The old man closed his eyes. As life carried away the rumblings of the town, and the heavens smiled their foolish, indifferent smile, he was alone, forsaken, naked, already dead [1, p. 124].

Albert Camus

Suffer on behalf of others [2, p. 31].

George Bernanos

Has anyone the right to abandon a human being? And even if he dies, shouldn't one do all one can to give him an easier death? [3, p. 67].

Jean Giono

On the wards of medical centers and in the broader society in general, dying and death are separated from the mainstream of human activity. Dying is excluded from social life through the isolation of children from death, by the absence of traditionally grounded social rituals to guide dying people and their loved ones, and by the growing expectation that dying should properly remain within the confines of an individual's private existence. Dying is excluded from the medical world in that its nidus is redefined from concern about death to symptom management and treatment modalities. Illness orientation and even palliative focus provide a framework by which the "big" issue of dying is retrenched and gives way to narrowly concentrated technical and medical interests. In this way, the powerful personal experience of confronting death is detached and excluded from the ordinary routine of medical work.

The American faith in science and technology and the shared cultural commitment to individualism are seminal forces which underlie the social isolation of dying in America. As discussed in Chapters 3 and 4, technocratic-individualism generates a frame of reference for everyday social living which is in contradiction to the realities of the human experience of dying. The images of denial and meaninglessness which typify our age profoundly affect the way in which Americans learn to think about death. It is within this context that dying is isolated from the positively esteemed, sought-after values and meaningful experiences in American society. Specifically, not only are ideas and images about dying and death culture-bound, but as these images become instruments of socialization, they function to influence an individual's perception of his or her own dying and facilitate or inhibit the ability of the dying person and surrounding community to meaningfully adjust to the experience of dying.

Images of dying and death arise in a specific connection to cultural and historical context. The medicalization of death has emerged as a structural reflection of the specific cultural images and circumstances of contemporary America. Medicalization of death, however, is not only reflective of the dominant images of dying and death in the technocratic social setting, but is one vehicle by which death and dying are transformed into tolerable social realities. The once prominent idea of death as a social, community, and natural process becomes redefined into a scientifically manageable and preventable phenomenon when death is medicalized:

> More than ever before, we can hope today, by the skill of doctors, by diet and by medicaments, to postpone death. Never before in the history of humanity have more-or-less scientific methods of prolonging life been discussed so incessantly throughout the whole breadth of society as in our day. The dream of the elixir of life and of the fountain of youth is very ancient. But it is only in our day that it has taken on scientific or pseudoscientific form. The knowledge that death is inevitable is overlaid by the endeavor to postpone it more and more with the aid of medicine and insurance, and by the hope that this might succeed [4, p. 47].

The thought of a person dying in modern civilization is filled with images of hospitals, machinery, drugs, professional staff, alienation, a sterile environment, and enormous suffering. In a way, these iconic realities of the dying patient's life have become standardized symbols reflecting the peculiarities of medicalized dying. The salient point to be emphasized is that medicalization is both a reflector of and contributor to primary ways of death in the modern technocratic society. Additionally, medicalization of the dying process isolates patients from their own dying experience. The medical education of student doctors, the professional activity and norms of medical work, along with the technologically-based professional orientation of the profession function to disengage dying, as a human experience, from the professional frame of reference which defines the mainstream of physician activity. As seen earlier, there are a variety of means by which physicians transform the personal issues of dying into medicalized concerns.

Closed-awareness contexts where truth is hidden, obscured, or sugar-coated are very much used as a means of isolating dying and its experiences from the mainstream of physician-patient interaction. The technologically-based, save-at-all-costs orientation, as well as the avoidance-neglect and sympathetic-detachment orientations, are additional ways in which physicians disengage personal considerations from the clinical worldview. Consequently, the patient's experience of dying is excluded from the interactional dynamics of the physician-patient relationship.

The inconsistency of physicians' attitudes regarding how dying patients should be managed, the lack of norms to guide physicians in their interactions and communications with the dying, and the fact that physicians tend to relate to the dying patients in ways which doctors find most personally easy and emotionally comfortable further contributes to the isolation of the experience of dying. Dying is excluded from the shared professional culture of physicians, and, to the extent that physicians are the *de facto* umpires and arbitrators of medicalized death, the personalized sufferings of dying are defined as inappropriate content for physicians to address. Expressions of suffering threaten efficiency and businesslike accomplishment of work and must be curtailed.

In addition to dying being isolated from the interactional world of doctors and patients, the bureaucratic organization of the modern medical center excludes personal experiences with dying from its standardized organization of professional activity. Indeed, the values of affective-neutrality, efficiency, detachment, and rationality preeminently underlie the operation of the modern medical center. In this regard, from the viewpoint of institutional expectations, the dynamic, emotional state of human dying must be neutralized by bureaucratic organization and focus. In the bureaucratic view of things, the personal side of dying is too emotionally charged and cumbersome to address. It threatens efficiency and businesslike accomplishment of work. The affective state of dying is thereby excluded from the operational mainstream of bureaucratic medical activity. In this sense, dying is relegated to and contained in the individual patient's private or personal frame of reference. Thus, the human experience of dying is pushed farther and farther behind the scenes of medical work and isolated from the public arena of medical activity.

Curiously, however, a counter revolutionary movement is emerging. Its aim is to de-isolate dying from medical interest and cultural concern. This movement entails not just the grass roots hospice and death-with-dignity movement, but a growing coalition of professionals interested in palliative medicine.

Each year in the United States 2.5 million people die. Two-thirds of these individuals will die after prolonged suffering-filled struggles with chronic disease. Eighty percent of all deaths occur in the dehumanizing confines of hospitals, nursing homes, or other institutions. Most dying individuals and family members express distress and dissatisfaction. The picture presented in this book may be grim but it is representative of the severe condition of dying persons in contemporary America. Bearing out this point is a study that followed 9,000 patients in five different hospitals. The study, called SUPPORT, was funded by the Robert Wood Johnson Foundation. It confirmed the findings presented in this book, namely that there are substantial shortcomings in the medicalized treatment of dying persons. Specifically it found:

- the culture of technologized medicine is at odds with patients' needs and desires
- far too many patients suffer in unrelieved pain
- communication between physicians and patients is inadequate
- the high cost of medicalized dying has an alarming financial impact on many families.

As the authors summarize their findings, they appallingly conclude: "We are left with a troubling situation. The picture we describe of the care of terminally ill or dying persons is not attractive" [5, p. 1597]. In an associated study, the same group of researchers interviewed 3,357 family members of patients who had died in SUPPORT. The conclusion, once again consistent with the findings and analysis of this study, presents a desolate picture. It revealed a major divergence between patients' preferences for care and the medicalized focus of physician caregivers. In fact, care received was at odds with care desired, and family members believed that their loved ones preferred comfort but instead received life sustaining treatment [5]. We can imagine how disillusioned these loved ones must have been at the systematic indifference of physicians to the comfort needs of their dying patients.

In a culture already anxious about dying and its associated indignities, these studies sounded a national alarm. As a result, interest in the medical community and modern culture in matters related to end-of-life has increased. Two major components of this surge in interest are physician assisted suicide and medical palliation. Given the current state of dying in America, it is no wonder that advocates of assisted suicide are finding their message resonating throughout the culture. Despite the fact that most professional organizations, including the American Medical Association, American Nursing Association, and American Hospice Association, vociferously oppose physician assisted suicide, the majority of people in the country support its legalization. Jack Kevorkian has brought the topic to national notoriety in dramatic fashion. Oregon has legalized it and state courts in New York and California have struck down legal prohibitions against it. Timothy Quill, arguably the most persuasive and reasonable advocate for physician assisted suicide, agrees that doctor facilitated suicide is palliative. Its goal, he says, is the compassionate elimination of "severe, unrelenting, and intolerable suffering." He illuminates the point by recounting his involvement with one of his patients who decided she was ready to end her suffering by ending her life:

In her eyes, continuing life under such circumstances lacked any meaning
. . . her future now held only the terrifying prospect of increasing dependence, incapacity, and loss of integrity prior to death. Death was
far preferable to Diane than enduring the further dissolution of all
that had meaning to her, and there was nothing more that Comfort Care
could do to ease what was becoming an excruciating final decline
[7, p. 171].

It is beyond the scope of this study to debate the ethics and legalities of assisted
suicide. The essential point to be raised, however, is that physician assisted suicide is
a form of medicalized death. Or more correctly, it is part of a process of redefining
the medicalization of death. In this process, which I term re-medicalization of
dying, death is actually achieved by medical intervention. The ruling idea is that
physician assisted suicide is an appropriate medical solution to the problems of
dying. Inasmuch as Quill and others suggest that the goal is relief of suffering,
physician-assisted suicide essentially is palliation-by-killing. And, as the inten-
tional hastening of death is palliative and relieves suffering, a new form of
medicalization has emerged to control the dying process. In this way, physician-
assisted suicide does not eliminate medicalization of death. Instead, it extends the
ability of the profession to be in a position of authority over the end of life.

Paralleling the right-to-die movement is a growing national effort to palliate
death. As already suggested, the notions of "dying well" and "good death" are
beginning to be articulated and projected throughout the culture. Nationally supported campaigns, such as Project on Death in America, Last Acts, and the
Medicaring Demonstration Project are seeking to reshape the care that dying
persons receive at the end of life. Palliative care is growing as a specialty in
mainstream medical practice. These are laudable efforts involving the participation of exemplary and caring professionals. The crucial point to be understood,
however, is that most of the attempts to improve care of dying persons are taking
place within the jurisdiction of medicine. Palliation is extremely desirable. But it
is also a form of re-medicalization. And, as a mode of re-medicalization, it is an
incomplete response to the enormous suffering, psychosocial complexity, and the
problem of meaninglessness faced by dying persons and loved ones. If I am
correct, and the evidence is persuasive, any successful attempt to refashion the
modern ways of death must fully consider the role of the broader social forces of
technicism, materialism, individualism, meaninglessness, and spiritual yearning.
Additionally, pervasive changes must take place in the training, practice, and
organization of the profession of medicine before an effort to humanize and
improve the care of dying patients can succeed. Another shortcoming of the
re-medicalization movement is its failure to recognize that a dominant tendency of
the broader technocratic society is the drift away from community and moral
solidarity toward isolated individualism. Themes of moral estrangement, spiritual
isolation, and interpersonal fragmentation pervade contemporary society. They

are also salient in the popular and intellectual study of modern life. In Nisbet's eloquent words:

> To examine the whole literature of lament of our time—in the social sciences, moral philosophy, theology, the novel, the theatre—and to observe the frantic efforts of millions of individuals to find some kind of security of mind is to open our eyes to the perplexities and frustrations that have emerged from the widening gulf between the individual and these social relationships within which goals and purposes take on meaning. The sense of cultural disintegration is but the obverse side of the sense of individual isolation [7, pp. 9-10].

The historical sense of community, which flourished in predeveloped Western society, has been extensively discussed in the academic literature. For our purposes here, two major points are salient. First, traditional ties of community bound individuals together in a framework of moral imperatives, social rituals, and social stability. Second, in relationship to death and dying, community presence and traditional rituals of dying facilitated, or perhaps it would be more correct to say mandated, that dying be a culturally shared community experience. Thus, dying took place not just in the public presence of community but within a frame of reference that was characterized by standardized behaviors, common assumptions, and shared cultural meanings.

As Western society developed economically, industrially, and politically, community and tradition began to lose their base of authority. Again, two major points stand out. First, moral certainty, which is a by-product of communal living, is replaced by secular individualism. The result is that quests for meaning are increasingly divorced from a shared communal base and are more and more pursued by individuals independently of each other. The insecurities, spiritual and existential yearnings, moral dilemmas, and normlessness which typify our age not only reflect the absence of shared cultural meanings and norms, but are situations which increasingly challenge the individual in personal ways. Individuals, in order to cope with the demands of modern life, must respond to these situations on the basis of their personal resources and abilities. Second, in relation to death and dying, the human experience of dying has become isolated from shared, communal meanings. The result is that the meanings of dying are increasingly privatized and individualized. The absence of shared cultural norms and the individuation of meanings of dying isolate the dying patient, family, friends, neighbors, and the surrounding community from each other into private, encapsulated worlds of survival, coping, or indifference. The result clearly is increased alienation of the dying patient. This process also exacerbates the instabilities and normlessness of the dying experience by dividing the participants into privatized spheres of meaning and coping. The present palliative care re-medicalization movement ignores these facts.

The escalator social stigma of the dying process is a lamentable outcome of the social isolation of death. In a most fundamental way, the dying patient is isolated from the qualities which are valued in American culture, from those which provide a seedbed for self-esteem and self-affirmation, as well as those qualities which provide a base for interconnections and interactions with others. The pain and suffering that often typify the experience of dying are unmitigated by cultural legitimation. In the absence of culturally grounded meaning systems for suffering and pain, pain and suffering have become defined as clinical issues requiring therapeutic, medical management. In this way, the pain of dying is isolated from the web of social and cultural systems of meaning. I do not mean to overromanticize the role that culturally anchored support systems played for dying people in traditional, Western society. Unquestionably, in an age of death from infectious disease and pestilence, many people died very painful and agonizing deaths. Certainly, medical technology has achieved some significant results in controlling and managing the physical agony of the dying process. Yet, even in this age of hi-tech medicine, physical pain remains a salient—and very much feared—dimension of dying. The management of the pain of dying has passed from the hands of family, community, and social or religious rituals to medical technicians. When biomedicine fails to control the pain, the dying patient is left to face pain and associated suffering in an isolated and privatized world. In this framework of isolation and meaninglessness, coping and endurance are under-mined by indifference. In this way, while cultural reliance on the technological management of pain and suffering has positively contributed to reducing some of the physical agony of dying, it has simultaneously resulted in a heightening of emotional and social isolation of the dying patient.

The emotional, cultural, and social isolation of the dying patient is associated with the loss of self-esteem, identity deterioration, and blemishment. In our age of individualism, with increased value placed on self-development and expression, dying is the ultimate decimator of the American pursuit of personal well-being. Helplessness, vulnerability, despair, physical devolution, and sexual blemishment impact the dying patient in such a devastating way that profound social stigma emerges. The scenarios of personal terror recounted in Chapters 2 and 8 illus-trate not just the identity diminishment of dying persons but also their personal and social impotence. Traditional social rituals of dying, in a straightforward Durkheimian sense, provided a common base of participation and a sense of belonging. These rituals served to attach the dying person to the community of the living. In addition to generating a sense of group cohesiveness in the face of dying, traditional social rituals facilitated a sense of strength and transcen-dence, as the dying person became thickly attached to the moral order of the surrounding community. Also, it should be remembered that the traditional social rituals of death were both reaffirming of and reaffirmed by prevailing cultural values. In this way, the dying person was integrated into a cultural framework of meaning that provided for moral and social significance.

The absence of ritual, institutionalized interconnections with the community of the living, and the lack of culturally sanctioned meanings to dying leave the dying patient morally, socially, and personally diminished. This really is the underlying basis of escalator social stigma of dying, namely, the fact that personal and social death precedes biological death. Thus, the problem of meaninglessness asserts itself for dying patients not just in an abstract, existential way, but in ways that have concrete, deleterious effects the personal and social identity.

The fact of death is in the nature of being alive. More significantly, however, it is in the nature of humanity to be aware of the fact of mortality and to seek ways of coping with the inescapability fact of death. Indeed, since the beginning of the human race, human beings have had to come to terms with and find some means of adjusting to the biosocial facts of death. In American society today, the dominant patterns of responding to the inescapable problem of death include technological management of dying and the growing expectation that one should die a socially or personally dignified death. Social dying with dignity minimally means that one should not publicly distress others by one's dying. Maximally, dignified death means dying in a way that transforms the dying process into a final opportunity for self-enhancement, growth, and an individually inspired quest for meaning. It is in the latest conceptualization that the "good death" can be achieved.

As death in American society has become divorced from rituals and culturally legitimized systems of meaning it is increasingly characterized by meaninglessness, terror, devolution, normlessness, and stigma. As a result, new forms of controlling and managing dying and death have necessarily emerged. Modern management through death-with-dignity and technological manipulation of the dying process suppress and contain the tribulations of dying in a fashion that minimally disturbs and threatens the broader social world. In doing so, however, it increases suffering for dying persons and loved ones by intensifying their social isolation.

Personal dying-with-dignity places the burden of successful and appropriate death squarely on the shoulders of the individual. In this way, "good death" is isolated from collectively shared social codes, norms, and rituals. The quest for dying a good death leads the dying patient away from commonly based systems of meaning and toward private and isolated definitions. But, as I suggested earlier, it is also largely unrealistic in a society which excludes dying, suffering, and death from the course of everyday activity, to expect that individuals will be able to successfully make the social and psychological adjustments that are required for death-with-dignity. In this way, a lifetime of socialization for successful living in a narcissistic, technocratic social setting precludes and excludes most dying patients from a personally dignified and meaningful dying experience. This does not mean to assert that some individuals cannot heroically achieve a dignified death. Rather, it refers to normative societal patterns of dying wherein enormous suffering and meaninglessness prevail. There is no doubt that the patients in this study found personal dying-with-dignity to be unrealistic, problematic for their lives, and inconsistent with their medical management.

Redefining the process of dying into the contours of the sick role, together with the subsequent roller coaster journey of hope and despair, serves to exclude the personal difficulties of dying from the dominant frame of reference of physicians. The technological management of death is a powerful means of managing dying in the modern medical setting and of facilitating social dignity. In this way, technology has replaced tradition and ritual as the prevailing defense against death and dying. But, as the community of the living becomes less and less involved in the process of dying, not only is dying stigmatized and culturally denigrated, the psychological and social agony of dying individuals is increased. In an age where medicalized death has achieved an unparalleled sense of sterility, hygiene, and perhaps physical comfort, an emotional, personal, and social turbulence has simultaneously been unleashed. The turbulence that rages with respect to dying is typically ignored in the therapeutic and technological management of the individual patient's course of dying. The isolation that dying patients may feel is often so total that their suffering, fears, and even their very lives become increasingly invisible in a social setting where people have other things on their minds than suffering, dying, and death. This, perhaps, is the ultimate irony of modern civilization: In an era where the value of the individual has never been greater, the value of a dying person has never been more diminished. In an era where technology has contributed greatly to the diminishment of human pain and misery, the suffering and agony of isolated dying rages unmitigated. The despair of dying patients, trapped in various levels of chaos and complexity, is obvious throughout this book. Now it is up to you, the reader, to decide if we as a society are justified in despairing as well, and if we should be ashamed of the widespread indifference to the suffering of dying persons and loved ones.

REFERENCES

1. A. Camus, Irony, in *Lyrical and Critical Essays,* P. Thody (ed.), Vintage, New York, 1970.
2. G. Bernanos, *The Diary of a Country Priest,* Macmillan, New York, 1937.
3. J. Giono, *The Horseman in the Roof,* North Point Press, San Francisco, California, 1982.
4. N. Elias, *The Loneliness of the Dying,* Basil Blackwell, New York, 1985.
5. J. Lynn et al. (Principal SUPPORT Investigators), Care for Seriously Ill Hospitalized Patients—SUPPORT Investigators, *Journal of the American Medical Association, 274*:20, November 22/29, 1995.
6. T. Quill, *Death and Dignity,* W. W. Norton & Company, Inc., New York, 1993.
7. R. Nisbet, *The Quest for Community,* Oxford University Press, New York, 1953.

A Methodological Note

Sociology is an inherently controversial endeavor [1, p. 3].

Anthony Giddens

The social and cultural landscape is as much of the province of the sociologist—or novelist or poet—as the physical setting is of the painter [2, p. 43].

Robert Nisbet

Fieldwork, then, provides a mirror for looking at who we are as over and against who we would like to be. It provides us with soft data-observations, intuitions and comments—for rethinking some very hard questions about what it means to be a member of the society [3, p. 14].

Charles Bosk

One of the hallmarks of the sociological tradition is the penetration of official and orthodox explanations of social living. The discovery of non-obvious systems of meaning and insight that go beyond the smokescreen of official rhetoric or bureaucratic self-interest and which unveil patterns of human living, that are obscured and hidden by the cultural and social arrangements of society, are of central importance to the mission of sociology. In this way, as Berger aptly describes, sociology fulfills an important debunking function:

> We would contend, then, that there is a debunking motif inherent in sociological consciousness. The sociologist will be driven time and again, by the very logic of his discipline, to debunk the social system he is studying . . . The sociological frame of reference, with its built-in procedure of looking for levels of reality other than those given in the official interpretations of society, carries with it a logical imperative to unmask each other. This unmasking imperative is one of the characteristics of sociology particularly at home in the temper of the modern era . . . [4, p. 38].

Clearly, the debunking motif of sociology entails searching for unadmitted and hidden aspects of social life. It also carries with it a responsibility to confront and study unpleasant and unappealing aspects of social living. In this way, not only does sociology seek to debunk the hidden and taken-for-granted interpretations of social living, but it nurtures the development of a critical sensitivity in the exploration of salient issues that affect the condition of human life, especially in the modern societal context.

This critical sensitivity is at the core of what C. Wright Mills termed the sociological imagination [2]. In adopting the style of sociology which Mills advocated, I have sought in this book to explore dying as a public issue, defined in terms of the cultural and social facts of modern society. Indeed, I have sought to explore how the values of American culture, the institutional arrangements of the society as a whole and of the field of medicine in particular, have created a particular milieu which significantly influences the lives of dying individuals. In a certain sense, formulating the question of modern dying in terms of its dimensions as a public issue contains an ultimate irony. The more the troubles of dying individuals are framed by isolation, psychologizing, and privatization, the more these processes of individuation reflect a collective drift and pattern of modern death. In this way, the tendency to define and isolate each individual's death in a private world of coping is itself a manifestation of a public issue.

The result of my application of Mills' sociological imagination is a portrait of the modern dying patient as perceived from an admittedly critical viewpoint. Just as a landscape or portrait which takes form on a painter's canvas reflects the viewpoint of the painter, sociological portraits necessarily reflect the viewpoint of the sociological artist, that is to say, they have been transmuted and filtered through the scholar's perception, consciousness, and style [5].

Nisbet, in his classic book *Sociology As An Art Form*, discusses the role of art within the discipline and defines artistic sociology not as a fleeting fad but as being very much anchored in the classicism and historical tradition of the field:

> Far from least among sociology's contributions in the nineteenth century is the distinctive ways in which its practitioners saw the landscape in human affairs that had been so largely created by the two great revolutions. . . . Not quantitative, empirical science following any of the contrived prescriptions of current textbooks in methodology or theory construction, but the artist's vision, lies behind such concepts as mass society, Gemeinschaft, Gesellschaft, social status, authority, the sacred and the secular, alienation, anomie, and other signal reactions to the European social landscape in the nineteenth century that we properly associate with the development of sociology [5, p. 73].

I have sought in this book to paint an iconic portrait of the human experience of dying in the modern, medicalized social setting. In crafting a portrait of modern dying, the real life experiences of dying patients were essential. It was therefore necessary for me to enter into the backrooms of medicine, where I could observe and study the life circumstances of hospitalized, dying patients as unobtrusively as possible, so as to get close to the life circumstances of these dying patients as I possibly could. It was also important to understand the personal world of dying persons as members of the culture. In order to do this, I also ventured into their homes and private lives.

In adopting the strategies for observational research as set forth in the *Discovery of Grounded Theory* [6] and *Field Research: Strategies for a National Sociology* [7], observation and interviews were the two dominant mechanisms of accumulating a body of research materials on the human process of dying. The research materials were gathered at two urban medical centers with a strong teaching emphasis. I gained entrance into the professional and personal worlds of hospital dying, by associating myself with a faculty-oncologist who was receptive to the goals of my research plan. During the four-month exploratory phase of the study, I accompanied him on his daily rounds. This enabled me to begin to see patients every day to establish a sense of normalcy to my presence in the medical setting. It also provided the opportunity to begin to establish a sense of ease and comfort with patients, whom I would see at moments of great physical and emotional vulnerability. The development of this sense of faith and trust in me was essential to getting as close as possible to the world of dying patients, and was something that slowly developed. Once trust was achieved, the openness with which patients spoke to me and their lack of concern with maintaining behavioral appearances in front of me was rather striking. The painfully honest sentiments which are reflected by the words of the dying contained in this book are an indicator of the trust that I established with these patients.

During the fourteen months which constituted the main body of fieldwork, I spent my time on rounds, observing, listening, and talking to dying patients. My observations led me to witness the following situations/settings: physicians talking to each other in hallways, elevators, and stairwells about medical or non-medical matters; physicians formally and informally consulting about specific cases; patients being examined; patients relating to family members; physicians discussing X-rays and other test results; nurses and doctors relating to each other; and interns relating to attending physicians. By being able to integrate into the backrooms of medicine, two salient advantages occurred. First, I was able to see what the physician sees but the patient does not. For example, I saw, discussed, and was taught about the medical condition of each of the patients in the study through their X-rays. I was thus able to see the biological-technological underpinnings of physician activity, which take place in the backrooms of the hospital setting. Second, by spending time each day with patients, while they were admitted in the hospital, I was able to integrate into the human concerns and worldview of dying patients and their families. I was, therefore, the beneficiary of seeing and being a part of the human process of dying, from which physicians and other medical caretakers are isolated. This "double perspective" enabled me to examine the process of dying through the frame of reference of both physicians and dying patients.

Thirty-seven patients were in the hospital-only phase of the study. Nineteen of them were male, their ages ranged from twenty-two to ninety. All of the patients in the study were in advanced stages of cancer, i.e., they were at post-surgical and radiation treatment stages, and were subjectively defined by their attending oncologist as having a potentially fatal disease and only months to live. Some patients lingered on for unexpectedly long periods of time, while others died rather quickly—but all of them are dead. The results of this study were previously reported in *On Death Without Dignity: The Human Impact of Technological Dying.*

An additional thirteen patients were followed in different settings including home, clinic, and the hospital. Patients and families were interviewed with a focus on the meanings of facing life threatening illness, and the effectiveness of medical care in relieving their suffering. All of these individuals were also patients in an urban medical center.

I do not mean to imply that dying from cancer in a major, urban medical center is the only way of dying in American society. Clearly, people die from other chronic diseases or medical circumstances. Moreover, people die in nursing homes, community hospital, hospices, and at home. But, first of all, cancer does provide a model disease for studying the modern process of dying in that it represents a chronic illness trajectory, which increasingly typifies modern illness and dying. Also, the cultural meanings of cancer, so nicely portrayed by Sontag's *Illness as a Metaphor* [8], are such that the deepest fears and terrors of modern people about dying and death, are embodied in the human cancer experience. Second, I have elected to study dying in the setting of the urban medical center precisely because that environment is reflective of the most modern style of dying found in American society today. Thus, I have sought to create and portray an impression of dying in America that reflects the cultural and social drift toward modernity. I do not mean to imply, however, that variations of dying styles are not possible or do not occur within the modern framework.

A final methodological note is worth mentioning. The sensitivity of the topic of dying, its deeply personal implications, and the fact that I would regularly see patients during times of heightened vulnerability, helped to create a special and complex role for me in the lives of dying patients who participated in the study. There was a tendency on the part of the patients to begin to see me not only as a researcher but also as a source of support—someone who would offer comfort during times of emotional turmoil, someone they would generally see daily during the course of their hospital stay, someone they could complain to, etc. This was even more profound among the patients and families that I followed at home. They tended to become attached in a personal way, saw me as a confidant, often treated me as an intimate, and thought of me as a member of the family. Indeed, the more open and painfully honest patients were in the conversations with me, the more they identified me as being more that just a sociomedical researcher.

While the issue of establishing workable, amicable relationships with the people one is studying is critical in all types of naturalistic sociological research, the circumstances of dying and death make the development of such relationship especially necessary. In order to penetrate into the worlds and sub-worlds of dying patients, I found it essential to get close to their lives. The result was that I became a part of their lives. Although it is beyond my intent to write on the dilemmas of naturalistic research with dying people, the role of such research in the lives of dying persons and the way in which the study of the process of dying creates special issues for naturalistic fieldwork are important topics worthy of future consideration. But I can say this: The complexities, vulnerabilities, and deeply private nature of modern dying require a special connection between researcher and participant, if the study is to succeed in penetrating into the deeply painful and private dimensions of dying.

One of the cornerstones of successful social science research is that the people who are being studied will recognize themselves in the written account of the study [9]. If dying patients and their loved ones can see themselves in my portrait, I will have been successful in telling their story. If physicians who regularly work with dying patients can divorce themselves from their own professional worldview and see some of the human consequences of medicalized dying, I will also have succeeded. Additionally, if you, the reader, have been touched by this portrait of dying or have found that it provoked thought, reflection, or insight, I will have been successful in debunking and portraying the human and social nature of the modern dying experience. In this way, the study of dying may not be value-free, but it is always value-relevant and life-affirming.

REFERENCES

1. A. Giddens, *Sociology: A Brief but Critical Introduction,* Harcourt, Brace, Jovanovich, New York, 1982.
2. C. W. Mills, *The Sociological Imagination,* Oxford University Press, New York, 1959.
3. C. Bosk, The Fieldworker as Watcher and Witness, *The Hastings Center Report, 15*:3, 1985.
4. P. Berger, *Invitation to Sociology,* Doubleday and Co., New York, 1963.
5. R. Nisbet, *Sociology as an Art Form,* Oxford University Press, p. 73, 1977.
6. B. Glaser and A. Strauss, *Discovery of Grounded Theory: Strategies for Qualitative Research,* Aldine Publishing Co., Chicago, 1967.
7. L. Schatzman and A. Strauss, *Field Research: Strategies for a Natural Sociology,* Prentice-Hall, New Jersey, 1973.
8. S. Sontag, *Illness as a Metaphor,* Vintage Books, New York, 1979.
9. A. Strauss et al., *Social Organization of Medical Work,* (see the Preface and Methodological Appendix), University of Chicago Press, 1985.

Index